High-Intensity Participation

HIGH-INTENSITY PARTICIPATION

The Dynamics of
Party Activism in Britain

Paul F. Whiteley
and
Patrick Seyd

Ann Arbor
THE UNIVERSITY OF MICHIGAN PRESS

Published in the United States of America by
The University of Michigan Press
Manufactured in the United States of America
⊚ Printed on acid-free paper

2005   2004   2003   2002   4   3   2   1

A CIP catalog record for this book is available from the British Library.

Library of Congress Cataloging-in-Publication Data

Whiteley, Paul.
    High-intensity participation : the dynamics of party activism
in Britain / Paul F. Whiteley and Patrick Seyd.
        p.   cm.
    Includes bibliographical references and index.
    ISBN 0-472-10620-1 (cloth : alk. paper)
        1. Political activists—Great Britain.   2. Political
participation—Great Britain.   3. Political parties—Great
Britain.   I. Seyd, Patrick.   II. Title.
    JN1121 .W45   2002
    324.241'011—dc21   2001008277

Contents

❦

Chapter 1

High-Intensity Participation, Political Parties, and Democratic Politics

❧❀❧

THIS BOOK IS ABOUT HIGH-INTENSITY political participation, that is, participation that takes a lot of time and effort on the part of those who are involved in it. By the term "political participation" we mean activities by individuals aimed at influencing the policies or the personnel of the state and government. Thus participation of this type refers to activities such as campaigning, organizing, fund-raising, and attending meetings as well as seeking and achieving elected office.

The task of understanding why some people participate in politics while others do not is perhaps *the* central concern of political science. As is widely recognized in a large body of literature, citizen participation is at the core of democratic politics. A good deal of this literature is about voting, which is of course a fundamentally important means of influencing government. However, the study of voting behavior is not a good arena for understanding wider forms of political participation. This is because voting is a relatively low-cost activity, and consequently individuals' willingness to vote in an election only throws a limited light on the factors that motivate them to undertake high-intensity forms of participation, which is the focus of our concerns. It is also true that voting turnout has little variance; either people vote or they do not, and this fact gives only modest empirical leverage in understanding the determinants of participation in general (see Aldrich 1993).

Highly active participants are much more important to democratic politics than is often recognized. Individuals who run campaigns of various kinds, undertake voluntary activity in different types of organization, and, at the high end of the scale, stand for elective office literally run the system. Indeed democratic politics is impossible without them. Thus if explaining political participation is a core issue in political science, then explaining high-intensity participation is arguably the most important concern in this core area.

One of the key features of high-intensity participation is that it takes place both in orthodox institutions—such as interest groups, charities, political parties, and state institutions such as local authorities—and in unorthodox institutions—such as environmental protest groups, new social movements, and utopian communities. These are quite diverse forms, but their common thread is that they involve organizations. These may not be the classic bureaucracies of Weberian theory, but to varying degrees they involve shared values, a collective memory, mechanisms for the socialization of new recruits, mechanisms for enforcing decisions, and, to varying degrees, longevity.

High-intensity participation is impossible without institutions, since individuals acting alone cannot change state policies. To effect this change actors need an institutional framework within which collective action can be organized. Creating the cooperative behavior that under-pins collective action requires actors to have a stable set of expectations about each other, and this can only be fostered in institutions.

The institutions that provide the framework for collective action in this study are political parties. Political parties are the most important nonstate institutions in democratic politics, since, unlike other types of organizations such as interest groups, they aim to capture control of the state by running candidates for elective office. For this reason parties are one of the best vehicles for studying high-intensity participation.

If parties are important for democratic politics in general, they are par-ticularly important for the British system, with its uncodified constitution and executive dominance of the legislature. However, it is often forgotten that the Westminster system relies on strong political parties, without which executive dominance would be impossible. The party system is strong because two conditions are met. First, the parties really matter to voters, with partisanship being a strong force in electoral politics. Second, parties themselves are strong, having an active organizational base, ade-quate funds, and a professional structure that keeps them in existence between elections and that performs the key tasks of campaigning, orga-nizing, and recruiting. If electoral partisanship were to weaken greatly and the party organizations were to wither and die, the Westminster system would collapse.

This might seem like a strong conclusion, but it is supported by work in the social choice literature. If the issue spaces in a society are multidimensional and there is no partisanship with which to anchor voters, then social choice processes become chaotic (McKelvey 1976; Schofield 1978). This means that no party will be able to capture a stable majority of the electorate, since it can always be outflanked by rivals maneuvering along a new issue dimension.

These of course are abstract results in social choice, but they have concrete relevance to the British case. Party loyalty underpins stable government, and this is ultimately enforced by party members and the electorate. If Members of Parliament (MPs) were as loosely attached to their parties as U.S. congressmen are to their own, then the U.K. executive could never develop coherent programs or govern effectively. The final sanction used by governments to whip dissident MPs into line is the fear of deselection by their local parties and the resulting loss of their seats arising from the fact that the electorate will not support independents. In the absence of partisanship in the electorate and effective local party organizations, this ultimate sanction would not work.

In Britain, as in most advanced industrial democracies, it is possible to join a political party by paying an annual membership fee and agreeing to certain rather general principles espoused by the party.[1] Party members vary in their involvement from people who pay their subscriptions and do little else to those who are full-time politicians at the local or national levels. Members at the lower end of the participation scale are very similar to voters in terms of the amount of time they devote to politics. However, at the high end of the scale party members are very different from voters, and it is this type of high-intensity participation that is the focus of this study.

The key question to be addressed in this book is, Why are some individuals high-intensity participants while others are not? Thus most of our effort is spent on trying to explain individual-level behavior within an institutional context. Since understanding the institutional context is vital for explaining high-intensity participation, we begin by examining the British party system. This examination, which is the main focus of the rest of chapter 1, provides the reader with the necessary background for understanding the context in which such participation takes place.

Political participation can only be understood in terms of a theoretical model that explains why some people get involved in politics while others do not. In chapter 2 we review the main alternative theoretical models that have been used to try to explain political participation in the literature, evaluating the strengths and weaknesses of each perspective. This leads to a discussion in chapter 3 of how high-intensity participation might be measured and how we should go about testing which of these rival models provides the best explanation of such participation. The aim here is to determine which theory, or combination of theories, provides the best explanation of both low-intensity and high-intensity participation. Chapter 3 uses cross-section surveys of Labour and Conservative party members in Britain to test these alternatives within a static framework.

Chapter 4 extends the analysis of chapter 3 from that of a static cross-sectional perspective to that of a dynamic perspective using panel analysis. As is well known, panel surveys make it possible to investigate the causal dynamics of models with much greater validity than is possible in a cross-section analysis. The analysis in this chapter is focused on identifying an optimal model of high-intensity participation, that is, a model that provides the best explanation of this type of participation.

The evidence in chapter 4 also suggests that high-intensity participation is declining in the British party system. Having developed a model for explaining the dynamics of high-intensity participation, chapter 5 addresses the question of whether the decline can be reversed. The focus in this chapter is on the Labour party, which achieved a remarkable turnaround in its fortunes in the period 1994 to 1997 by reversing a long-term trend decline in membership. The issue examined in chapter 5 is whether this reversal of the decline in membership also implied a reversal of the decline in high-intensity participation.

Chapter 6 continues the theme of declining participation to address the question of why participation fails. This is particularly important given the evidence in chapter 4 that such participation appears to be in decline in the grass roots party organizations. The key issue is to examine whether the model that explains high-intensity participation can be reversed and used to explain why some people give up party politics altogether and drop out.

Chapter 7 changes the focus again, this time from party members to voters. The aim of this chapter is to investigate the extent to which the optimal model examined earlier can be adapted to explain low-intensity partisanship in the form of voting. In other words, we move away from high-intensity participation to examine the dynamics of voting behavior and partisanship over time. Since the evidence in chapter 2 suggests that low-intensity and high-intensity participation within a political party can be explained by rather similar models, the aim of chapter 7 is to see whether an adapted version of the model can explain voting behavior outside the institutional setting of the political party.

The final chapter examines the implications of these findings for the study of political participation in political science and also for the party system in general and the British party system in particular. As well as speculating about high-intensity participation in the future, this chapter examines some of the implications of the theoretical findings for the Westminster model of parliamentary government. We have suggested that high-intensity participation takes place only within an institutional context; in the rest of this chapter we examine the role of political parties in Britain in order to furnish the institutional context for the study.

The Importance of Parties in Britain

With the emergence of mass, electoral politics in Britain at the end of the nineteenth century, the political party came to be regarded, almost universally, as one of the fundamental institutional features of representative democracy. Parties became the primary means by which opinions were structured into some form of coherent political program that would both guide government and enable the ruled to hold the rulers to account. Arguments might have prevailed at times since then over particular features of the party system—for example, the respective roles of party leaders and party activists in determining party policies (McKenzie 1955; Minkin 1978)—but there was no question of the extensive public support, at both the mass and elite levels, for the party as a significant institution in the political system.

Twenty-five years ago a committee of inquiry established by the British government to examine financial aid to political parties, the Houghton Committee, provided survey evidence of strong public support for parties. In a representative, national survey of the electorate carried out for the committee, 86 percent of respondents agreed that parties "are essential to our form of national government"; 84 percent agreed that "in general, the parties are a good thing for Britain"; and 65 percent agreed that "they are the only way to represent the public's views" (HMSO 1976: 232–33). In its report, the committee concluded that "the existence of political parties is an essential feature of our system of parliamentary democracy" (19) and outlined various reasons why it believed that parties were essential. These reasons provide a useful summary of the functions of parties as they have operated in twentieth-century Britain.

First, the committee stated that parties are "the agencies through which the electorate can express its collective will" (18). The committee did not elaborate further upon this, nor on any other of its statements, but clearly what its members had in mind was that parties provided the electorate with alternative policy choices at elections.

Second, the committee argued that parties perform an aggregative role in society. Parties, it stated, provide "the framework within which differing political views can be formulated, debated and translated into practical political programmes, and the many demands and efforts of smaller groups in society can be aggregated and merged into a small number of workable alternative political programmes" (18). In other words, diverse political demands are aggregated by parties into broad political programs that form the basis of legislative behavior. The third point, which follows from this, is that parties provide "the essential basis for stable government in an elected Parliament" (18). Thus, policy outcomes are more predictable because parties oblige individual legislators to take political responsibility for their actions, whether popular or unpopular.

Without parties to enforce loyalty, individual legislators are more likely to seek benefits and avoid costs in their legislative actions, thereby avoiding difficult political decisions and increasing the likelihood of political gridlock. Hence, the weakness of party in the United States makes governing more difficult because members of both Houses of Congress lack the organizational means of sharing the costs as well as the benefits of government (see Arnold 1990).

Fourth, parties provide the means for "selecting and nominating candidates for election to Parliament" (HMSO 1976: 18) and "an orderly framework within which political leaders can emerge, develop, and strive for political office" (18). Parties, therefore, provide a forum in which candidates for public office can be sifted and assessed, and this process continues as would-be leaders make their way up the parties' organizational hierarchy. Furthermore, would-be leaders develop the arts of bargaining and compromise, both necessary aspects of leadership in liberal democracies. So, parties are arenas for political learning.

Fifth, parties are "the means whereby members of the general public are able to participate in the formulation of policies," and, finally, parties perform an educative role "to promote and maintain political awareness within society at all levels" (18).

In addition to these six reasons advanced by members of the committee in support of parties, we could add another, namely, that parties help organize disappointment. Defeat in an election or on policy issues is a frequent phenomenon in political life, and a party helps people of similar views to adapt, reorganize, and restructure collectively in the face of such adversity.

Twenty-five years after the Houghton Committee report it is unlikely that a similar committee of inquiry would write such a powerful and positive report on parties.[2] Recently parties in Britain have received a bad press. They have been linked with corruption, with the abuse of patronage, and with the initiation of policies for purely factional advantage. There has been extensive press coverage of illegal activities in local government and of cronyism in appointments to quasi-nongovernmental organizations (or quangos) and in the awarding of political honors, all cases in which parties have inappropriately exploited their powers. There have been numerous stories of financial irregularities in party funding, eventually leading to the establishment of the Committee on Standards in Public Life to examine the whole issue.

Disillusion with parties has developed within the political elite. For example, it was reported that the participants to the 1993 Anglo-German Koenigswinter conference, an annual meeting of a section of both countries' political elites, acknowledged that their parties "had run out of ideas, alienated public opinion, [and] were in need of new inspiration and leaders" (Guardian, March 20, 1993). In May 1993 the British Broadcasting Corporation (BBC) broadcast a radio program, "When the Party's Over," in which many of the contributors criticized parties; again in November 1993 it broadcast a television program in which a prominent journalist, Martin Jacques, asserted that parties were outdated and an outmoded means of political expression. Oxford academic Vernon Bogdanor, a critic of the modern form of parties, wrote an article in the Times arguing that the mass party was now outdated (Times, September 27, 1993). Finally, Mulgan (1994) claimed that parties were outdated institutions, more appropriate for the nineteenth century than for the twenty-first century.

Whether these doubts among parts of the British political elite regarding the performance of parties are shared by a wider public is debatable. The Houghton Committee's specific survey questions, referred to earlier, have not been repeated, thus certain indirect measures—such as party identification, voter turnout at general elections, and party member-

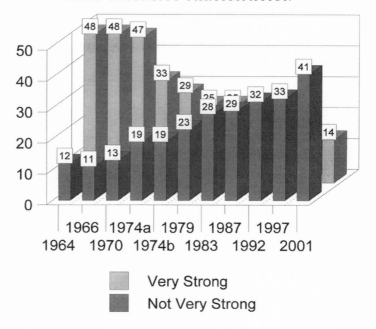

Fig. 1.1.   Trends in the strength of party identification in Britain, 1964–2001.
(Data from British Election Study Surveys.)

ship—have been used by academics attempting to assess the mass public's
views of parties (Webb 1995). The evidence from these alternative measures, however, is somewhat mixed.

Data from the British Election Studies show that over the past thirty
years the majority of people still identify with a political party, but, as
figure 1.1 reveals, the intensity of this identification has declined. The
number of respondents with a very strong attachment to a party has
declined from 48 percent in 1964 to 14 percent in 2001, and those with a
not very strong attachment has grown from 12 percent in 1964 to 39 percent in 2001. There is, however, a debate on the validity of the party
identification measure, focusing on the extent to which it measures public attitudes about a specific party's policies and leadership at a particular
moment of time rather than about parties in general (Brynin and Sanders
1997; Bartle 1999). Hence, this evidence must be interpreted with care.

Since 1945 electoral turnout has fluctuated from a high of 84 percent
in 1951 to a low of 59 percent in 2001, and as is clear from figure 1.2 a

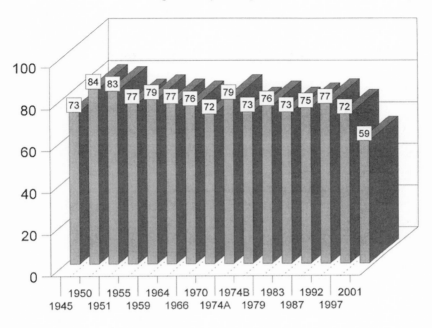

Fig. 1.2. Electoral turnout in general elections, 1945–2001

downward trend is apparent in this baseline measure of political participation. To some extent turnout figures are a reflection of the efficiency
and accuracy of the voter registration process.[3] As a consequence, the
month of the year in which a general election is called will affect the
turnout figure.

Finally, individual membership of both Conservative and Labour parties has declined since the late 1940s and early 1950s, when they both had
large memberships. At that time, membership record keeping was the
responsibility of constituency officers, most of whom were volunteers and
amateurs, which leads one to doubt the accuracy of the numbers published. Only with the introduction of national membership records by the
Labour party in the late 1980s, by the Liberal Democrats from their formation in 1988, and by the Conservative party in the late 1990s can one
feel more confident of their greater accuracy. Notwithstanding that point,
there is a trend decline in both parties' membership, which can be
observed in table 1.1.

The trends in table 1.1 are relatively clear. However, that between 1994 and 1997 the Labour party significantly increased its individual membership suggests that decline is not some inevitable feature of modern society and politics but can be influenced by a party's own recruitment strategies. For much of the postwar period both the Labour and Conservative leaderships displayed only limited interest in their membership. Only after its 1983 election defeat did the Labour party begin to give a higher priority to membership recruitment; but it was under Tony Blair that a more active mobilization-recruitment strategy was initiated. This will be discussed more fully in chapter 5.

Party identification, electoral turnout, and party membership have often been used by those suggesting that parties in Britain are in decline as surrogates for any more specific questions on the public's attitudes about parties per se. We believe, however, for the various reasons given earlier that this evidence is both too limited and too vague. Of greater value is the specific question on the public's attitude about parties asked in the 1997 British Election Study, which asked respondents to grade their feelings on a five-point scale about whether they regarded parties as necessary to make the political system work. We see in table 1.2 that some 76 percent of respondents in the election study were strongly supportive of parties (i.e., graded one or two) and only 5 percent were critical of parties (i.e., graded four or five) (British Election Study 1997). This evidence suggests that mass-level support for parties remains high. We conclude therefore that, although parties should not be complacent about

TABLE 1.1   Trends in Individual Membership of the Labour, Conservative, and Liberals/Liberal Democrat Parties

Year	Labour	Conservatives	Liberals/Liberal Democrats[a]
1953	1,005,000	2,805,000	—
1960	790,192	1,750,000	243,000
1974	691,889	1,500,000	190,000
1983	295,344	1,200,000	145,258
1992	279,530	500,000	100,000
1998	387,776	204,000[b]	—

Source: Labour = Labour Party National Executive Reports; Conservative Party and Liberals/Liberal Democrats = Katz and Mair 1992: 847; Webb 1994: 113; Butler and Butler 1994: 132; Webb and Farrell 1999: 48.

[a]Note that the Liberal Party became the Liberal Democrats in 1988.

[b]The 1998 figure for the Conservatives is based on the numbers participating in the ballot on the party's European strategy.

TABLE 1.2. Public Attitudes toward Parties in 1997

"Some people say that political parties are necessary to make our political system work in Britain. Others say that political parties are not needed in Britain. Using this scale where would you place yourself?"

Parties are . . .		
Necessary	1	43%
	2	33%
	3	18%
	4	3%
Not necessary	5	2%
Don't know/No response		1%

Source: British Election Study 1997.

the public's support for them as institutions and although that support may have diminished over time, they are still recognized as important features of democracy. To that extent parties retain their tenacious hold on political life at both elite and mass levels in Britain.

In 1950 a group of American political scientists produced a report, "Toward a More Responsible Two-Party System" (APSA 1950), in which they argued the need to replace the prevailing American party system—which they described as "two loose associations of state and local organizations with very little national machinery and very little national cohesion" (25)—with a "responsible party" (22) system. They defined "responsible parties" using various criteria. In their view responsible parties are cohesive organizations with national programs "drafted at frequent intervals by a broadly representative convention" (10); a "more program-conscious" (70) national party membership "in which individuals support this program rather than personalities, patronage and local matters" (10); "strong and active campaigning organizations in the constituencies" (21–22); and a "permanent, professional staff" (50). The type of responsible party the APSA committee had in mind was based upon the British, Canadian, and Australian party systems.[4]

Fifty years after the publication of the APSA report it is interesting to examine whether the responsible party model still applies to Britain. The committee examined five key features of this model: programmatic goals, party membership, internal party democracy, party activism, and the professional party bureaucracy. To evaluate British parties in the light of these characteristics a number of different questions must be addressed: First, are the parties still programmatic in the sense of setting out a clearly defined set of policy alternatives that the electorate can choose between? Second, do they recruit program-conscious members who democratically participate in the formulation of the party programs? Third, do parties have strong and active constituency organizations that support the national structure and ultimately enforce party cohesion? Finally, do their professional bureaucracies provide an institutional memory and sustain the wider organization?

The literature on party organization emerging since the APSA report tends to contradict the responsible party model. The "catch-all" party model stresses the importance of electoral success, which is sought at the expense of programmatic coherence (Kirchheimer 1966). The "cartel" party thesis argues that parties are increasingly becoming agencies of the state, suggesting that parties are no longer autonomous (Katz and Mair 1995). Finally, the "electoral-professional" model with its emphasis on centralized control by the leadership appears inconsistent with internal party democracy (Panebianco 1988). Are these models more appropriate descriptions of the British party system in the twenty-first century than is the responsible party model? Since at the time of the APSA report the Conservative and Labour parties dominated party politics, we intend to concentrate on these two parties in our response to the questions just mentioned, but some references to the Liberal Democrats will be made where appropriate.[5] We examine each of the criteria in the APSA report in turn.

Parties and Programmatic Goals

There are two senses of the term "programmatic goals," one very general and the other more specific. The first refers to party representation of the cleavage between capital and labor, owners and workers. This interpretation is best exemplified by Samuel Beer (1965) in his study of the party system, *Modern British Politics*, in which he argues that the emergence of a "collectivist politics" in the twentieth century produced Tory and Socialist democracy. Beer claims that "party has distilled the interests and aspirations of a class into a comprehensive social philosophy" (87) and that "the voter has a choice of two coherent and distinctive programs" (88). Both party programs and voters' loyalties reflected the dominant role of class in British politics. However, one must be careful not to exaggerate this form of programmatic cleavage in Britain, because without working-class electoral support the twentieth century would not have been the "Conservative century" (Seldon and Ball 1994). Furthermore, socioeconomic changes from the 1950s onward have rendered this interpretation increasingly redundant, as parties' programs and electoral appeals have developed beyond their traditional cleavages.

It was this development in Britain and in other industrialized European states that prompted Kirchheimer (1966: 184) to argue that "mass-integration" parties, such as the Labour party, were becoming "catch-all" parties. He argued that, whereas mass-integration parties had previously limited their electoral appeal to specific sections of the population, catch-all parties were adopting broader societal goals that transcended the interests of one particular class. In addition, Kirchheimer suggested that in this new type of party the powers of the leadership were being strengthened while those of the individual members were being downgraded.

The problem with Kircheimer's argument regarding parties' electoral appeal is that neither Conservative nor Labour parties ever appealed solely to one specific, class-based section of the population. We have already made the point that the Conservative party always required working-class supporters to win elections, the "angels in marble" as they were described by McKenzie and Silver (1968: 74). Similarly, the Labour party's electoral strategy from 1918 onward avoided appealing solely to one particular class; it aimed to win the support of all workers "by hand or by brain" (Cole: 18).

The second use of the term "programmatic goals" refers to parties' specific policy commitments, the most significant of which are contained within their election manifestos. Manifestos constitute "an authoritative statement of the policy concerns of the collective leaders of the parties and that defines and guides the presentation of issues in the media, through which party priorities get to the electorate" (Klingemann, Hofferbert, and Budge 1994: 26). Manifestos are used by parties to send messages to the voters and also to the government machine.

In recent elections manifestos have grown considerably in size (Topf 1994: 153). However, some claim that they now put more emphasis on glossy images and, as a consequence, have become more bland. Furthermore, the manifesto pledges are ambiguous, often involving political fudges, and there is little relationship between manifestos and election campaigns (Weir and Beetham 1999: 100–110).

Parties clearly avoid taking too precise a position in their manifestos on some issues; nevertheless, the emphasis parties place upon issues varies, and this indicates their relative priorities. Klingemann and his colleagues argue that their research on election manifestos between 1945 and 1987 confirms that parties adhere to a distinct and consistent left-right agenda, concluding that they "find support for the seemingly naive claim that what was written in these documents *before* elections was a good aid to predicting the actions of governments *after* the elections" (Klingemann, Hofferbert, and Budge 1994: 20).

Twelve months after the Labour party's 1997 general election victory, the government published an annual report listing its legislative achievements, and it included the following statement: "This list summarizes the current state of progress on each of the 177 manifesto commitments up to 1 May 1998. Of these, 50 have already been kept or done, 119 are under way and on course, and only 8 have yet to be timetabled" (TSO 1998b: 96). This statement demonstrates the importance that the contemporary Labour party attaches to its election manifesto. The manifesto is regarded as the party's contract with the voters to deliver on its promises and, as such, is used as a means to overcome bureaucratic inertia or intraparty opposition. When Peter Mandelson stated, after the Labour party's 1997 general election victory, that "Labour Members of Parliament have been elected to carry out the manifesto for which we have received an overwhelming mandate from the public" (*Guardian*, May 17, 1997), he was suggesting that Labour MPs had contractual obligations to support the government in its implementation strategy.

Labour is no different in this regard from its major party rival. The Conservative party's origins as a nineteenth-century elite, cadre organization meant that its parliamentarians found the idea of election manifestos, and the accompanying concept of public mandate, an alien form of politics. Nevertheless, the twentieth-century history of the Conservative party is one of adaptation to modern political behavior in order to maintain its electoral hegemony. Election manifestos have been an important aspect of its appeal for popular support. Until 1945 these were issued as personal appeals from the party leader, but after 1950 they were issued in the name of the party.

Clearly parties shift in their programmatic commitments. For much of the 1980s the Conservative and Labour parties contradicted the Downsian (1957) model as they abandoned two-party consensus and developed very distinctive and polarized positions. Norris writes, "One of the most striking trends in British politics is how the major parties were sharply polarised during the early 1980s on classic economic and social issues, such as public ownership versus privatisation, unilateralism versus multi-lateralism, and Britain's role within and outside Europe" (1993: 1). The Conservative party's four consecutive electoral successes between 1979 and 1992 forced the Labour party into a steady modification of the program that it had adopted in the early 1980s. After 1983 the Labour party first shifted away from public ownership and then, much more comprehensively, replaced its collectivist commitments with a liberal political economy such that, by the time it fought the 1997 general election, it had abandoned its traditional social democratic attachment to redistribution by means of taxation and public expenditure. At that general election, both major parties occupied a similar political terrain in which they were committed to private enterprise, market principles, and consumer choice. Nevertheless, a careful examination of the parties' 1997 election manifestos (Budge 1999) reveals significant differences along the left-right spectrum between Labour and Conservative parties. What is also revealed is that the Liberal Democrats, for the first time in over thirty years, were no longer positioned between Labour and Conservative parties but were to the left of the Labour party. The point is, however, that although political choices may have been limited for electors the parties remained programmatic rather than pragmatic and catch-all, albeit with a different set of commitments than in the previous decades.

One further point regarding the programmatic nature of British parties is that modification or adaptation of party programs does not happen solely as a result of a leader's sudden shift of opinion. For example, it took Neil Kinnock and his leadership team a considerable time to shift the Labour party away from some of the electorally unpopular policies it had adopted in 1983 (Hughes and Wintour 1990). It was Kinnock's long-term reforms that provided the base from which Blair's reforms between 1994 and 1997 could proceed. Similarly, with the Conservative party, although Margaret Thatcher became leader in 1975, her party only gradually moved toward her distinctive beliefs (Gamble 1994).

A consequence of the programmatic nature of British parties, and of the fusion of executive and legislative powers, has been the disciplined voting behavior of MPs. Their election to the House of Commons as party representatives, and thus as standard-bearers for a party program, has obliged them to sustain or oppose the executive's actions according to whether they are on the government or opposition back benches. Cohesive voting behavior of MPs along party lines has been a prominent feature of the twentieth-century legislature (Norton 1975, 1980). However, that disciplined voting has been declining as a consequence of various factors, including the styles and capabilities of party leadership, the impact of the issue of British membership in the European Union (EU), and the social and cultural changes occurring among parliamentarians and party activists (Norton 1980). Nevertheless, disciplined party voting remains a significant feature of the responsible British party system as compared with the weaker American party system.

We now turn to a second feature of the responsible party model—membership.

Party Membership

It might be thought that the APSA committee's attachment to the importance of a participatory, programmatic party membership is outdated. Parties appear to be less interested in recruitment, and some academic research has argued that members are increasingly irrelevant. For example, Mair has suggested that "the party on the ground . . . is becoming less important or . . . is in decline" (1997: 124).

We noted earlier that since the early 1950s party membership has declined. During the 1950s and 1960s Conservative and Labour leaders showed little concern over this trend. Periodic recruitment campaigns initiated from the 1960s onward were more symbolic than real, essentially because both leaderships were largely convinced of the unimportance of members. The development of a new communications technology, television and advertising in particular, meant that, as long as parties could obtain the money for election campaigning, they did not feel the need for human resources. Members were regarded as a less efficient means of communicating with voters than was the television "fireside chat" or the mass advertising campaign. This attitude was strongly influenced by an academic consensus that members were unimportant in influencing electoral outcomes (Butler and King 1966; Epstein 1967; Butler and Kavanagh 1988).

However, after almost forty years of relative party indifference to members, a transformation in attitude has occurred in which both Labour and Conservative party leaderships have openly and publicly committed themselves to the expansion of membership as an important feature of their political strategies. Labour declared a target of half a million members by 2001 (Labour Party 1998), and, similarly, the Conservative's target was one million members by "the Millenium" (Conservative Party

1997: 26). However, after the Labour party expanded membership from 305,000 in 1994 to 405,000 in 1997, recruitment stalled after the 1997 election.[6] It is noticeable, though, that Prime Minister Blair has constantly emphasized the importance of members as part of his long-term governing project (see, for example, *Guardian*, May 1, 1998). Similarly, the Conservative party, after a disastrous hemorrhaging of its membership during the 1990s, attempted to reproduce Labour's recruitment successes. That it did not achieve the ambitious goals for recruitment of new members does not detract from the higher priority attached to this effort in comparison with the past.

The reasons for this switch to a determined membership recruitment strategy are fourfold. First, the electoral benefits of an active membership became more apparent in the 1990s. Research has revealed that locally active members who engage in contacting voters through delivering leaflets and canvassing and who participate in mounting election-day organization to ensure voter turnout produce highly significant effects on constituency outcomes in general elections (Denver and Hands 1997; Johnston and Pattie 1997; Seyd and Whiteley 1992; Whiteley, Seyd, and Richardson 1994). The Labour party took note of the claims that an active membership brought beneficial electoral consequences.[7]

The best example of the electoral benefits of an active membership occurred in the 1997 general election, when the Liberal Democrats more than doubled their number of MPs in the House of Commons while at the same time their share of the national vote declined. This was largely due to targeted, local campaigns in which its local activists played a significant role (Whiteley and Seyd 1999).

Second, members enhance a party's political legitimacy. A large and increasing membership suggests popular support. Recruitment of new members became a major feature of Blair's leadership, enabling him to claim that Labour spoke for a broad community of people, in contrast to the Conservative party's diminishing and narrow constituency. One of the reasons for the former Conservative leader William Hague's wanting to recruit new Conservative members was to provide him and his party with a source of political legitimacy. It was a means by which he could demonstrate that his personal qualities of leadership were attractive, and it enabled him to claim that the Conservative party was attracting a broader and more representative level of support. Similarly, the reemergence of the Liberal Democrats as a significant force in British politics has been closely identified with its claim to have strong links in local communities.

Third, all parties are now keen to demonstrate their democratic credentials by extending membership participation into party decision making. New structures and procedures have been created to enable members to play a significant role in intraparty affairs. In such circumstances new members are an added attraction if they are more inclined to support the leadership than existing members and activists. Labour's experience between 1979 and 1983, when the party had come under the powerful influence of left activists, and subsequently came very close to electoral collapse, played an important part in Kinnock's, and then John Smith's, commitment to membership recruitment. Their introduction, and subsequent development, of one-member, one-vote procedures emphasized the important role of individual members in reducing the collective role of the trade unions and also in weakening activists' powers. Blair's use of ballots of all individual members on some policy issues is based upon his belief that the inactive members are more likely to support his objectives.

Finally, members are an important source of party funding. An essential feature of the British party system has been its voluntaristic nature, one consequence of which has been that parties have received only limited state aid and have been reliant for the bulk of their income upon donations from corporate bodies, such as companies and trade unions, as well as individuals. The corporate sector has provided the overwhelming proportion of Conservative and Labour party income. However, recent controversies regarding the funding of both parties, and possible corrupt practices, have raised some public concern.

In response to these concerns the government set up the Neill Committee (TSO 1998a) to examine party funding that proposed a greater degree of transparency in party finances, such that from the year 2000 all donations to parties of over five thousand pounds at the national and one thousand pounds at the local level must be publicly declared. Another response by both Conservative and Labour parties has been to place a greater emphasis upon the role of their members as subscribers and fundraisers, as the Liberal Democrats have been forced to do out of necessity.[8] The ever-rising expense of maintaining the day-to-day activities of a party and the need to mount sophisticated and costly election campaigns require large sums of money, and members as either donors or fund-raisers have assumed a greater significance.

From 1988 onward the Labour party devoted considerable resources to broaden its income base by developing fund-raising efforts, membership initiatives, and financial services. In 1997 its National Executive Committee reported that the party had raised £1.6 million by individual donations in 1991, rising to £2.0 million in 1992, and to £10.0 million in 1997 (Labour Party 1997).[9] One of the consequences was to reduce the party's dependence upon trade union funding. Whereas, in 1978, 86 percent of the party's gross income had come from trade union affiliation fees, by 1991 the figure had been reduced to 50 percent (HMSO 1993: 87) and to 30 percent by 1997 (TSO 1998a: 32). The party's deputy general secretary claimed in evidence to the Neill Committee that "40 per cent of the party's funding was made up of small donations" and that "some 70,000 members pay a monthly subscription [i.e., a donation]" and "a further 500,000 people make a donation each year" (TSO 1998a: 32). The party's individual members have become an important source of income, as they provide contributions over and above their membership subscriptions.

The Conservative party seemingly has been less dependent upon its members for raising money. However, it is hard to estimate this precisely since the party has not been obliged to publish financial accounts and it has been unwilling to divulge much financial information, even to its own members. Membership subscriptions until 1999 were paid to local Conservative associations rather than to national party headquarters. However, a quota scheme, established in 1948, requires constituency associations to provide funds to central party headquarters, calculated on the basis of the Conservative share of the vote in each constituency. What is clear is that the amount of money raised by local parties and then channeled through to headquarters by means of this quota scheme declined in the 1990s (Pattie and Johnston 1996). In part, this was the consequence of a declining membership (Whiteley, Seyd, and Richardson 1994), but it was also a means by which local associations could show their political displeasure with the party leadership.

In the 1990s the Conservative party's financial problems were acute. Its income and expenditure accounts for the year ended March 1995 revealed liabilities of £19 million, and of these, £11 million was accounted for by a bank overdraft. Its need, therefore, of substantial donations from its supporters was considerable. It transpired that some of its most substantial donors came from overseas. Between 1992 and 1997 the party accepted forty-seven overseas donations worth a total of £16.2 million (TSO 1998a: 33). Nevertheless, the chairman of the Conservative party, Norman Fowler, claimed in evidence given to a House of Commons select committee that the party had raised £26 million in 1992–93, of which £18 million had been raised in the constituencies (HMSO 1993: 51). What was unclear from Fowler's statement was how much of the money was raised by local members. But it has become clear that local associations are important in providing the national party with interest-free loans. While the total sum is not known, the Neill Committee records a loan figure of £3 million, with £1.2 million being provided by local associations in 1997 (TSO 1998a: 33). Thus even a party that in government was able to attract large corporate donations has revealed its need for members' subscriptions and fund-raising income.

So far we have demonstrated the importance that both party leader-ships attach to their members. In this sense these parties continue to fulfill one of the essential requirements of the responsible party model. But the APSA committee went further by stressing the importance of "a program-conscious party membership" to ensure that the influence of personality, patronage, and locality was reduced. Do the parties recruit members com-mitted to distinct principles? And do their principles change over time? Are there differences between inactive and active and newly recruited and long-standing members? Many of these questions will be answered in later chapters, but here we will deal with whether members are in fact program-conscious.

Our research reveals that Labour, Conservative, and Liberal Democrat members hold distinct opinions and that underlying these are distinctive ideological principles. In 1992 we wrote that Labour members "are criti-cal of the market economy, and prefer more public intervention and the public provision of services; they believe that the bargaining rights of trade unions should be maintained; and, finally, they dislike Britain's pos-session of nuclear weapons, and want to cut overall spending on defence" (Seyd and Whiteley 1992: 118). Furthermore, Labour members' attitudes are significantly structured around four underlying dimensions—a general left-right dimension, a redistribution dimension, a dimension concerned with political principles, and, finally, one concerned with internal and external democratic reforms (120–24).

Conservative members hold a variety of opinions that do not divide precisely into neatly defined categories, but there are three underlying dimensions to their attitudes. First, there is a traditionalism dimension, which is wary of social and political change; second, an individualistic dimension, characterized by a preference for the market provision of col-lective goods; and, third, progressivism, in which government accepts responsibility for managing the economy and alleviating poverty (White-ley, Seyd, and Richardson 1994: 132–42).

Among Liberal Democrat members there is a modest amount of attitude structuring around four underlying, ideological indicators (Seyd and Whiteley 1999). Lifestyle and economic libertarianism are two such factors; the first links attitudes on a wide range of personal issues, such as sexuality, abortion, drugs, and censorship, and the second revolves around limited state intervention in economic and social affairs. Interestingly, the two are not closely correlated, such that support for freedom of the individual on lifestyle issues does not imply support for free-market solutions to economic and social problems. The third element, in contrast to the second, reflects a social democratic commitment to redistribution, expressed in terms of governments raising the level of taxes and spending more money on such public services as health and education. Finally, there is a distinct European element to Liberal Democrats' opinions, articulated in support of various aspects of further EU integration.

We conclude this examination of the second feature of the APSA's report on parties, dealing specifically with membership, by suggesting that individual members remain a vitally important aspect of the British party system.

A third feature of the APSA report was the committee's commitment to internal party democracy. It recommended that the party program "be drafted at frequent intervals by a broadly representative convention," that local party groups should "meet frequently to discuss and initiate policy," and that leaders should maintain contacts with their members. The committee's commitment was to the principle of a bottom-up party in policy-making. To what extent does this prevail?

Internal Party Democracy

Five years after the publication of the APSA report McKenzie (1955) concluded his comprehensive study of power within the Conservative and Labour parties with the argument that "the distribution of power within the two parties is overwhelmingly similar" (582) and that although neither leadership could afford to ignore its members both were primarily "the servants of their respective parliamentary parties" (590). In this view the claims by both parties that internal party democracy prevailed were much exaggerated. The APSA committee's idea, therefore, of members initiating or drafting polices was one that McKenzie suggested neither occurred in practice nor should occur.

McKenzie's conclusions have since been challenged by Minkin (1978) and Kelly (1989), who both argue that he underestimated the role of members as policymakers within the Labour and Conservative parties respectively. Nevertheless, the powerful oligarchical tendencies to which Robert Michels (1902) first drew attention have been reinforced over recent decades both by modern campaigning technologies and by the requirements of policy-making. Both time and specialism are resources at a premium, and both can result in the strengthening of the powers of party leadership.

The proliferation of news outlets, the arrival of twenty-four-hour news stations, and the revolution in news-gathering techniques require immediate political responses that inevitably centralize party decision making and allow for only limited consultation. Flexible and speedy responses are required by party spokespersons, and the time for widespread consultations on anything but the most general aspects of policy is almost impossible. Peter Mandelson, onetime Labour party communications director, has written, "You cannot conduct the campaign through democratic debate and consensus. The judgements are too fine and too quick" (MacIntyre 1999: 135). Kavanagh (1995: 108) writes that "the centralization of decision-making in the hands of the leader and those around him and the adoption of public relations, are interconnected."

The importance of political image has grown. Image requires party unity, strong leadership, and stage management. Political marketing has resulted in the expansion of both the numbers and the influence of the professionals—political consultants, public relations advisers, pollsters, speech writers, and advertisers. Scammell notes:

> The tier of specialist communications and marketers has never been greater in British politics, never better-known and arguably never more influential. This is a trend which is unlikely to diminish, despite fluctuations according to the personal taste of party leaders and managers. The consequences appear more far-reaching for Labour than for the Conservatives. The need for clear goals and the demands of disciplined communications imply a stronger leadership grip over the party as a whole and a diminution of the role of party conference. (1995: 19)

There is also an increased premium on specialist knowledge necessary to deal with policy matters. The complexity of policy means a greater reliance upon professionals, whether from the civil service or the think tanks, rather than upon "amateur" members (Denham 1996; Kandiah and Seldon 1996).

Both Labour and Conservative parties have introduced specific party reforms, which may either strengthen or weaken the powers of their leaders. Perhaps the most significant of these reforms has been the introduction of membership ballots to elect the leaders, a procedure that the Liberal Democrats adopted in 1988. The parties have also introduced leadership-initiated plebiscites on policy proposals and constitutional reforms. For the Labour party this has meant the abandonment of its century-long attachment to delegatory democracy and for the Conservative party an explicit and formal recognition of the role of members within the party. Critics of both the Blair and Hague leaderships argue that these ballots, by empowering all members rather than just activists, strengthen the power of the leaders (e.g., Coates and Kerr 1998; Charter News 1998).

Mair supports these critics and claims that the empowerment of individual members bypasses the knowledgeable activists and enfranchises those who "are at once more docile and more likely to endorse the policies (and candidates) proposed by the party leadership" (1997: 149). He suggests that "democratization on paper may . . . actually coexist with powerful elite influence in practice" (150).

The evidence, however, of the impact of this direct democracy on the distribution of power within the parties is mixed. As the leadership desired, membership ballots in the Labour party overwhelmingly approved the reform of clause 4 of the party constitution in 1994, which dealt with the public ownership of industry, and agreed with the proposed general election manifesto in 1996. But on the other hand, notwithstanding the leadership's powerful campaign against Ken Livingstone, members in London voted overwhelmingly for him to be the party's candidate for mayor of London. They have also endorsed other leadership critics by voting for them in the elections for the National Executive Committee of the party. Furthermore, our survey evidence reveals that inactive Labour members' opinions are not that different from those of active members, and therefore they may not be automatically more supportive of the leadership, as Mair claims (see Seyd and Whiteley 1992; Whiteley, Seyd, and Richardson 1994). Hence whether these members are likely to be more docile and supportive of the leadership than the activists is doubtful.

Up to this point the Conservative party has conducted four ballots, the first confirming Hague as party leader and approving the principles of party reform in 1997, the second approving party reform in 1998, and the third approving the principle of an anti-European strategy in 1998. In these three, members supported their former leader. The fourth ballot was to elect their new leader, Iain Duncan Smith, in September 2001.[10]

In addition to the introduction of membership ballots, the Labour and Conservative parties have modified their internal procedures and practices in such a way as to affect the balance of power within their respective organizations. The Labour party's loss of four consecutive general elections encouraged an "office at any price" mentality, particularly after 1992. Part of the leadership's explanation of Labour's poor electoral record was intraparty divisions; it believed that unity at all levels was necessary, and in this objective it was supported by the majority of the party's parliamentarians and individual members as well as by most leaders of the affiliated trade unions. The leadership acquired the powers to expel members deemed to have brought the party into disrepute, to determine short lists for the selection of by-election candidates, and to appoint rather than elect the chief whip. None of this occurred without some dissent, but, by its sophisticated use of political communication techniques, the leadership was able to undermine its critics and even to restrict the number of outlets for them to express their dissenting opinions.

During the years when Labour was in opposition—first under Kinnock's leadership and then more so under Blair's—control of party policy was increasingly centered around the parliamentary party and the shadow cabinet, at the expense of the National Executive Committee. Even the collective participation of the shadow cabinet tended to diminish as, after 1994, the Tony Blair–Gordon Brown axis developed in importance.[11]

In addition, the formal role of the annual conference in policy-making has been downgraded, although it retains ultimate sovereign authority. A new structural framework has been established, as can be seen in figure 1.3, with a joint policy committee, charged with the "strategic oversight of policy development" (Labour Party 1997b: 8); a national policy forum, charged "with overseeing the development of a comprehensive policy programme from which will be drawn the manifesto for the next election" (14); and eight commissions to develop specific areas of policy.[12]

The reasons for introducing a more continuous, discursive form of policy-making were, first, that the conference as a public arena needed to be used by the newly elected Labour government more as a forum to publicize its achievements than as a place where party divisions might gain publicity and, second, that the previous policy-making process was felt to be deeply flawed. The reform document, "Partnership in Power," explicitly acknowledged this latter fact because "very few of the party's members participate in the party's policy discussions" (Labour Party 1997b: 5), and, furthermore, because "complex issues are given very little time for debate,

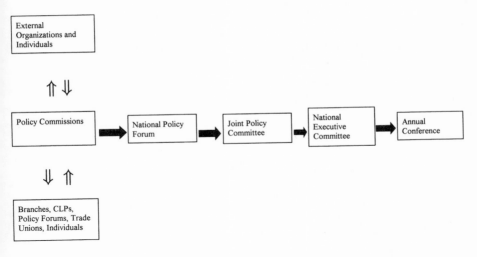

Fig. 1.3. Labour's new policy-making system

there is a tendency for Conference to have the same debates year in year out, very few delegates have the opportunity to participate directly in debates, the debates are focused around composite resolutions which delegates see for the first time on the Monday of Conference, and there is little interaction with party spokespersons" (7).

There are features of the new policy-making structures that tilt the balance of power away from the individual member, for example, the leadership's greater control of the proceedings at the annual conference. On the other hand, there is also potential for member involvement and influence in the network of local and national policy forums. Only after years of practice and the production of election manifestos will a more definitive judgment on the balance of power between leadership and members be possible.

By contrast, the Conservative party has traditionally accorded considerably more formal power to its leaders than has the Labour party (McKenzie 1955). The party's roots as a nineteenth-century cadre organization (Duverger 1954) have meant that during the 1980s and 1990s the combination of a party in government for eighteen years, a historic ethos of grass roots deference to leadership, and a structure that legally gave sole responsibility for the party and its finances to the leader resulted in the Conservative party's remaining overwhelmingly a top-down organization. A simple illustration of this point is that until 1997 it was the only British parliamentary party in which individual members were accorded no formal, direct role in the election of the leader.

But the Conservative party became increasingly divided during its eighteen-year period in office, and leadership became a more difficult task over time. To some extent the divisions were contained during Thatcher's early electoral successes, but during her period as leader, and more so after John Major succeeded her, the party became divided from top to bottom. Major's lack of authority within the party eventually forced him in 1994 into the extraordinary tactic of resigning as leader and challenging his critics to run against him, that is, to "put up or shut up." However, the leadership's lack of formal powers to discipline critics within both the parliamentary party and the extraparliamentary party made its task of maintaining party unity almost impossible (Whiteley and Seyd 1998).[13]

Less than a year after the Conservatives' comprehensive election defeat in 1997, and the subsequent election of Hague as leader, the party agreed to "a leap in the dark" as significant as Disraeli's acceptance of an expansion of the electorate in 1867 (Blake 1966). In March 1998 the party's Central Council approved the most far-reaching reforms of the twentieth century. For the first time in its history the Conservative party now exists in a constitutionally defined manner. The three previously dis-tinct elements of the party—parliamentary, national union, and central office—have now been merged. The National Union of Conservative and Unionist Associations has been abolished. For over one hundred years the party's principle organizational feature had been to allow members to select parliamentary candidates but then to isolate the parliamentary party and the party leadership from their pressures. Now, however, the new constitution specifically states that "the Party shall consist of its members" (Conservative Party 1998: 4) and that these members have been given the right to elect their party leader if and when she or he resigns or if 15 percent of the parliamentary party succeeds in a no-confidence motion.

As with the Labour party's recent reforms, Conservative reforms are too recent for a definitive judgment to be made about whether they strengthen the powers of a Conservative leader. Only close observation of the practice over the next few years will resolve this issue. Nevertheless, the formal recognition that the membership is the party, and the ceding of the right to elect the leader to these members, must shift power away from the parliamentarians to some extent. Whether this power goes to the members or to the leader is open to debate. The Conservative Charter Movement, a longtime campaigning organization for greater democracy within the party, has no doubts that the reforms will strengthen the powers of the leader. It argues that "the essence" of the reform is "absolute control from the top, unencumbered to the views of those beneath" (Charter News 1998: 1). On the other hand, there are claims that both efficiency and democracy have been strengthened by these reforms.

A fourth feature of the responsible party model, according to the APSA committee, was "strong and active campaigning organizations in the constituencies." Constituency-based organizations have been a significant part of the structure of all parties since the emergence of the mass electorate in the late nineteenth century. Parties have required human resources to fight elections, and, as a reward for their campaigning, members have been given the powers within their constituency parties to select parliamentary candidates and to send resolutions to party conferences.

Party Activism

Local parties have played a major role in sustaining the cohesion of Britain's two major parties. Leaders have depended upon the collaboration of constituency parties in imposing sanctions upon critics and rebels, in particular by refusing to re-adopt such people as the party's representatives in future elections. With few exceptions, constituency parties have performed this cohesion-sustaining role (Ranney 1965). The notable exceptions include local parties' support for some prominent Labour left rebels in the 1950s and Conservative Euro-skeptic rebels in the 1990s. What is apparent is that the autonomy of local parties is being curtailed and that the power of the parties at the center is increasing relative to the locality. Here we provide four examples of this increasing power.

First, membership recruitment used to be a local responsibility, but the establishment of a national membership by Labour in 1989 and by the Conservatives in 1998 has strengthened both parties at the center. It enables leaders to deal directly with members rather than to rely upon local intermediaries who may not be efficient or share the leaders' opinions and objectives. Furthermore, it means that membership income now comes directly to the center, part of which is then redistributed to constituencies, enabling the leadership to use the distribution of money as both a carrot and a stick in their dealings with local parties.

Local Labour parties have historically been more bound to the center by party rules compared with local Conservative associations. The historic right of local Conservative associations to manage their own affairs has made them a significant force in intraparty politics. Their ability to retain money at the local level and to conduct election campaigns as they felt appropriate caused the Conservative central office a good deal of concern. But the approval of a new constitution in 1998 that created a national membership, authorized the national collection of members' subscriptions, and introduced annual efficiency audits of all associations, with the threat of suspension and central control of those deemed to be inefficient, will transform intraparty relations. The Charter Movement claims that constituency associations will be placed under "unfriendly and draconian rule" (Charter News 1998: 3).

Second, central parties are now intervening more in the choice of by-election candidates because of the considerable media interest in the campaigns and their outcomes. Some recent local by-election disasters have persuaded party leaders of the need to ensure that their message will be well and efficiently communicated.[14] In 1988 Labour's National Executive Committee assumed the powers to draw up the short list of candidates for selection by the local party in by-elections and thus to exclude any possible problem candidates. In 1990 its powers were further increased with a rule change that enabled it, in the event of a by-election, to depose an already selected candidate it judged unsuitable and to impose a new one. Similar such powers have now been acquired by the Conservative leadership.

As we have already noted, the selection of parliamentary candidates has always been the most significant reward for local members. Their powers of selection, however, have always been to some extent limited by the center's establishing some parameters to their choice. The compilation by party headquarters of "an approved candidates list" and the power of final endorsement have given the centers some control over this locally exercised power. Labour has used these powers more extensively than have the Conservatives to determine the outcome of some selections. For example, prominent left-wing candidates were not endorsed prior to both the 1992 and 1997 general elections.[15] Critics of the current Blair leadership argue that it has increased its control over candidate selection in two ways: first, by establishing a system whereby the chief whip reports to local parties on the behavior of all Labour MPs during the lifetime of a Parliament; and, second, by establishing panels of approved personnel from whom local parties can choose their candidates for the Scottish and Welsh devolved assembly elections in 1999. It also refused to allow members to rank order the lists of party candidates for the elections to the European Parliament in 1999 and to allow members the sole choice of the candidate for the election of the city mayor in London.

Third, in general elections, party headquarters are now targeting potentially winnable constituencies and concentrating the bulk of their efforts in these areas (Butler and Kavanagh 1998: 210). Additional resources, such as finance, training, literature, and personnel, are provided for these constituencies, which then have to perform to centrally determined objectives. However, legal restrictions on local campaign expenditure and the limited number of professional staff at party headquarters mean that such a strategy still relies to a great extent upon local party activists.

The fourth, and final, example of the relative increase in the powers of the center at the expense of the locality is Labour's increasing intervention in Labour-controlled local authorities to curb what it perceives as left-wing extremism. The traditional autonomy of parties in local government (Gyford 1983) has been steadily eroded. Liverpool was the first local authority in which the leadership intervened to change local policies and practices by the Marxist-dominated leadership. Similar interventions have occurred in Lambeth, Islington, and Stoke. Often the leadership has accused Labour councillors of bringing the party into disrepute as the means of forcing them from office.

Professional Staff

The final feature of the APSA committee's responsible party model was the "need for permanent, professional staff" (APSA 1950: 50). As we pointed out earlier, British parties are voluntary organizations funded primarily by donations. Maintaining a professional staff is expensive, and the size of these staffs reflects the fact that for much of the postwar period the Conservative party has been the richest of the parties. Hence it employed more staff both at the center and in the regions and constituencies than did the Labour party (Katz and Mair 1992).

As table 1.3 indicates, there has been an overall decline in the number of professional staff employed by the parties over time. The Conservative

TABLE 1.3. Party Staffing in Britain

	Conservatives		Labour		Liberal Democrats	
Year	Central	Subnational	Central	Subnational	Central	Subnational
1964	97	580	50	248	19	74
1970	95	431	50	167	12	22
1979	—	350	—	128	17	—
1983	—	—	—	104	20	11
1987	100	291	71	95	25	8
1993	148	240	90	—	—	—
1998	167	221	179	150	35	5

Source: Conservative Central Office; Labour Party Personnel Department; Labour Party NEC Organization Committee minutes; Liberal Party Annual Reports; Liberal Democrats' Information and Personnel Offices. For further details see Webb 2000.

Note: Subnational staff includes both regional office staff (employed by national party headquarters) and party agents (usually paid for by local party organizations).

party, as noted earlier, has traditionally been able to afford most staff, but it has not been immune to financial cuts and has been forced to reduce its full-time staff in the same way as the Labour and Liberal Democrat parties have done. It is also apparent in all three parties that staff are increasingly employed at the headquarters rather in the constituencies.

One further point is that the introduction in 1974 of limited state funding of the parliamentary activities of opposition parties has concentrated staff in the parliamentary parties. This concentration of party staff at the parliamentary level has been further reinforced by the growth in MPs' salaries, which has enabled them to employ full-time researchers and thus to help strengthen their powers relative to the grass roots members.

Discussion

To sum up, considerable changes have taken place within both the Conservative and Labour parties since the APSA report was first published fifty years ago. Nevertheless, the parties remain programmatic organizations, albeit within an altered set of policy parameters; they remain relatively cohesive organizations whose members are attached to certain basic principles; and they remain voluntary organizations dependent upon the commitment of their members, even if there are differences in the powers given to members and, therefore, in the scope for internal democracy.

As we mentioned earlier some researchers have argued that the responsible model of parties has been replaced by the cartel or the electoral-professional parties. Mair in particular takes the view that parties have become "semi-state agencies" (1997: 106). Thus ostensible competitors collude and cooperate, in a similar way to economic cartels, in sharing state resources. They have become increasingly reliant upon the state for communications, staffing, finance, and patronage. Their goals are limited to effective management, and their campaigns are capital-intensive, professional, and centralized. Furthermore, they distinguish less between members and nonmembers, so that party supporters are involved in decision making. This type of party is vertically, rather than horizontally, organized such that members belong to a national rather than a local party. Finally, there is more of an atomistic sense of politics in such a party, and members exercise their rights as individuals rather than as delegates (Mair 1997: 108–14).

Mair notes the paradoxical role of the individual members in the cartel party. They are an important provider of party funds and of personnel for state bodies, a general legitimizer for the party in the community, and election campaigners. Yet their powers are weakening as democratization coexists with powerful centralizing tendencies. The atomized individual member has been given increased powers, for example, by leadership ballots, yet he or she is offered only limited choice. Mair claims that members, therefore, are "increasingly involved in legitimizing the choices of the party in public office" (1997: 149).

It is doubtful whether this cartel party model is wholly appropriate to Britain, as Mair himself acknowledges. In Britain state resources, such as finance, communication facilities, personnel, and patronage, are not extensive, and the relative absence of state funding means that parties remain essentially voluntary bodies. Nevertheless, centralizing tendencies have occurred that may well affect the incentives for high-intensity participation.

Panebianco (1988) claims that parties have become electoral-professional organizations, increasingly dominated by campaign, marketing, and policy professionals. Professional opinion pollsters, fund-raisers, advertisers, and journalists, all located in party headquarters, have become key personnel in any party. The introduction of the term "spin doctor" in our vocabulary is a recognition of this fact. Parties have always been concerned with managing public opinion in as favorable a manner as possible (Windlesham 1966; Kavanagh 1995). But parties now put greater resources into the use of such professionals, and the consequence is that the campaigning role of party activists has diminished. Kavanagh (1998: 42) suggests that "the targeting of key voters in marginal seats is increasingly conducted from the centre, via direct mail or telephone canvassing, rather than by local activists. . . . What matters less than ever to each political party is its strong partisans." Weir and Beetham (1999: 66–67) argue in similar fashion, claiming that "high-tech has replaced the 'poor bloody military' of local activists delivering leaflets and canvassing door-to-door in the old hit-and-miss way," and they go on to assert that campaigns "are now prepared, disciplined and systematic, guided by marketing and media professionals and governed by more and more centralized decision-making."

But the nature of election campaigning in Britain is more complex than that suggested by Panebianco and others who claim the emergence of the electoral-professional party. It is important to distinguish three features of an election campaign. First, there are the national campaigns directed and run by the central party headquarters that include the press conferences, leaders' speeches, party election broadcasts, and advertising. Second, there are the attempts by central party headquarters to direct local campaigns by targeting specific marginal constituencies. Third, there are the purely local campaigns mounted by the parties in the constituencies across the length and breadth of the United Kingdom that are organized and run by local activists. It is certainly the case that electioneering in constituencies now involves a wide range of labor-saving devices, including opinion polling, telephone canvassing, direct mail shots, and electronic mail communications. The computer has revolutionized the constituency campaign. Nevertheless, the role of local activists remains important, even in the case of the nationally targeted marginal constituency campaigns, because their skills cannot be entirely purchased. If a local party wishes to contact a significant proportion of its electors, averaging seventy thousand in a British constituency, in order to identify supporters, it will require local activists to carry out these tasks. Some of this work can be done by paid volunteers working either at the center or in the localities, but the bulk of the work still remains at the local level to be undertaken by devoted amateurs.

Reference has already been made to the extensive targeting strategies of all parties at the 1997 general election. But party headquarters still have to persuade local activists to come out and work and then to work where required. There is evidence that members will not work on elections unless both political and structural incentives are provided, and, furthermore, members have their own local attachments and priorities and are unwilling to be redirected in the manner that targeting assumes. Analyses of the 1997 general election suggest that the Liberal Democrats benefitted most, the Labour party less so, and the Conservatives least from their targeting efforts (Denver, Hands, and Henig 1998; Whiteley and Seyd 1999).

Rather than the "cartel" or the "electoral-professional party" being the appropriate term to describe the British party system in the twenty-first century, the "plebiscitarian party" may be more apt. In such a party the pattern of communication is often vertical rather than horizontal and has less to do with debate and discussion and more to do with marketing. Often communication between leaders and their members and supporters takes place outside of the established party structures, primarily through sympathetic newspapers. The structure of such a party is one in which the rally replaces the conference. In such a party the number of identifiers is important for legitimation reasons, but more emphasis is placed upon supporters rather than on members.[16] As a consequence, the barriers to membership are lowered to encourage supporters.

The discussion in this chapter provides the institutional background against which we can examine high-intensity participation. We will return to these topics again in chapter 8, where we examine the future of the party system. But for the moment it is sufficient to note that these developments in the party organizations since the APSA report have important implications for high-intensity political participation within the parties. The picture is complex, but on balance internal party democracy and thus the incentives for political action have declined. In the rest of the book we will examine the implications of this for high-intensity participation.

Chapter 2

Theories of Participation
and High-Intensity Participation

✤

IN THE PREVIOUS CHAPTER WE EXAMINED the changes to the British party system in the last fifty years since the APSA report on the responsible party model. We have suggested that these changes have implications for high-intensity participation in political parties. The picture is, however, mixed both at the level of the electorate and in relation to party members. There is some evidence, on the one hand, of partisan dealignment but also, on the other, of party strength, as demonstrated by the outcome of the 2001 general election. In that election the three major parties took 94 percent of the vote in Great Britain (British Election Study website, 2001). It is interesting to note that only one independent MP was elected to the House of Commons in 2001.[1] Similarly, while there is evidence of a postwar decline in the party membership, in the strength of party identification in the electorate, and in the share of the vote of the two major parties, Britain's political system is nonetheless still dominated by parties.

British government continues to be very much party government. Moreover, the two major parties raise and spend more money than ever before, and as we have seen they are both in the process of reviving their grass roots membership and revitalizing their party organization. At the same time there are clear centralizing tendencies within the parties that have served to move the system away from the original responsible party model, even if the new system cannot be accurately described as a cartel party model. Clearly, there are challenges to the parties in Britain, but they still dominate the political landscape. So is the British party system in decline or merely in transition? And what do these changes mean for high-intensity participation?

To answer these question we need a coherent theory of political participation. In the absence of such a theory, the meaning of the evidence is ambiguous. If we do not know why people support a party by voting for it, joining it, and in some cases working many hours for it, then we are unlikely to be able to determine what the developments in the party system discussed in chapter 1 mean for high-intensity political participation in the future.

The problem of providing such a theoretical explanation is made all the more acute by the fact that the dominant model of political participation in political science—the civic voluntarism model (see Verba, Schlozman, and Brady 1995)—predicts that participation in the British party system should be increasing, not declining, over time. This prediction is discussed more fully later in this chapter, but in the light of the fall in turnout in the 2001 general election compared with its predecessor (see fig. 1.2) and the evidence on party activism discussed later, there is clearly a problem with this model.

A similar problem occurs in relation to rational choice accounts of political participation. As is well known, rational choice theory has difficulty explaining why anyone should vote in an election or join and become active in a political party. On the face of it, in this theoretical framework the British party system should not be in decline because it should not have developed in the first place! Obviously, there is an important task of theoretical clarification to be undertaken before the evidence can be weighed and before the question as to what the changes in the party system mean for high-intensity participation can be answered.

This chapter is devoted to examining the alternative theoretical explanations of political participation that exist in the literature. The task is to evaluate their theoretical coherence, the empirical predictions they make about citizen involvement in politics, and their success or otherwise in explaining party support and high-intensity participation. The aim is to examine the strengths and weaknesses of each approach, before estimating them empirically in chapter 3. This chapter prepares the groundwork for an analysis that identifies the best models for explaining high-intensity participation in the Labour and Conservative parties.

There are five theoretical approaches or models of political participation that have developed in the political science literature. They can be described in abbreviated form as the civic voluntarism model, the rational choice model, the social-psychological model, the mobilization model, and the general incentives model. Each is influenced by a different research tradition, and we examine them in turn.

The Civic Voluntarism Model

The most well-known and widely applied model of political participation in political science was originally referred to as the resources model and had its origins in the work of Sidney Verba and Norman Nie (1972) in their influential research on participation in the United States. It was subsequently applied by the authors, their collaborators, and others to explain participation in other countries, including Britain (Verba, Nie, and Kim 1978; Barnes and Kaase 1979; Parry, Moyser, and Day 1992; Verba et al. 1993). The central ideas of the civic voluntarism model of participation are captured in the following quote:

> We focus on three factors to account for political activity. We suggested earlier that one helpful way to understand the three factors is to invert the usual question and ask instead why people do not become political activists. Three answers come to mind: because they can't; because they don't want to; or because nobody asked. In other words people may be inactive because they lack resources, because they lack psychological engagement with politics, or because they are outside of the recruitment networks that bring people into politics. (Verba, Schlozman, and Brady 1995: 269)

The authors of this quote define the resources aspect of this model in terms of "time, money and civic skills" (271). The psychological engagement aspect is defined principally in terms of the individual's sense of political efficacy (272), and, finally, the recruitment networks aspect is defined as "requests for participation that come to individuals at work, in church, or in organizations—especially those that come from friends, relatives, or acquaintances" (272).

In the earlier versions of this model, the emphasis was on the resources aspect of participation. The authors explained:

According to this model, the social status of an individual—his job, education, and income—determines to a large extent how much he participates. It does this through the intervening effects of a variety of "civic
attitudes" conducive to participation: attitudes such as a sense of efficacy,
of psychological involvement in politics and a feeling of obligation to
participate. (Verba and Nie 1972: 13)

Thus resources were paramount in the original version of the model,
although psychological attitudes always played an important role in
explaining participation as well. These civic attitudes are rather more
important in recent versions of the model, although it is still true to say
that resources are the dominant factor in explaining participation (Verba,
Schlozman, and Brady 1995: 270).

Verba and his colleagues developed the first empirical typology of different modes of participation and classified citizens into six different
groups on the basis of the types of activities they undertook (Verba and
Nie 1972: 118–19). There are, first, the inactives, who as the name suggests do little or nothing; second, the voting specialists, who vote regularly but do nothing else; third, the parochial participants, who contact
officials in relation to specific problems but are otherwise inactive: fourth,
the communalists, who intermittently engage in political action on broad
social issues but are not highly involved; fifth, campaigners, who are heavily involved in campaigns of various kinds; and, finally, the complete
activists, who participate in all kinds of activities.

When the same model was subsequently applied to the task of providing a cross-national explanation of political participation, it allowed the
authors to examine differences in participation engendered by different
political institutions and cultural settings. The later work stressed the distinction between individual and group resources in promoting participation, arguing that "organization—and we might add ideology—is the
weapon of the weak" (Verba, Nie, and Kim 1978: 15). In other words,
groups bound together by ideological ties are able to overcome the lack of
individual resources of their members, and this promotes the participation of their members in politics. In effect, the authors were arguing that
institutions facilitate participation.

This theoretical model has been widely cited and replicated, and it is
probably the most important model of political participation in the literature today. However, it does face problems. The first problem relates to
the use of socioeconomic status as a predictor of participation and civic

values. It is well established that participants are generally higher-status individuals than are nonparticipants; for example, Verba and his collaborators show that high-status individuals are overrepresented in the category of very active participants and underrepresented in the category of inactives (Verba and Nie 1972: 131–33).

What the model fails to explain, however, is why large numbers of high-status individuals do not participate in politics. In other words, while participation is associated with social status, the latter is nonetheless a relatively weak predictor of participation, because many high-status individuals do not get involved in politics. This problem for the model can be seen in Verba and his collaborators' (1995) most recent work on participation in the United States. In the theory, family income is treated as a good proxy measure of socioeconomic status in the American context, but nonetheless it has a very weak influence on participation.[2]

This latter point explains the paradox referred to briefly at the start of this chapter. If socioeconomic status is such an important determinant of political participation, then societies that are gradually becoming more middle class and better educated over time should experience increased rates of participation. The increase in white-collar occupations at the expense of blue-collar occupations and the tremendous growth in higher education in many advanced industrial countries are now well documented (see Dalton, Flanagan, and Beck 1984; Abramson and Inglehart 1995). However, there is no evidence of increased political participation in these countries, and in the case of the United States both voting turnout and participation in voluntary organizations have actually declined rather than increased (Brody 1978; Putnam 1995; Miller and Shanks 1996).[3]

If we apply the model to Britain, there is clearly a problem in explaining why participation in the 2001 British general election was significantly lower than, for example, in the 1979 election, since during the intervening twenty-two years a massive expansion had occurred in higher education.[4] Again, the model would have to explain the trends in party membership noted in chapter 1, which, with the sole exception of the Labour party between 1994 and 1997, are downward, not upward.

A second problem with the civic voluntarism model is actually identified by Verba and his colleagues themselves. They write:

The SES model is weak in its theoretical underpinnings. It fails to provide a coherent rationale for the connection between the explanatory socioeconomic variables and participation. Numerous intervening factors are invoked—resources, norms, stake in the outcome, psychological involvement in politics, greater opportunities, favorable legal status, and so forth. But there is no clearly specified mechanism linking social statuses to activity. (Verba, Schlozman, and Brady 1995: 281)

They go on to suggest that a focus on broader resources, such as the amount of spare time the individual has available in the average week and his or her financial resources, helps to deal with this problem. However, it is difficult to see why this should be true, since, if individuals are rich and have plenty of leisure time, there is still no reason why they should spend their money or free time on political activities rather than on vacationing, playing sports, or watching television.[5]

The key problem with the resources model is that it focuses exclusively on the supply side of the equation and neglects the demand side aspects. Thus individuals supply more participation if they have the resources or a psychological sense of efficacy. What is missing is any understanding of why individuals have a demand for participation, of what incentives they have to get involved in politics. Many high-status individuals have no such incentives, which explains why they do not participate. While resources allow one to understand the supply of participation, it is necessary to consider the incentives for participation, or the demand side of the equation, to understand why individuals get involved in politics. We turn to this issue later.

The Rational Choice Model

Rational choice theory has played an important role in the analysis of political participation ever since Downs's seminal work, *An Economic Theory of Democracy* (1957). There is a lively and sometimes rancorous debate between advocates of rational choice approaches (Tsebelis 1990; Aldrich 1993; Jackman 1993) and their opponents, who deny the relevance of rational choice accounts (Hindess 1988, Lowi 1992; Eckstein 1992). The rational choice model is summarized succinctly by Downs in the following terms:

A rational man is one who behaves as follows: (1) he can always make a decision when confronted with a range of alternatives; (2) he ranks all the alternatives facing him in order of his preferences in such a way that each is either preferred to, indifferent to, or inferior to each other; (3) his preference ranking is transitive; (4) he always chooses from among the possible alternatives that which ranks highest in his preference ordering; and (5) he always makes the same decision each time he is confronted with the same alternatives. (Downs 1957: 6)

It is well known that rational choice theory applied to the task of explaining political participation faces a key problem, the so-called paradox of participation, first highlighted by Olson (1965). This is the proposition that rational actors will not participate in collective action to achieve common goals because the products of such collective action are public goods. Public goods have two properties: jointness of supply and the impossibility of exclusion (Samuelson 1954). Jointness of supply implies that one person's consumption does not reduce the amount available to anyone else, and the impossibility of exclusion means that an individual cannot be prevented from consuming the good once it is provided, even if he or she did not contribute to its provision in the first place. The classic textbook example of a collective good is national defense—if one person "consumes" national defense this does not reduce the amount available to anyone else, and if that person refuses to pay their taxes to fund defense spending, they cannot be prevented from consuming it.[6]

Olson's insight was to note that the policy goals and programs, which are the "products" of a political party, are public goods, and consequently rational actors have an incentive to free ride on the efforts of others and to let them do the work to provide such goods. Consequently, a voluntary organization like a party would get no assistance from the rational self-interested individual in the absence of other types of incentives to participate (Olson 1965: 9–11). In addition, Olson points out that this problem is much more acute in large groups than it is in small groups. In the case of a small group it may well be rational for a single individual to provide the collective good, since it is possible that the benefits to that individual exceed the costs of providing the good without any assistance from other people (22–24).

There have been four broad approaches to dealing with the paradox of participation within the rational choice framework (Whiteley 1995). The first approach is to appeal to threshold arguments; when the costs of collective action are very small, as they are in the case of voting, then an individual may well ignore them because they are below a threshold of significance (Barry 1970; Niemi 1976). The difficulty with this approach is that it solves the paradox by abandoning the rational choice framework: if costs and benefits are so trivial that actors do not bother to calculate them, then the theoretical explanation for voting is no longer a rational choice explanation.

The second approach has its origins in game theory and is based on the idea that if no one is expected to vote, then an individual who actually does vote will have a decisive effect on the outcome of an election. In this case it is clearly rational for the individual to participate (Meehl 1977). However, if everyone else participates, then it ceases to be rational, since the individual will no longer be decisive in determining the outcome. From this perspective payoffs depend on the interrelationship between the strategies that the different actors pursue.

More generally, the collective action problem is often modeled as a prisoner's dilemma game, and theorists have developed "folk" theorems that examine the conditions under which collective action is rational in this game. The dilemma arises from the fact that if the game is played only once it is rational for the individual to free ride on others and not participate, regardless of the strategy the opponents pursue. Unfortunately, the result of this course of action is inferior to the outcome that can be achieved if everyone cooperated and worked together to provide the public good.

Theorists have concentrated on establishing the conditions under which it is rational to cooperate and thereby avoid the dilemma (Taylor 1976; Palfrey and Rosenthal 1985; Axelrod 1984). These conditions are various; first, individuals should not discount the future too much since myopia reduces the payoffs of cooperative action; second, they should participate in a repeat game and not just a one-shot game, so that the benefits of cooperation can build up; third, they should be uncertain about when the game ends, since by backward induction certainty restores the noncooperative equilibrium;[7] finally, they should be able to punish noncooperative behavior on the part of others. If these conditions are met, then cooperation brings higher returns than noncooperation.

Unfortunately, these conditions only apply to two-person games and not to N-person games of the type required to study participation in a large organization like a political party. This is largely because it is difficult, if not impossible, to identify and hence sanction free riding in the N-person game (Axelrod 1997: 41). Since the active members of a political party have no sanctions to induce the inactive members to get involved and share the burden of work, free riding cannot be punished.

Equally, there are few, if any, incentives for individuals to avoid myopia in politics, since their own involvement makes no material difference to the outcome of an election or to the changing of the policy goals of their preferred party. This means that the conditions for cooperation that emerge from this literature generally do not apply to political participation.

The third approach to the collective action problem introduces altruistic concerns into the calculus of participation. Mueller (1989: 362), for example, suggests that voters will take into account the utilities of other voters when deciding whether they should participate in an election. He describes this as a Jekyll-and-Hyde view of human nature, with part of the motivation for participation being altruistic and part being self-interested. Margolis (1982: 82–95) develops a similar argument.

Altruism is quite compatible with rational choice theory (see Elster 1983), but it fails to solve the paradox of participation. Altruism implies that an individual will accept costs without receiving corresponding benefits, but there is still the question of whether the individual's participation will make any difference to these outcomes. It is simply irrational to incur costs if by doing so individuals make no difference to outcomes, regardless of whether they are motivated by altruism or self-interest.

Chong (1991) captures this problem in his analysis of participation in interest groups as an assurance game, in which individuals are altruistic and therefore are not predisposed to free ride on the efforts of others. In this situation, the collective action problem does not go away because participants are still unsure whether enough other people will participate to make such participation effective, although it does mitigate the problem to some extent. However, if altruists believe that there are not enough people to ensure that collective action crosses a threshold of effectiveness, then they will not participate. Again, this implies that, apart from the case of collective action by small groups, political participation generally is not rational.

Finally, the fourth approach to the collective action problem is the one used by Olson, an appeal to selective incentives as the explanation of collective action. These are private incentives unrelated to the collective goods produced by the group. This approach has been used to explain the paradox of participation applied to voting. For example, Riker and Ordeshook (1973: 63) list a series of selective incentives that individuals have for voting, including "The satisfaction of complying with the ethic of voting," "The satisfaction of affirming allegiance to the political system," and "The satisfaction of affirming a partisan preference." Since individuals who do not vote do not receive these benefits, they are selective incentives.

Green and Shapiro (1994) in their critique of rational choice applications in political science are scathing about this particular approach. They write:

> Aside from being a post hoc explanation (and an empirically slippery conjecture in any event), the notion that civic duty shapes voter participation raises more empirical problems than it solves. For one, it is unclear why civic duty should fluctuate from one sort of election to another within the same region, producing sharply different turnouts for Presidential elections, national off year elections, statewide elections, and local elections. (52)

In Olson's account, selective incentives for joining a trade union involve things such as subsidized insurance, free legal advice for members, and discounts on various purchases. These seem to provide plausible incentives for joining such organizations for some individuals, and therefore the selective incentives idea has validity. However, it is not clear that it can be applied to explaining away the paradox of participation, particularly when applied to voting, where such incentives are largely absent. On the other hand, as we shall argue later, this idea is quite important for understanding high-intensity participation.

Overall, while rational choice accounts of participation have value, the various attempts to explain away the paradox of participation all face difficulties. One author has suggested that the problem of explaining turnout is the "paradox that ate rational choice" (Grofman 1995). Rational choice accounts of participation orientate research onto the demand side of the political participation equation. Individuals are motivated by considerations of self-interest when they get involved in politics. Moreover, the absence of any serious discussion of incentives is a major flaw of the civic voluntarism model of participation. However, it is also clear that a purely rational choice account provides an incomplete explanation of political action.

The Social Psychological Model
• ☞ •

The third broad theoretical approach to the analysis of political participation comes from the social psychological literature and has been particularly important in understanding unorthodox forms of participation, such as protest behavior and rebellious collective action (Muller 1979; Finkel, Muller, and Opp 1989; Muller, Dietz, and Finkel 1991; Finkel and Opp 1991). There are several variants of the social psychological model, but we will focus on the expectations-values-norms theory discussed by Muller (1979: 23–31), which is based on the work of Fishbein and his collaborators (Fishbein 1967; Azjen and Fishbein 1969).

The underlying theory is concerned with explaining the relationship between attitudes and behavior. Fishbein's work started from the point that traditional social psychological theories, which aimed to explain behavior from attitudes, did not appear to work very well, since the relationships appeared to be very weak (Azjen and Fishbein 1969: 14–27). His solution to this problem was to focus closely on measuring the individual's attitudes toward the behavior rather than toward the objectives of that behavior. Applied to the task of modeling the link between attitudes and political participation, this meant that citizens should be asked about their attitudes toward various types of protest behavior rather than about their attitudes to unjust laws or political events that might have triggered this behavior. Fishbein believed that such attitudes, together with other factors, make it possible to predict behavior fairly accurately. He explained that "the theory identifies three kinds of variables that function as the basic determinants of behavior: (1) attitudes toward the behavior; (2) normative beliefs (both personal and social); and (3) motivation to comply with the norms" (Fishbein 1967: 490).

Thus the expectations-values-norms theory explains behavior in terms of two broad classes of factors: expected benefits and social norms. On the one hand individuals are seen as utilitarians who calculate the benefits of different courses of action, although in this model no distinctions are made between the private and collective benefits of political action. On the other hand they are seen as actors embedded in networks of social norms and beliefs, which provide internal and external motivations to behave in certain ways.

Muller operationalized the theory using a series of indicators related to the question of modeling aggressive political participation (1979: 69–100). He writes:

> Attitudes about behavior are defined as the individual's beliefs about the consequences of his behavior multiplied by their subjective value or utility to him. Normative beliefs refer to an individual's own belief in the

justifiability of his behavior as well as to his perception of significant others' (parents, peers) expectations about it. Motivation to comply with the norms reflects such factors as an individual's personality and his perception of the reasonableness of expectations of others. (25)

As far as the cognitive aspects of participation are concerned, the expected benefits of participation are weighted by the individual's sense of political efficacy. In other words individuals will participate if they believe that this will bring them benefits, providing that they also believe that participation is effective. Thus even if an individual expects high rewards from participation, he or she may not get involved if their sense of political efficacy is rather low.

With regard to social norms, these are two types: internal or private norms and external or public norms. Private norms are the internalized values that the individual brings to the act of participation, such that a person will participate if he or she feels that political action is normatively justified. For example, if a person feels a law to be unjust, this will stimulate him or her to participate in protest activity designed to change the law. Such private norms are largely a product of socialization that operates over a longtime scale and are influenced by the early experiences of the individual.

Public norms are determined by the attitudes of other people whose opinions they value. Hence if other people whose views are important to them are supportive of participation, this will further motivate them to be active. Thus a key feature of such public norms is that they are enforced by other people, who express approval or disapproval of the behavior of the individual concerned (see Elster 1989: 97–151). Thus party members motivated by social norms respond to the perceived opinions of significant others, or individuals whose opinions they respect and value. This again is a social psychological variable.

Muller and his associates have introduced the idea of a "unity principle," that is, a norm that all members of the group should contribute to collective action if the collective good is to be provided (Muller and Opp 1986, 1987; Finkel, Muller, and Opp 1989). They describe this norm as "calculating Kantianism." When faced with the possibility of free riding on the efforts of others, group members ask themselves, "What if everyone did that?" Since the answer is that the collective good would not be provided if everyone tried to free ride, they choose to participate. In this way group norms influence participation.

Measurement issues play a prominent role in the social psychological model of participation. The models arising from this approach have been used with some success to account for unorthodox types of participation in various democratic systems (see Marsh 1977; Barnes and Kaase 1979). But in common with the other theoretical approaches, this does face problems. In a sense, the weaknesses of the rational choice model are the strengths of the social psychological model and vice versa.

The first problem is that the notion of utility is not very well defined theoretically in the social psychological model. It is interesting that a distinction is made between private and public norms in this model, but there is no equivalent distinction drawn between private and public utilities or the benefits that derive from political action. As we saw earlier, this is a crucial distinction in rational actor models of participation. In the social psychological model, equal weight is given to actions that benefit society as to actions that benefit the individual. It is implicitly assumed that individuals will participate to oppose a social injustice of some kind, even if it is not clear that they will benefit personally from this course of action. The paradox of participation highlights the problems of treating collective benefits in the same way as individual benefits and shows how these variables can be antagonistic to one another in some situations. This is a valuable insight that the social psychological models ignore.

There is another problem with this social psychological approach, which again is highlighted by rational choice theory. As we have seen, political efficacy plays an important role in these theories, but it is subjective efficacy, not objective efficacy of the type found in rational choice accounts. The problem is that there appears to be evidence of a big gap between subjective and objective political efficacy. For example, we know that the objective probability of an individual making a difference to the outcome of an election or to changing national policy goals is effectively zero, and yet the evidence suggests that many people think they can change these things and consequently have high levels of subjective political efficacy.

When asked to respond to the following statement in the 1992 American National Election Study survey—"People like me don't have any say about what the government does"—some 57 percent of electors disagreed with the statement (ICPSR 1992), even though it is objectively true for all but a handful of individuals. In Britain some 31 percent of respondents to the 1992 British Election Study survey disagreed with the same statement (ESRC 1992). This result shows that, although Britain is smaller than the United States, many of its citizens have a feeling of political efficacy.

The hiatus between subjective and objective efficacy might, on the face of it, be explained by the fact that voters think collectively, not necessarily individually, when responding to this question. Thus they are answering the question in terms of their perceptions of the influence of people like themselves, not merely in terms of themselves as individuals. This is an interesting idea, and is explored more fully later, but it cannot be the sole basis for making decisions about participation. This is because the individual has no control over such collective or group influence; they can speak for themselves but not for the group. Given this point, it is irrational for them to feel a sense of personal efficacy solely because they believe that the electorate as a whole is politically effective. In other words, political efficacy must be grounded in an objective measure of their own political influence, even if it is affected by identifications with a group. If it is not grounded in this reality, then the disturbing implication follows that citizens participate in politics because they are deluded into thinking that they can make a difference in outcomes.

Thus a key problem with social psychological models is that they pay no attention to the rationality of decision making. We made the point earlier that rational choice models provide an incomplete account of political participation, but a similar point can be made about social psychological models. Their lack of attention to the objective basis of political influence is a serious omission that needs to be rectified if they are to provide an adequate account of participation. Perceptions of group influence may matter, but so must perceptions of individual influence, and the latter must be based on an objective reality, not on subjective perceptions alone.

The Mobilization Model

The mobilization model asserts that individuals participate in response to the political opportunities in their environment and to stimuli from other people. Put simply, some people participate because the opportunities for them to do so are greater than for other people and also because they are persuaded to get involved by other people. The model can be linked to the resources model, as Verba, Schlozman, and Brady point out in the ear-

lier quote illustrating the reasons why most people do not become political activists.[8]

The opportunities for participation are obviously linked to the
resources model since individuals with high socioeconomic status are
more likely to have access to political parties, interest groups, or campaign
organizations than are low-status individuals, because those kinds of institutions are more commonly found in the communities in which high-status individuals live (Verba, Schlozman and Brady 1995: 337–43). Since
the opportunities for participation are not uniform across the population,
an interaction between resources and opportunities mobilizes some individuals to get involved. Social pressures to participate are linked to
resources too, since, if high-status individuals are more likely to participate, this promotes a norm of participation among such people that is not
found among low-status individuals.

The bulk of the evidence to support the mobilization model comes
from research on the relationship between campaigning and turnout in
elections. Much of this research is based in the United States, and one of
the earliest papers on the subject, involving a study of electoral turnout in
Gary, Indiana, set out the methodological framework within which subsequent work has been done. In this paper Cutright (1963) pointed out
that the key problem was to identify the effects of mobilization separately
from other factors in explaining electoral participation. Their research
showed that campaigning by Democratic and Republican precinct com-
mitteemen made an important difference to the vote, controlling for a
variety of other variables, such as voters' socioeconomic status. Thus
these effects worked independently of resources (see also Cutright 1963;
Wolfinger 1963; Crotty 1971).

The first study to use the American National Election Study data by
Kramer (1970) showed that canvassing at the precinct level had a
significant effect on turnout in national elections over the period 1952 to
1964. The most recent work in the United States that looks at the impact
of party organization on the vote at the county level for presidential and
congressional elections in the 1980s showed, not surprisingly, that a party
able to contest seats at all levels did much better than a party unable to do
this (Frendreis, Gibson, and Vertz 1990; see also Huckfeldt and Sprague
1992; Wielhouwer and Lockerbie 1994). This finding reinforces the dual
character of mobilization, which is most effective when it combines persuading people to participate with providing them an opportunity to do
so. Rosenstone and Hansen (1993) have the most comprehensive mobi-

lization model and in particular focus on the role of voluntary organizations in mobilizing participation in the United States, using data on group membership in the American National Election Studies.

Research on electoral mobilization in Britain reinforces these findings. Research that uses campaign spending as a surrogate measure of campaign activity shows that the latter has a significant influence on voting behavior over time (Johnston 1987; Johnston, Pattie, and Johnston 1989; Johnston and Pattie 1995; Pattie, Johnston, and Fieldhouse 1995). Survey-based research using Labour party members (Seyd and Whiteley 1992; Whiteley and Seyd 1992, 1994) or surveys of constituency agents from all the main parties (Denver and Hands 1985, 1997) also find significant relationships. Finally, in an ingenious field experiment Bochel and Denver (1972) found that campaigning had a significant influence on voting turnout in local elections in Scotland. All these findings support the mobilization model.

The mobilization model does, however, cause problems for the other three theoretical models of participation. In the case of the resources model, it distorts the estimates of the relationships between socioeconomic status and participation, because it implies that participation to a significant extent causes itself. Leighley explains, "the standard socioeconomic model assumes that positive civic orientations are causally prior to acts of participation. Yet we know that certain types of participation enhance numerous political attitudes, including political efficacy and sophistication" (1995: 186). This implies that the model linking resources and attitudes to participation in a recursive chain of causation is misspecified and may well exaggerate the influence of the former on the latter (see also Finkel and Muller 1998). A specification that allows for a two-way interaction between civic attitudes and participation is required, and this is commonly neglected in the standard analysis of participation.

Mobilization is also quite problematic for rational choice accounts of participation, since these assume that individuals have already acquired enough information to decide whether they are going to participate. In this situation, mobilization would only move the rational actor to get involved if it provided new information relevant to the cost-benefit calculus of choice. It is not clear why canvassing, for example, which provides highly biased information from strangers and should be heavily discounted for that reason, should induce individuals to participate.

The mobilization model also causes difficulties for social psychological accounts of participation. As we have seen social norms are an important mechanism for influencing behavior, but they are activated by significant others, or people who the individual knows and respects. Again, it is not clear why citizens should be persuaded to participate by a stranger who knocks on their door or calls them on the telephone.

The mobilization model clearly highlights aspects of political participation neglected by the other models. But it is in some ways the least well developed of the theoretical models of political participation, and it leaves many unanswered questions, most particularly, that of why people should change their behavior in response to the efforts of others to persuade them to do so. The point that the social environment in which some people live is more favorable to participation than it is for others is well taken. But overall the mobilization model cannot provide a complete theory of participation.

Up to this point the review of these theoretical perspectives has highlighted the advantages and disadvantages of their distinctive approaches. But we have concluded that none of them can provide a comprehensive account of political participation. In the next section we examine the general incentives model, which is a synthesis of these accounts and as such aims to provide such an account.

The General Incentives Model
· *☉* ·

The general incentives model of participation was introduced specifically to explain the incidence of high-intensity types of participation, such as canvassing, attending meetings, and running for office, activities that are the focus of our concerns (see Seyd and Whiteley 1992; Whiteley, Seyd, and Richardson 1994; Whiteley et al. 1994; Whiteley and Seyd 1998). As mentioned, the theory derives from a synthesis of rational choice and social psychological accounts of participation.

The essence of the theory is that actors need incentives to ensure that they participate in politics but that we need to consider a wider array of incentives than narrowly defined individual incentives that appear in rational choice models. Thus the Olson model, while plausible and insightful, is too narrow to give an adequate account of why people should join or be active in a political party. However, this point does not ignore the central insight of Olson's theory, which is the idea that individuals become politically active in response to incentives of various kinds.

We referred to selective incentives earlier, and these may be important for understanding why some people join and become active in a party. Selective incentives are of three types: process, outcome, and ideological.

Process incentives refer to motives for participating that derive from the process of participation itself. Various authors have referred to a number of different motives that might be counted under this heading. Tullock (1971) has written of the entertainment value of being involved in revolution; Opp (1990) writes about the catharsis value of involvement in political protest. For some people, the political process is interesting and stimulating in itself, regardless of the outcomes or goals. High-intensity participation is a way of meeting like-minded and interesting people, and for some this is motive enough for getting involved. Selective outcome incentives refer to motives concerned with achieving certain goals in the political process, but goals that are private rather than collective. A potential high-intensity participant might harbor ambitions to become a local councillor, for example, or the local mayor or even to be elected to the House of Commons. Others might want nomination from their party to become a school governor or a local magistrate. Yet others might be interested in business connections that party membership can bring, particularly in areas where the party is strong in local government. It has long been recognized that political leaders or entrepreneurs can be exempt from the paradox of participation because they have incentives, such as interesting, well-paid jobs and elective office (Salisbury 1969).

One of the distinctive features of political parties is that they are vehicles for achieving elected office, something that is not generally true of protest groups or lobbying organizations. Thus elected representatives have to serve an apprenticeship within their party organization before they can be chosen for elective office. From this perspective activism can be regarded as an investment that must be made if the individual has ambitions to develop a future career in politics. Thus outcome incentives measure the private returns from participation associated with developing a political career as an elected representative of the party. This is clearly an important selective incentive for activism.

A third type of process motivation is ideology, the explanation for this being rooted in the so-called law of curvilinear disparity (see May 1973; Kitschelt 1989). This is the proposition that rank-and-file members of a political party are likely to be more radical than the party leadership or the voters. Thus there is a curvilinear relationship between ideological radicalism and the position of the individual within the organizational hierarchy of a party. In the case of the Labour party this would mean that the members were to the left of both the voters and the party leadership, and in the case of the Conservative party it would mean that they were to the right of them.

This is an interesting idea, but it has not been very well grounded theoretically. In the context of the present model, we would explain it in terms of process motives for involvement. Thus ideological radicalism should motivate individuals to join a party because it allows them to interact with like-minded people and give expression to deeply held beliefs. Their involvement is prompted by similar motives of the active churchgoer—membership of the church allows religious people to give expression to their beliefs as well as to become part of the congregation.

It can be seen that a number of incentives exist to promote political participation, which are independent of the collective incentives that create the paradox of participation. However, these selective incentives are really only applicable to a potential high-intensity participant. For those people who regard their party membership as a private matter, not to be discussed or shared with other people, it is difficult to see how they can be motivated to join by selective incentives.

Collective incentives are based on the provision of collective goods, the policy goals of a political party. Thus individuals motivated by collective incentives may believe that their party will reduce unemployment, improve health service, defend the nation, promote the interests of people like themselves, and generally implement policies that they favor. Whether they join the party depends on whether they see it collectively as a vehicle for achieving those goals. Collective incentives to join or be active in a political party are of two kinds: positive and negative. Individuals will participate not only because they want to promote particular policy goals but also because they oppose the policy goals of other parties. On the one hand Labour party members may be motivated to get involved because they support some aspect of Labour party policy; alternatively they may participate because they oppose Conservative policies. Thus positive incentives involve promoting collective goods, whereas negative incentives involve opposing collective "bads."

Clearly, such motives are subject to the free-rider problem in that individuals might be tempted to let other people do the work to advance such policy goals. In a purely individualistic world in which people do not think in solidaristic terms, this would restrict participation greatly, as we pointed out earlier. But if people think in solidaristic terms, then they will participate because they feel they want to contribute to a collective effort.

Thus the group consciousness of the type discussed earlier in connection with social psychological models of participation is recognized as an important component of this model.

We conjecture that individuals think of the group welfare, as well as their own welfare, when making a decision to participate. The most obvious example of such group thinking occurs in the family, where the relevant question is very often not, What is best for me? but rather, What is best for all of us? If this idea is applied to the task of explaining party membership and party activism, then it implies that one reason some individuals join is because they believe that their party collectively can make a difference to outcomes. They still undertake a calculus of costs and benefits, but it is focused at the level of the party as a whole and not just at the level of the individual. If they reach the conclusion that their party can make an important difference in the lives of people with whom they identify, then they will join and may become active. The corollary of this is that, if they decide the party cannot make a difference, then they will not join or become active.

However, as mentioned earlier, individual efficacy matters also, and there has to be an objective basis to such feelings. Thus it is important to examine the question of whether an individual makes a difference to outcomes in relation to these collective goods and bads. If an individual party member makes no difference to outcomes, then he or she is deluded into participating, no matter how much that individual desires the collective goal.

It can be rational for an individual to join a party in pursuit of collective goals of the type that involves the paradox of participation. The key to this is the relationship between the costs and benefits of party membership. Rational individuals may perceive that their own contribution to the collective good is small, but collective action will still be rational for them if they also see the costs as being very small as well. In other words it is the perceived difference between costs and benefits that matter, not some exogenously defined measure of the benefits alone. In this situation, becoming a member without receiving selective incentives makes sense, providing that the individual believes he or she is making a nonzero contribution to the collective good.

Earlier discussion made the point that the individual's ability to influence national party policies is effectively zero, but this is not true of local party politics. Within a branch party or a local constituency party, one individual can make a difference to policy outcomes, even though that difference might be rather small. Parties in Britain are organized on a decentralized constituency basis, and local parties still retain important powers over the recruitment of candidates for local and parliamentary seats, and in relation to local policy-making, which makes participation rational. This point carries the important implication that, if parties weaken the powers of their local branches or if the political system itself is too overcentralized, this will diminish the incentives for participation.

Our surveys of Labour and Conservative party members revealed that an average of forty-six individuals in the former party and forty-five individuals in the latter devoted ten or more hours to party activity in the average month in each of the 634 constituencies in Britain (Seyd and Whiteley 1992: 228; Whiteley, Seyd, and Richardson 1994: 249). Among this relatively small group of highly active people, a single individual can clearly make a difference to outcomes, such that there is an objective basis to the individual's feelings of efficacy. Of course for these people costs are also high, but it is conceivable that their individual contributions to the collective good exceed those costs, making participation rational. Thus individual political efficacy at the local level provides the objective basis for subjective efficacy, which will then carry over to the national political level.

In addition to personal efficacy, a sense of group efficacy can also motivate participation. This is an aspect of "civic culture" in which parties are seen as key institutions in motivating participation by voters as well as by party members (see Almond and Verba 1963: 105; Muller and Opp 1986, 1987). Such group incentives for participation are not compatible with a rational actor model of participation, since as we mentioned earlier the individual is not in a position to influence the political effectiveness of a national organization such as a political party. For this reason, it is not rational for them to evaluate their own participation in relation to the performance of the group as a whole (see Whiteley 1995). However, from a social psychological perspective, the group solidarity engendered by success does provide an incentive to participate, independently of other factors.

Another set of factors that explain participation within the general incentives framework are motives based on emotional or affective attachments to a party. These motives also lie outside the standard cost-benefit model of decision making, with its emphasis on cognitive calculations, and are rooted very much in the social psychological research tradition. Such motives have long been discussed in the literature on party identification, since the early theorists saw partisanship as an affective orientation toward a significant social or political group in the individual's environment (Campbell et al. 1960); they have also been discussed in relation to economic voting (Conover and Feldman 1986) and in the American literature on residential voting (Marcus 1988). Even a formal theory of expressive voting has been developed postulating that voters are motivated by a desire to express support for one candidate or policy outcome over another, independently of whether their vote influences outcomes (Brennan and Buchanan 1984; Carter and Guerette 1992). Similarly, Frank (1988) has developed what he terms a "commitment" model in which actor's emotional predispositions override their short-run calculations of self-interest and allow them to cooperate with each other to solve collective action problems.

Accordingly, we reason that some people will be motivated to join by an expressive attachment to their party, which has little to do with the benefits they might receive from membership, either at the individual or collective levels. Such motives for joining are grounded in a sense of loyalty and affection for the party, which is unrelated to cognitive calculations of the costs and benefits of membership.

Overall, the general incentives theory of political participation postulates that a number of distinct factors are at work in explaining why people join a political party or become active once they have joined. These are selective and collective incentives, group motivations, and affective or expressive motives. Some of these factors are grounded in rational choice theory, but the theory goes beyond a narrow rational choice conception of participation to examine broader motives for involvement, derived from the social psychological theoretical tradition.

This model deals with the shortcomings of the other theoretical approaches to participation discussed earlier. Unlike the resources model the general incentives model focuses on the demand side of the equation and the incentives for participation. While the resources model is both theoretically obscure and rather weak at predicting participation, particularly high-intensity participation, the general incentives model is theoretically well grounded and has a superior ability to predict high-cost types of participation, such as party activism (Whiteley 1995).

The general incentives model incorporates the theoretical concerns of the rational choice approach, with its focus on the costs and benefits of decision making, but without the narrow perspective and the blindness to more general social psychological processes that influence participation.

Finally, while it includes key social psychological variables, the general incentives model addresses the weaknesses of the other models in their neglect of the question of individual rationality. A theory that relies exclusively on behavior that is not rational in the conventional sense is a weak vehicle for explaining party membership and high-intensity participation.

Having outlined the rival theoretical models of political participation, in the next chapter we go on to examine which of these models appears to be empirically optimal for explaining participation in British political parties. It is possible that one of the models is best or that a hybrid that incorporates elements of more than one model is most suited to explaining participation in this context.

Chapter 3

Testing Rival Models

❧❦❧

THE AIM OF THIS CHAPTER IS TO EVALUATE the alternative theories of participation discussed in chapter 2 and to apply this evaluation to the task of explaining political participation in the British party system. Clearly, the starting point of the analysis is to define participation in this context, in particular high-intensity participation. As we pointed out in chapter 1, all too often debates about political participation, particularly in the rational choice tradition, have been dominated by the analysis of voting behavior and explanations of voter turnout (Riker and Ordeshook 1968; Ferejohn and Fiorina 1974, 1975; Silberman and Durden 1975; Palfrey and Rosenthal 1985; Uhlaner 1989). But as Aldrich (1993) points out, this provides only a relatively weak test of theories of participation because voting is such a low-cost activity.

The advantage of studying party members and party activists is that the variation in participation is much greater among this group. At one end of the scale party members get involved in low-intensity forms of participation such as donating money and voting in party ballots. In this respect these members are very similar to voters. At the other end of the scale some members get involved by working for campaigns, running the party organization, raising money, organizing elections, and running for elected office, both within and outside the party. These are the high-intensity participants. One interesting question is whether these two types of participation form a single continuum, with low-intensity forms leading naturally to high-intensity forms of participation. Alternatively, the two types of participation could be quite distinct, with party members being involved in one but not necessarily the other. This is one of the topics to be examined in this chapter.

The chapter is divided into four sections. We begin by developing political participation scales using data from our 1989–90 survey of Labour party members and our 1992 survey of Conservative party members in Britain. The details of these surveys are discussed in the appendix. The scales include a wide range of political activities common to both parties, varying from low-intensity to high-intensity activities. Needless to say, the scales have considerably more variance and are more reliable than the dichotomous voting turnout variable often used to model participation.

In the second section we specify rival specifications of the theories discussed in chapter 2, identifying the variables required to test the alternative perspectives. The third section is a methodological discussion designed to briefly examine the encompassing approach to the testing of rival theories, a strategy for theory building that arises out of recent work in applied econometrics (see Mizon 1984; Hendry and Richard 1990). The fourth section is devoted to applying this strategy to the task of evaluating the alternative theories of participation, using data from the surveys. This examination prepares the groundwork for a discussion of the dynamics of participation in chapter 4.

Measuring Participation

In earlier work (Seyd and Whiteley 1992; Whiteley, Seyd, and Richardson 1994) we identified three different aspects of political activism or political participation in parties. The first aspect related to levels of contact between party members. Obviously highly active party members are likely to have a lot of face-to-face contact with each other at the local level, but it would be a mistake to think that contact is synonymous with activism. It is quite possible, for example, for party members to be relatively inactive but to have regular contact with other members either socially, through their families, or because activists call on them to donate money, to sign petitions, to remind them to vote on election day, or to collect their membership subscriptions. Clearly contact is a necessary but not sufficient condition for activism.

In table 3.1 the contact dimension is measured in 1989–90 for Labour and in 1992 for the Conservatives. It can be seen that markedly different rates of contact were experienced by the average member in the two parties. Roughly, Conservative party members were about twice as likely to have no contact at all with other members in comparison with Labour party members. A similar picture emerges in relation to attending meetings, an important indicator of contact often used as a key measure of high-intensity participation. In this case Labour party members were about four times more likely to attend meetings frequently than were Conservatives.

The second dimension of participation relates to campaigning. This involves fund-raising, organizing membership recruitment drives, arranging meetings, and running local election campaigns. For a general election, the "long campaign," or the eighteen months leading up to a general election, is particularly important (Miller et al. 1990). The work of the general election campaign itself is relatively short, typically five or six weeks, but it is also very intensive.

Key indicators of the campaigning dimension appear in table 3.2. These measures are not comprehensive in that they focus primarily on election-related activities and ignore campaigning linked to local or national policy issues. Nonetheless, they are reasonably good indicators of the amount of campaigning occurring at the grass roots level. Again, Labour party members were more involved in campaigning activities than were Conservatives, with the single exception of donating money. Gen-

TABLE 3.1. The Contact Dimension of Party Activism (in percentages)

"Thinking back over the last year, how often have you had contact with people active in your local branch or constituency party?"

	Labour	Conservatives
Not at all	10	22
Rarely	17	30
Occasionally	29	21
Frequently	44	27

"Thinking back over the last year, how often have you attended a party meeting?"

Not at all	36	66
Rarely	14	14
Occasionally	20	8
Frequently	44	12

Note: Data are from Labour party members in 1989–90 and Conservative party members in 1992.

erally the data show that a significant proportion of party members were involved in campaigning activity, and this is true in both parties.

The third dimension of activism is the representation dimension. This is the activity of holding elective office, either within the party organiza-tion or in outside bodies such as the local council, a National Health Ser-vice (NHS) trust, or the governing body of a local school. This type of activity is classically high-intensity participation, since the meetings of party committees or local council committees can take up a great deal of time, particularly if the party controls the local authority. Not surpris-ingly, the representation dimension of activism involves a much smaller proportion of the party members than do the other dimensions. As can be seen in table 3.3, 30 percent of the Labour party members had stood for office within the party organization on at least one occasion within the previous five years, compared with only 11 percent of Conservatives. The corresponding figures for running for office outside the party organization are, not surprisingly, smaller for both parties. This end of the participation scale comprises the very active members who devoted many hours of their time to party activities in the average month.

We proceed by investigating whether these different measures can all be captured in a single scale. Thus the participation scale is built from the responses to the variables in tables 3.1 through 3.3. Nine of the variables

TABLE 3.2.   The Campaigning Dimension of Party Activism
(percentage who have done this at least once in previous five years)

	Labour	Conservatives
Displayed an election poster	90	51
Signed a petition supported by the party	94	49
Donated money to the party	82	85
Delivered leaflets	83	39
Canvassed voters	66	25

TABLE 3.3.   The Representation Dimension of Party Activism
(percentage who . . .)

	Labour	Conservatives
Stood for office in party in last five years	30	11
Stood for outside office in last five years	15	6
Currently hold office in party	14	8
Currently hold office on outside body	15	7

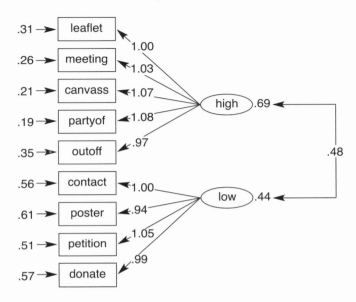

Fig. 3.1. The high- and low-intensity participation scales for Labour party members. *Leaflet* = delivering leaflets; *meeting* = attending a meeting; *canvass* = canvassing voters; *partyof* = running for office in the party; *outoff* = running for office outside the party; *contact* = had contact with activists; *poster* = displayed an election poster; *petition* = signed a petition; *donate* = donated money to the party.

in these tables were measured in four-point scales,[1] such that a measurement model was constructed using these indicators with the LISREL8W maximum likelihood estimation procedure (see Jöreskog and Sörbom 1993). The chi-square goodness-of-fit statistics indicated that a two-factor model fitted better than a single-factor model for both parties, and the results of this analysis appear in figures 3.1 and 3.2.[2]

Figures 3.1 and 3.2 contain the maximum likelihood estimates of the two underlying activism scales, labeled "low-intensity" and "high-intensity" participation respectively. They are derived from nine of the variables in tables 3.1 through 3.3. Each of the observed indicators is represented by an abbreviated label in a box in the diagram, the details of which appear in figure 3.1. The maximum likelihood estimates of the effects of each observed variable on the underlying scale appear on the arrows, and they are all statistically significant at the usual levels.

It is clear that, although the earlier theoretical discussion suggested

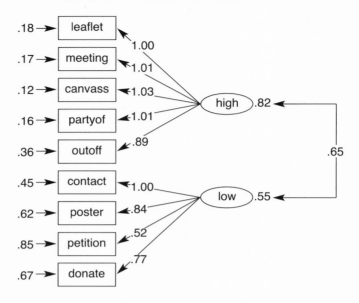

Fig. 3.2. The high- and low-intensity participation scales for Conservative party members. The indicators are the same as those in figure 3.1.

that participation can be described in terms of three dimensions, empirically the results suggest that two dimensions are adequate for understanding different aspects of participation. The low-intensity scale measures activities that involve modest costs in the way of time or effort. Putting up a poster in a window, signing a petition, or making a donation are all important from the point of view of the party and election campaigning, but they are easily accomplished without much time and effort.

In contrast, the high-intensity scale refers to high-cost activities such as attending meetings, canvassing, and running for office, the kinds of activities that keep the party organization going and that help to ensure that elections are won and campaigns are successfully conducted. The two scales are not independent of each other, since the correlations between them that appear in the figures are moderately high; the correlation for Labour party members is 0.48 and for Conservatives is 0.65. Thus it is reasonable to think of participation in the grass roots parties in terms of these two linked dimensions rather than in terms of the three dimensions discussed earlier.

In the light of this discussion we examine the specifications of the alternative models of participation discussed in chapter 2 next. Once the predictor variables in these models are identified, we go on to model the determinants of both the low-intensity and high-intensity participation scales.

Specifying the Determinants of Participation
• ❦ •
The Civic Voluntarism Model

In our discussion of the civic voluntarism model in chapter 2, we observed that the authors explained participation in terms of individuals' resources, their psychological engagement with politics, and recruitment processes that bring them into political activity (Verba, Schlozman, and Brady 1995: 272). In the light of that discussion we can specify a civic voluntarism model of party activism and apply it to the task of explaining variations in activism in the Labour and Conservative parties. For the moment, activism will be defined in terms of both low-intensity and high-intensity participation. These will be distinguished from each other later. The model can be specified as follows:

$$A_i = a_j + b_1 p_i + b_2 R_i + b_3 ED_i + b_4 SC_i + b_5 INC_i + b_6 FT_i + u_i \qquad (1)$$

where
A_i is individual i's level of activism in the Labour party.[3]
p_i is individual i's sense of personal efficacy.
R_i measures if the individual was asked to join the party by friends, family, or work colleagues.
ED_i is individual i's educational attainment.
SC_i is individual i's occupational status.
INC_i is individual i's income.
FT_i measures if individual i works full-time.
u_i is the residual, with $E(u_i) = 0$, $E(u_i u_j) = \sigma^2$, where $i = j$, 0 otherwise.

The first predictor in this model measures the psychological engagement aspects of the civic voluntarism model. As mentioned in chapter 2, this aspect of the model is defined principally in terms of the individual's sense of political efficacy (Verba, Schlozman, and Brady 1995: 272). The

Likert-scaled indicators used to capture this dimension of participation appear in table 3.4.[4]

It can be seen in table 3.4 that the sense of personal efficacy measured by the two statements is quite high, particularly among Labour party members. The average party member feels a reasonably strong level of civic engagement that should, according to the civic voluntarism model, promote activism. The variables are coded so that a high score is given to individuals who feel a strong sense of efficacy.[5]

The recruitment aspect of the civic voluntarism model is captured in table 3.5, which measures the percentage of party members recruited by family, by friendship networks, or in the workplace. It can be seen that this form of recruitment is not very important for either party, although it is more important for the Conservatives than for Labour. To be fair, these figures may understate the role of such recruitment networks in the civic voluntarism model, since in the model the authors stress the importance of requests for involvement from all types of people. However, they do emphasize the particular importance of friends and family as agents for recruiting new participants into politics (Verba, Schlozman, and Brady 1995: 272).[6] One important feature of the recruitment variable is that it represents the mobilization model of participation discussed in chapter 2, which stresses the importance of significant others in motivating the individual to participate. Accordingly, when it comes to estimating effects, we can regard the mobilization model as being nested within the civic voluntarism model.

Table 3.6 measures the resources aspect of the civic voluntarism model. As the quote in chapter 2 suggests, resources can be evaluated in terms of time, money, and civic skills. In the case of time, individuals who work in full-time occupations are less able to participate than are part-timers, the retired, or individuals in full-time education, so this is used as a proxy measure of the time variable. It is measured by a dummy variable scoring one if the individual is in full-time employment and zero otherwise.

TABLE 3.4.   Indicators of Psychological Engagement or Personal Efficacy (percentage who strongly agree or agree)

	Labour	Conservatives
"People like me can have a real influence on politics if they are prepared to get involved."	74	57
"When party members work together they can really change Britain."	92	75

The money dimension is measured by a six-point income scale, and civic skills are measured by occupational status and educational attainment, the latter being the key indicator in the American version of the model (Verba, Schlozman, and Brady 1995: 19). The social class indicator is based on the Hope-Goldthorpe occupational classification scale (see Goldthorpe 1980) and is coded using the five-point version of the scale. Thus white-collar professionals or members of the salariat score one and blue-collar workers score five. Educational attainment is measured by means of a dummy variable that scores one if the individual is a graduate and zero otherwise.

As can be seen in table 3.6 Labour party members are more likely to be in full-time occupations than are Conservatives, largely because so many of the latter are retired. Despite this fact, Conservatives tend to be more

TABLE 3.5. The Recruitment Aspect of Civic Voluntarism (percentage of party members recruited by members of their family, friends, or workmates)

Labour	Conservative
7	12

TABLE 3.6. Indicators of Resources in the Civic Voluntarism Model (in percentages)

	Labour	Conservative
In full-time employment	52	27
Not in full-time employment	48	73
Under £10,000 per annum	38	27
£10,000 to £15,000	18	18
£15,000 to £20,000	15	14
£20,000 to £30,000	17	19
£30,000 to £40,000	8	10
Over £40,000	4	13
Salariat	49	55
Routine nonmanual	16	18
Petty bourgeoise	4	13
Foreman and technician	5	6
Working class	26	8
Graduate	29	12
Nongraduate	71	88

affluent, although it is noteworthy that about one-quarter of them are in the lowest income category. The social class scale shows that Conservatives are more likely to be white-collar professionals than are Labour party members, although the difference between the two parties is not large. However, only about one-quarter of Labour party members are members of the working class, and for the Conservatives this group makes up less than 10 percent of the sample. Thus participation in British political parties is dominated by the middle class. Nearly 30 percent of the Labour party members are graduates, compared with only 12 percent of Conservatives, again reflecting the fact that Conservatives tend to be a lot older than Labour party members and have consequently missed out on the expansion of higher education in Britain, which has occurred particularly over the last twenty years.

As mentioned earlier, the central focus of the civic voluntarism model is resources, and practically all of the variables in the model measure different aspects of resources. In contrast, the key focus in rational choice accounts of participation are incentives, and these are discussed next.

The Rational Choice Model

As the discussion in chapter 2 indicates, the main problem for rational choice accounts of participation is dealing with the paradox of participation first formulated by Olson (1965). Following Olson's work, a rational choice model of party activism can be specified as follows:

$$A_i = a_j + b_1 (p_i * B_j) - b_2 C_i + b_3 O_i + b_4 P_i + b_5 ID_i + u_i \tag{2}$$

or alternatively in additive form:

$$A_i = a_j + b_1 p_i + b_2 B_j - b_2 C_i + b_3 O_i + b_4 P_i + b_5 ID_i + u_i \tag{2a}$$

where A_i and p_i are the same as in model (1), although the interpretation of p_i is rather different, as we explained earlier. In this model efficacy has to be based in objective reality and cannot be merely seen as a psychological attitude. The other variables are:

B_j are the collective benefits resulting from the expected implementation of the party's program.

C_i are the costs of participation.
O_i are selective outcome incentives from participation.
P_i are selective process incentives from participation.
ID_i are selective ideological incentives from participation.

The distinction between the collective and private benefits arising from political activity is central to this model (see Olson 1965). Collective benefits, B_j, are the public goods associated with the policy goals pursued by the political parties. The essential idea here is that party members have a greater incentive to be active if their party is pursuing policies that closely accord with their own policy preferences, in other words if their policy goals are congruent with the goals of the party as a whole. The theory predicts that greater policy congruence should promote greater participation.

As mentioned earlier, such collective benefits give rise to the problem of free riding, and as a consequence in a purely rational choice account few party members would be motivated to participate by such incentives.[7] However, we hypothesize that such incentives are an important influence on the individual's decision to participate. This implies that our working hypothesis is that the free-rider problem is not a serious impediment to participation in practice, since members are not narrowly rational in their behavior.[8]

In the traditional specification of this model, the collective benefits measure is weighted by personal efficacy, p_i, although the model can also be specified in an additive form. Empirical tests will determine whether the additive version of the model (2a) is preferable to the interactive version (2). Personal efficacy is measured by the same indicators used in the civic voluntarism model set out in table 3.4, although the interpretation of the variables differs between the two models. In rational choice accounts feelings of efficacy have to be grounded in objective reality, while this is not true of the civic voluntarism model. However, in measurement terms, the variables are the same in both models.

Table 3.7 contains the policy indicators that are used to define the collective benefits scale. The indicators touch on the key issues of redistribution, health care, trade union rights, and public spending, which have been at the forefront of British politics for many years. The first indicator of collective benefits relates to the issue of poverty. Relative poverty significantly increased over the years of Conservative incumbency from

1979 to 1997, indicating that this was a low priority for the Conservatives, despite the fact that many of their party members support spending on poverty.[9] Following this logic, Conservative party members who discount the importance of poverty have a greater incentive to be active than do members who attach considerable importance to the relief of poverty, since their preferences are congruent with the policy goals of the party. The reverse would be true of Labour, which in opposition and in the run-up to the general election of 1992 argued that alleviating poverty would be a high priority for a Labour government.[10] Thus Labour members who thought that the government should definitely spend more on poverty scored five, while Conservatives who thought this scored one.

The second and third indicators relate to health care and the growth of private medicine in Britain. Because the postwar Labour government founded the NHS, Labour party members tend to be particularly hostile to policies that undermine the NHS. The Conservative government implemented a number of policies designed to promote private health care in Britain,[11] so again Conservatives who attach little priority to the NHS have more of an incentive to participate than do Conservatives who want to strengthen the NHS.

In contrast, Labour's manifesto expressed strong support for the NHS and stressed the need to improve resources for it.[12] By the same logic Labour party members who attach a high priority to spending on the NHS have a greater incentive to be active than do those who attach a lower priority to this objective. Thus Labour members who definitely supported spending on the NHS and definitely opposed the growth of private medi-

TABLE 3.7.   Collective Benefits Measures in the Rational Choice Model
(percentage who think definitely or probably should)

"Please indicate whether you think the government should or should not do the following, or doesn't it matter either way?"

	Labour	Conservatives
Spend more money to get rid of poverty	99	81
Put more money into the National Health Service	99	80
Encourage the growth of private medicine	4	52
Reduce government spending generally	21	60
Give workers more say in the places where they work	94	64
Introduce stricter laws to regulate trade unions	12	66

cine scored five for each of these indicators. Conservatives with the same profile of opinions scored one for each of the indicators.

The fourth collective benefits measure is an indicator of attitudes toward cuts in government spending, which also discriminates between the parties. The Labour party has been traditionally committed to high levels of public spending, particularly on the welfare state, and the Conservatives have been committed to cuts in spending. Thus the 1992 Labour party manifesto stated, "We therefore believe . . . that for liberty to have real meaning the standards of community provision must be high and access to that provision must be wide" (Labour Party 1992: 7). In contrast the Conservative manifesto stated, "Our policy is to reduce the share of national income taken by the public sector" (Conservative Party 1992: 6).[13] Thus Labour members who definitely supported such cuts scored one, whereas Conservatives with the same views scored five.

The fifth and sixth indicators of collective benefits relate to trade union and workers' rights in Britain. Again, this relates to clear policy differences between the parties, because the Conservatives embarked on a series of trade union laws after they were first elected that in the words of one writer aimed to "(a) reduce the scope of regulations designed to protect labour, and (b) increase the scope of regulations controlling trade union behaviour" (Crouch 1990: 322). Thus the Conservatives took vigorous action to undermine the organizational strength of trade unions when they were in office. In contrast Labour, with its long tradition of links with the trade union movement, stressed the importance of giving employees rights in the workplace, including the right to trade union recognition (Labour Party 1992: 13). Thus Labour members who definitely supported workers' rights and definitely opposed stricter laws on trade unions scored five for each measure. Conservatives with the same views scored one for each of the measures.

To sum up, Conservative party members who favored cuts in spending on poverty, government support for private health care, reductions in government spending, and more restrictions on trade unions and workers' rights have a greater incentive to be active than do Conservatives who oppose these policy objectives, and they thus score five for each indicator. The reverse interpretation applies to Labour party members, such that members who support spending programs, the NHS, and workers' rights should have a greater incentive to work for the party than should members who disagree with some, or all, of these policy goals. For both parties

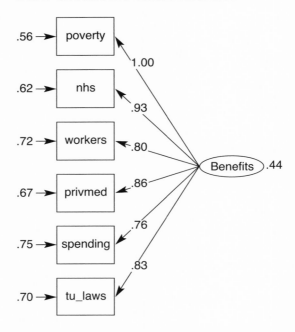

Fig. 3.3.   The collective benefits scale for Labour party members. *Poverty* = spend-ing on poverty; *nhs* = spending on the National Health Service; *workers* = give workers more say; *privmed* = encourage private medicine; *spending* = reduce gov-ernment spending; *tu_laws* = introduce stricter trade union laws.

high scores denote policy congruence or agreement with the party policy goals, and low scores denote the opposite.

The degree of policy agreement or disagreement among the party members can be seen in table 3.7. There is a strong consensus in both par-ties about the need to spend money on poverty and the NHS and, in the case of Labour, the need for enhanced workers' rights. Thus on the face of it policy agreement provides a greater incentive for Labour party members to be active than it does for the Conservatives. However, the caveat to this argument is that the Conservatives were in government during the period 1984 to 1992 when the surveys were conducted, and therefore in a position to deliver on policy promises. In contrast Labour supporters had to discount their evaluation of policy congruence by taking into account the fact that the party was in opposition and was thus unable to deliver on policy promises.

The maximum likelihood estimates of the collective benefits scales for

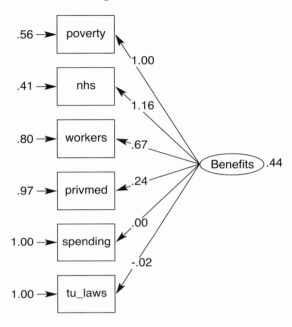

Fig. 3.4. The collective benefits scales for Conservative party members. The indicators are the same as those in figure 3.3.

Labour and the Conservatives appear in figures 3.3 and 3.4. It can be seen that for Labour all of the indicators have a significant relationship with the underlying scale; however, for the Conservatives it appears that, although the relief of poverty, NHS funding, and workers' rights all have significant relationships to the scale, the other measures do not. Thus attitudes toward government spending in general, private medicine, and trade union laws are unrelated or weakly related to the scale. This may reflect the fact that Conservatives have less coherent ideological beliefs than do Labour party members. In the light of these findings we will utilize all six indicators of collective benefits for Labour and the three significant indicators for the Conservatives in the subsequent analysis.

Table 3.8 contains the indicators of perceptions of the costs of participation, which aim to measure the extent to which respondents feel that campaigning for a political party is both tiring and time-consuming. A high perception of costs should inhibit political activism, so respondents in both parties who strongly agree with these statements score five for each measure.

A second type of motivation for participation in the rational choice model derives from selective incentives, or the private returns from involvement. It will be recalled from the discussion in chapter 2 that these incentives represent Olson's (1965) solution to the free-rider problem. Table 3.9 contains indicators of selective incentives in the rational choice model. The indicators of outcome and process incentives are Likert-scaled statements, and the indicators of ideology are nine-point scales of a type that has frequently been used in the comparative analysis of ideology (see, for example, Barnes and Kaase 1979). Respondents in both

TABLE 3.8.   Indicators of Perceptions of Costs in the Rational Choice Model (percentage who strongly agree or agree)

	Labour	Conservatives
Attending a party meeting can be pretty		
tiring after a hard days' work.	72	69
Working for the party can be pretty boring at times.	76	43

TABLE 3.9.   Indicators of Selective Incentives in the Rational Choice Model (percentage who strongly agree or agree)

	Labour	Conservatives
Outcome incentives		
A person like me could do a good job as		
a local (party) councillor.	49	27
The party would be more successful if more		
people like me were elected to Parliament.	35	23
Process incentives		
Being an active party member is a good		
way to meet interesting people.	68	59
The only way to be really educated is to		
be a party activist.	44	36
Ideology[a]		
Percentage in three left-wing categories for party	39	8
Percentage in three right-wing categories for party	15	44
Percentage in three left-wing categories for Britain	68	2
Percentage in three right-wing categories for Britain	10	61

[a]Indicators of ideology are nine-point scales.

parties who strongly agree with the indicators of outcome and process incentives score five for each measure. In the case of ideology, the expectation is that left-wingers are more active in the Labour party and that right-wingers are more active in the Conservative party, an interpretation consistent with the curvilinear disparity thesis discussed in chapter 2.

The data in table 3.9 suggest that outcome incentives are more important for Labour party members than for Conservatives, with small but fewer significant differences between the two parties in relation to process incentives. Thus nearly one-half of the Labour members thought that they could do a good job as a local councillor, compared with just over one-quarter of Conservatives. Close to seven out of ten Labour members thought that party activism was a good way to meet interesting people, compared with six out of ten Conservatives. In relation to ideology, not surprisingly, Labour party members coded themselves in the left-wing categories of the ideological scales and Conservatives in the right-wing categories.

Social psychological models of participation are also preoccupied with incentives, as the earlier discussion indicated. But social norms and the desire of the individual to conform to such norms are also key issues in this theoretical approach, which is discussed next.

The Social Psychological Model

As we mentioned in chapter 2 social psychological models of participation have tended to focus on unorthodox participation and to stress the importance of social norms as well as the expected benefits from participation. We can specify the social psychological model as follows:

$$A_i = a_j + b_1(p_i * EB_i) + b_3N_i + b_4E_i + u_i \tag{3}$$

or the additive version:

$$A_i = a_j + b_1p_i + b_2EB_i + b_3N_i + b_4E_i + u_i \tag{3a}$$

where
    A_i and p_i are the same as in model (1).
    EB_i are the expected benefits from participation.
    N_i are social norms that promote participation.
    E_i are expressive or affective factors that promote participation.

Personal efficacy appears in this model as it does in the previous models. In the social psychological model it can be interpreted as a normative justification for participation, such that an individual who believes that he or she can be influential is seen as justifying participation privately to themselves. As we mentioned in the discussion in chapter 2, this variable says nothing about the objective validity of such a belief.

Similarly, the expected benefits measure differs from its equivalent in the rational choice model in that it focuses on attitudes to the behavior in question rather than attitudes to expected outcomes from that behavior (see Fishbein 1967: 490). Thus the questions should be about the immediate benefits resulting from different acts of participation rather than about the policy gains or losses that might occur from participation, possibly in the long run. Indicators of this type appear in table 3.10.

There are considerable differences between Labour and Conservative party members in their perceptions of the effectiveness of particular types of activity. Part of these differences is due to small differences in question wording,[14] but they are also the result of differences in the perceptions of the members about which political actions are effective. Respondents who thought that a particular activity was very effective scored four, and those who thought it was not at all effective scored one.

Table 3.11 measures the influence of social norms on the individual's attitudes toward party activism. In the case of Labour, such norms were measured by two Likert-scaled statements, which both related to their perceptions of the status of party activists in the minds of other people. Party members who strongly agreed with the statements scored one, and those who strongly disagreed scored five. As the data suggest most Labour respondents thought that the public sees party activists as extremists and

TABLE 3.10. Indicators of Expected Benefits in the Social Psychological Model (percentage who think activity is very effective or effective for Labour and is influential to a large extent or to some extent for the Conservatives)

	Labour	Conservatives
Displaying an election poster	68	23
Donating money to party funds	87	56
Delivering party leaflets during an election	87	45
Attending a party meeting	63	31
Canvassing voters on behalf of the party	89	41
Standing for elected office within the party	75	32
Standing for elected office at a local or national election	83	45

that their work is very often not recognized. This was a direct way of measuring members' perceptions of the social norms surrounding party activity. The implication is that their perceptions that most people have a poor image of party activism should deter such activism.

In the case of the Conservatives an alternative approach was adopted, that of asking them how a significant other person in their lives would react to two Likert statements, both of which asked about the images of party members. As can be seen in the table Conservatives thought that their significant other would disagree with the proposition that party activists are extremists. Similarly, they believed this person would think that party members are respected in the local community.[15] Accordingly, Conservatives who strongly disagreed that party members are perceived as extremists and strongly agreed that they are perceived as respected figures in the local community scored five for each measure.

Table 3.12 contains the indicators of expressive or affective motives

TABLE 3.11. Indicators of Social Norms in the Social Psychological Model (percentage who strongly agree or agree)

	Labour
Many people think party activists are extremists.	75
The amount of work done by ordinary party members is very often unrecognized.	85
	Conservatives[a]
Many Conservative party activists are extremists.	17
On the whole, members of the local Conservative association are respected figures in the local community.	70

[a]For Conservatives, the preamble to the Likert statement said: "Think about those people whose opinions are especially important to you, for example, your spouse, friends, or colleagues. Consider the person whose opinions you most respect: would you say that they agree or disagree with the following statements?"

TABLE 3.12. Indicators of Expressive Attachments in the Social Psychological Model (strength of attachment to their party) (in percentages)

	Labour	Conservatives
Very strong	55	33
Fairly strong	38	50
Not very strong	6	14
Not at all strong	1	4

for participation in the social psychological model. They are the intensity of partisanship indicators that have been used in the American and British Election Studies for many years (see Campbell et al. 1960; Butler and Stokes 1974). In the present context these indicators measure the individual's emotional attachment to his or her party, and the strength of this attachment should be an important influence on his or her participation in the social psychological model of participation. For both parties respondents who are very strong identifiers score four and those whose identification is not at all strong score one.

The General Incentives Model

The last of the models examined in chapter 2 is the general incentives model, which can be regarded as a hybrid model that includes rational choice and social psychological variables. The general incentives model can be specified as follows:

$$A_i = a_j + b_1(p_i * B_j)\, b_2 C_i + b_3 O_i + b_4 P_i + b_5 ID_i + b_6 G_i + b_7 E_i + u_i \qquad (4)$$

or in additive form:

$$A_i = a_j + b_1 p_i + b_2 B_j - b_2 C_i + b_3 O_i + b_4 P_i + b_5 ID_i + b_6 G_i + b_7 E_i + u_i. \qquad (4a)$$

All of the variables in this model have been defined previously, with the exception of G_i, a measure of group efficacy. The essential idea here is that individuals are motivated to be active if they believe themselves to be part of a highly successful organization that is able to achieve its goals.

The indicators of group incentives to participate appear in table 3.13.

TABLE 3.13. Indicators of Group Incentives in the General Incentives Model (percentage who strongly agree or agree)

	Labour	Conservatives
The party leadership doesn't pay a lot of attention to the views of ordinary party members.	39	43
Parties in general are only interested in peoples' votes, not in their opinions.	51	—
Voting is the only way people like me can have any say about how the government runs things.	—	76

The measures tap into the sense of the effectiveness of group action by party members acting together and not just as individuals. Roughly 40 percent of the members of both parties agree with the proposition that the party leadership does not pay a lot of attention to party members. In the case of the second indicator, which concerns the effectiveness of political action, the wording of the Conservative measure is different from that of the Labour measure. Accordingly, respondents who strongly disagreed with the statements scored five, and respondents who strongly agreed scored one. Thus the highest scores went to those respondents who thought that parties are effective and that the party leaders are responsive to their members. Perceptions of group effectiveness are clearly different from the perceptions of individual efficacy examined in table 3.4.

Given that the measures in the various models have now been defined, in the next section we go on to examine the methodological strategy aimed at determining which model provides the best account of party activism.

The Encompassing Approach to the Testing of Rival Theories

The discussion in the previous section indicates that personal efficacy is common to all of the models, although it has a different interpretation in rational choice and social psychological accounts. Similarly, the general incentives model shares many variables with the rational choice and social psychological models, although there are also significant differences among these models.

The standard political science approach to evaluating alternative models has been to use a goodness-of-fit measure such as R^2 or the t-statistic associated with a particular estimate. However, applied econometricians are increasingly skeptical of the value of these measures in the absence of clearly specified alternative models (Charemza and Deadman 1992: 14–30). In an influential article Leamer argues:

> Diagnostic tests such as goodness of fit tests, without explicit alternative hypotheses, are useless since, if the sample size is large enough, any maintained hypothesis will be rejected. . . . Such tests therefore degenerate into elaborate rituals for measuring the sample size. (1983: 39)

Recent developments in applied econometrics have created an alternative "encompassing methodology" that is explicitly designed to test rival theories and avoid this criticism (Mizon 1984; Granger 1990; Hendry 1995). Encompassing methodology involves the idea that the best theory should be able to account for, or incorporate, the results of rival theories by outperforming them in various diagnostic tests.

The approach starts with the theoretical construct of a data generating process (DGP), which is the mechanism underlying the observed data (Granger 1990). The DGP is usually very complex and can only be approximated in practice by the models that are estimated. In this situation the best methodological approach involves testing rival models against each other to see which is the best at approximating the DGP. If one model is better than another it should encompass the alternative; that is, it should be able to predict or account for the results of an alternative model as well as predict phenomena that the rival model is unable to predict. No one model is likely to give a perfect representation of the DGP, but the aim of empirical research should be to try to identify the best of a set of alternative models.

One important distinction is found between nested and nonnested models; a model is nested within another when parameter restrictions placed on the latter produce the former. For example, model (2) is nested within model (4), such that tests of the hypothesis that coefficients b_6 and b_7 in model (4) are equal to zero will allow the researcher to establish whether the latter can be reduced to the former, thus providing a more parsimonious representation of the DGP without loss of explanatory power. Similarly, the mobilization model is nested within the civic voluntarism model.

In contrast, models (3) and (4) are nonnested because they contain different variables, making it impossible to obtain one specification by restricting the parameters of the other. In this situation, we can start with a global model, or a model containing all the variables that appear in both, and then impose restrictions on this to determine if one or another of the original models, or some hybrid combination of the two, provides the best representation of the DGP. In any exercise of this kind one model may encompass another or none of the models may encompass each other. In the latter case the individual models may represent elements of a more general model, perhaps even the global model, which encompasses them all.

The exercise of starting with a global model and restricting its parameters to identify the best model is an aspect of the general-to-specific modeling strategy advocated by Hendry (1995) and others. It runs counter to the traditional political science approach of building simple models to begin with and then making them more elaborate subsequently. The traditional strategy, exemplified in an extreme form by stepwise regression techniques, is considerably inferior to the general-to-specific approach since it invalidates the test statistics and leads to misspecification errors that are unlikely to be identified by the model-building strategy (see Spanos 1990).

A final issue of considerable importance in encompassing methodology is the question of whether predictor variables are endogenous or exogenous, that is, whether they are determined by other variables in the model or determined by factors entirely outside the model. In the case of the civic voluntarism model, variables such as class and income are clearly exogenous, since there is no sensible theoretical support for the proposition that participation determines socioeconomic status; the causal process clearly runs from socioeconomic status to participation. But the personal efficacy variable in the model is more problematic; clearly, participation may determine personal efficacy, despite that the specification defines the relationship in the other direction.

The standard way of dealing with interactions of this type in cross-sectional data is to specify two equations, one for activism and one for efficacy, to estimate the effects. However, as is well known, such specifications require instrumental variables, or variables that are significant predictors in only one of the interactive equations, if the model is to be identified (see Pindyck and Rubinfeld 1991: 292–96). Such instruments are not always available, or they may not be adequate to identify links. A much better way of identifying such interactions is to use panel surveys or time series data. We examine this issue in chapter 4.

In the light of these various points, we next examine the relationship between the four models that have been set out.

Testing Rival Theories of Participation

Given that there are two participation scales for each party, we begin by examining the rival theories applied to the task of explaining variations in the low-intensity scale for Labour members. This is done in table 3.14.

Table 3.14 contains the maximum likelihood estimates of the rival models discussed earlier applied to the task of explaining the low-intensity participation dimension. The various measurement models are not shown for reasons of space, but all of the coefficients in these measurement models are statistically significant. In addition to the familiar R^2 statistic, there is a chi-square statistic (χ^2) attached to the civic voluntarism, social psychological, and rational choice models. This measures the reduction in the goodness of fit of the global model caused by constrain-

TABLE 3.14. Rival Models of Low-Intensity Participation for Labour Party Members (maximum likelihood estimates)

	Civic Voluntarism	Social Psychological	Rational Choice	General Incentives
Personal influence	0.43**	0.20***	0.15***	0.14*
	(16.6)	(8.4)	(3.5)	(1.9)
Full-time employment	0.02	—	—	—
	(1.5)			
Household income	0.02	—	—	—
	(1.6)			
Social class	−0.03**	—	—	—
	(2.5)			
Educational attainment	0.02*	—	—	—
	(1.8)			
Recruitment to party	−0.02***	—	—	—
	(3.0)			
Group influence	—	—	—	−0.05*
				(1.9)
Collective benefits	—	—	0.11***	0.13***
			(8.4)	(5.7)
Costs	—	—	0.11***	0.10***
			(4.6)	(3.0)
Outcome incentives	—	—	0.12***	0.10***
			(9.6)	(6.7)
Process incentives	—	—	0.14***	0.09
			(3.4)	(1.3)
Ideology	—	—	−0.07***	−0.05***
			(4.5)	(3.6)
Expected benefits	—	0.08***	—	—
		(8.3)		
Social norms	—	−0.03***	—	—
		(3.9)		
Expressive incentives	—	0.17***	—	0.12***
		(16.8)		(11.2)
R^2	0.17	0.30	0.33	0.36
χ^2	24.6***(5 df)	11.7***(2 df)	80.7***(6 df)	—

*$p < 0.10$; **$p < 0.05$; ***$p < 0.01$

ing the values of the model under consideration to equal zero. In this way we can test whether the model explains anything at all when its rivals are taken into account. For example, the chi-square statistic increases by 24.6 for the gain of 5 degrees of freedom when the variables unique to the civic voluntarism model were set to zero in the global model. This is a statistically significant change,[16] meaning that the goodness of fit of the global model deteriorates significantly if the civic voluntarism model is ignored.

This means that some or all of the variables in the civic voluntarism model are required to properly model low-intensity participation. This also implies that the rational choice and social psychological models do not encompass the civic voluntarism model. It is worth noting that the traditional political science model building strategy would have preferred the social psychological model to the civic voluntarism model merely because of its higher R^2 statistic.

Having identified that some or all of the variables in the civic voluntarism model are required in an encompassing model, it is noteworthy that the latter explains only a modest percentage of the variance and that only four of the variables are significant. These are personal influence, social class, education, and recruitment. The estimates suggest that party members who have high levels of personal efficacy, are middle class, graduates, and were not recruited by friends, family, or workmates are more likely to score highly on the low-intensity participation scale than are members lacking these characteristics. Oddly, the recruitment variable has the opposite sign to that predicted by the civic voluntarism model, which implies that members who were recruited by family and friends have less contact with the party rather than more, as the theory would suggest.[17] It is also the case that neither time nor income appears to be significant influences on low-intensity participation, a finding that is not that surprising given the low-cost activities that make up the scale.

It may be recalled that the recruitment variable represents the mobilization model that is nested within the civic voluntarism model. That the sign is the opposite to that predicted by the mobilization model, and also that other variables are important in the civic voluntarism model, means that the latter encompasses the former. Thus the civic voluntarism model unequivocally does a better job at explaining contact than does the mobilization model. More generally, the civic voluntarism model is not encompassed by the other models, but it does appear to produce one perverse effect, relating to political recruitment, when it is applied to the task of explaining contact.

The social psychological model is a significantly better fit than the civic voluntarism model. Moreover, the signs of the predictors are consistent with theory, such that personal efficacy, expected benefits, social norms, and expressive incentives all stimulate low-intensity participation.[18] It is also the case that the other models do not encompass the social psychological model, since the goodness of fit of the global model significantly deteriorates if it is removed.

Turning to the rational choice model, the additive version is estimated in table 3.14, and it is clearly not encompassed by the other models in view of the chi-square statistic. Moreover, with one exception the signs of the predictor variables are consistent with theory and the R^2 statistic is larger than the other two models. Thus personal efficacy, collective benefits, outcome, process, and ideological incentives all significantly influence low-intensity participation.

As mentioned earlier, personal efficacy has to be consistent with objective efficacy, which is problematic even for low-intensity activities such as donating money or signing a petition. It is hard to make the case that a single individual can be effective in changing policy goals or policy outcomes by getting involved in low-intensity participation. Thus although the effect is significant, its meaning is not clear in a purely rational choice model.

The other variables all have signs consistent with theory, such that congruence between the respondent and the party on policy objectives promotes participation, as do the selective outcome and process incentives. It is noteworthy that the effect of the ideology scale is negative, indicating that left-wingers are more involved in low-intensity participation than are right-wingers, a finding consistent with the law of curvilinear disparity discussed in chapter 2.

One puzzle is that the effect of costs on participation is positive rather than negative in the rational choice model. Thus respondents who perceive that participation carries high costs are nonetheless more involved in low-intensity participation than are their counterparts. Such an effect has appeared in earlier research (Muller and Opp 1986) and can be interpreted in psychological rather than in cost-benefit terms; members scoring highly on the low-intensity participation scale are simply more aware of the potential costs of participation than are their inactive counterparts, but this does not deter them from participating. As mentioned earlier, since the low-intensity participation scale does not contain high-cost types of participation, the meaning of the indicators used to measure the cost variable may be rather abstract in any case. On the other hand a positive sign on the cost variable is inconsistent with a purely rational choice theory of participation, in which perceptions of costs should deter action.

It is possible of course that the multiplicative version of the rational choice model (3) is superior to the additive version (3a). Accordingly, a multiplicative version of the model was estimated, but it proved to be inferior to the additive version.[19]

Since we know that the rational choice model is not encompassed by the other two models, this must also be true of the general incentives model because the former is nested within the latter, and so the encompassing test is omitted in this case. Incorporating expressive incentives and the group influence variable into the rational choice mode significantly increases the R^2, so the general incentives model clearly encompasses the rational choice model. Expressive incentives are largely responsible for this improvement in fit, since the group incentives variable is barely significant in the larger model. Moreover this variable has a negative effect on the low-intensity participation scale, indicating that respondents who are likely to agree with the indicators in table 3.13 are more involved than those who disagree. Again, this is much more consistent with a social psychological model than a rational choice model.

Table 3.15 contains the estimates of the rival models of the high-intensity participation scale, or the high-cost types of political participation associated with campaigning and running for office set out in tables 3.2 and 3.3. There are important similarities and differences between the models in table 3.15 and the models in table 3.14. In the case of the civic voluntarism model, personal influence, social class, education, and recruitment are statistically significant with the same signs as in the earlier table. However, full-time employment and household income are now significant predictors of activism but with the opposite signs to those predicted by the civic voluntarism model.

Thus individuals with high incomes tend to be rather less active than are those with low incomes, other things being equal, and individuals in full-time occupations are more active than are those in part-time occupations or in no occupations at all. Clearly, these are anomalous results in terms of the civic voluntarism theory, casting some doubt on its validity in the case of high-intensity types of participation.

In contrast the social psychological model of high-intensity participation is very similar to the equivalent model in table 3.14, although the magnitude of some of the effects differs. Thus the indicator of efficacy or personal influence is less important and the indicator of expected benefits is more important than in the low-intensity model. Perhaps it is not surprising that evaluations of expected benefits play a more important role in influencing decisions about high-intensity participation in comparison with low-intensity participation. A similar point can be made about the rational choice model of high-intensity participation; it is very similar to

TABLE 3.15. **Rival Models of High-Intensity Participation for Labour Party Members (maximum likelihood estimates)**

	Civic Voluntarism	Social Psychological	Rational Choice	General Incentives
Personal influence	0.48***	0.09**	0.80**	0.38***
	(14.5)	(2.1)	(2.4)	(3.8)
Full-time employment	0.12***	—	—	—
	(7.5)			
Household income	−0.05**	—	—	—
	(2.7)			
Social class	−0.05***	—	—	—
	(2.7)			
Educational attainment	0.06***	—	—	—
	(3.5)			
Recruitment to party	−0.03**	—	—	—
	(2.6)			
Group influence	—	—	—	−0.02
				(0.9)
Collective benefits	—	—	0.11***	0.13***
			(4.2)	(3.7)
Costs	—	—	0.7***	0.00
			(6.8)	(0.3)
Outcome incentives	—	—	0.38***	0.39***
			(19.4)	(17.4)
Process incentives	—	—	0.12***	0.53***
			(8.6)	(5.5)
Ideology	—	—	−0.05***	−0.03*
			(2.8)	(1.8)
Expected benefits	—	0.31***	—	—
		(12.5)		
Social norms	—	−0.09***	—	—
		(7.9)		
Expressive incentives	—	0.26***	—	0.16***
		(20.3)		(11.3)
R^2	0.10	0.24	0.31	0.41
χ^2	21.2***(5 df)		196.0***(6 df)	—

$*p < 0.10$; $**p < 0.05$; $***p < 0.01$

the low-intensity participation model, except that personal influence and outcome incentives are much more important than in the latter.

The goodness of fit of the general incentives model of high-intensity participation is rather better than the equivalent model of low-intensity participation, and this is largely explained by the role of selective incentives. The latter are significant but rather weak in the low-intensity model but are strong in the high-intensity model, particularly process incentives. Thus mixing with other like-minded individuals and harboring ambitions for a political career are both powerful motives for participating in high-cost types of activities. Not surprisingly, they play a much less significant role in explaining low-intensity participation.

The estimates for the low-intensity models for Conservative party members appear in table 3.16, and it can be seen that they share many of the features of the Labour models; thus the social psychological model is practically the same as in table 3.14, except that social norms are not significant. Similarly, the rational choice model is rather similar to the Labour case, except that outcome incentives are not significant and costs deter participation rather than enhance it, as in the Labour model. A similar point can be made about the general incentives model, although in this case group incentives have a positive effect on low-intensity participation and respondents on the right of the political spectrum are more involved than are those on the left. Again, this finding is consistent with the curvilinear disparity thesis.

The civic voluntarism model of low-intensity participation for the Conservatives differs most clearly from the equivalent Labour model. It may be recalled from table 3.14 that social class, education, and recruitment influenced low-intensity participation in the Labour model. In contrast, out of these variables only education is a significant predictor in the Conservative model. Moreover, the sign of the education variable is negative, suggesting that less educated Conservatives are more involved than are highly educated Conservatives, other things being equal. Another difference relates to full-time employment, which is a significant predictor of low-intensity participation in the Conservative model, although it was not significant in the Labour model; respondents in full-time employment tend to be more involved with the Conservative party than do others.

Overall, it appears that the general incentives model of low-intensity participation encompasses the rational choice model for the Conservatives. It is also the case that the social psychological model is encompassed by the other models, since the reduction in fit is not significant when it is removed from the global model. This means that social norms and the expected benefits are superfluous in modeling the determinants of low-intensity participation for Conservative party members.

Table 3.17 contains the estimates of the models of high-intensity participation for the Conservatives, and once again there are important similarities with the Labour models; the social psychological, rational choice, and general incentives models are very similar for both parties, although

TABLE 3.16.   Rival Models of Low-Intensity Participation for Conservative Party Members

	Civic Voluntarism	Social Psychological	Rational Choice	General Incentives
Personal influence	0.13***	0.10***	0.05*	0.01
	(10.5)	(3.6)	(1.9)	(0.6)
Full-time employment	0.07***	—	—	—
	(6.3)			
Household income	−0.02	—	—	—
	(1.5)			
Social class	0.02	—	—	—
	(1.4)			
Educational attainment	−0.05***	—	—	—
	(3.7)			
Recruitment to party	−0.02	—	—	—
	(1.3)			
Group influence	—	—	—	0.07***
				(5.1)
Collective benefits	—	—	0.09***	0.05***
			(3.7)	(2.3)
Costs	—	—	−0.04***	−0.03**
			(2.7)	(2.2)
Outcome incentives	—	—	−0.24	0.13***
			(0.6)	(0.5)
Process incentives	—	—	1.30***	0.94***
			(3.0)	(4.2)
Ideology	—	—	0.14***	0.12***
			(9.6)	(8.6)
Expected benefits	—	0.45***	—	—
		(12.6)		
Social norms	—	0.01		—
		(0.5)		
Expressive incentives	—	0.06***	—	0.04***
		(4.5)		(2.9)
R^2	0.11	0.35	0.20	0.24
χ^2	33.4***(5 df)	1.3(2 df)	86.2***(6 df)	—

*$p < 0.10$; **$p < 0.05$; ***$p < 0.01$

perceptions of personal influence appear to play a less important role in explaining high-intensity participation in these models for Conservatives than they do for Labour. Selective incentives clearly play a very important role in explaining participation in both parties, as do expressive incentives. The major difference between the two parties relates to the goodness of fit of the social psychological model, which is much higher for Conservatives than it is for Labour. In particular, expected benefits are

TABLE 3.17. **Rival Models of High-Intensity Participation for Conservative Party Members**

	Civic Voluntarism	Social Psychological	Rational Choice	General Incentives
Personal influence	0.28***	0.10***	0.03	0.01
	(15.5)	(7.0)	(1.5)	(0.6)
Full-time employment	−0.14	—	—	—
	(0.7)			
Household income	−0.01	—	—	—
	(0.5)			
Social class	−0.02	—	—	—
	(0.9)			
Educational attainment	0.10***	—	—	—
	(4.3)			
Recruitment to party	−0.02	—	—	—
	(0.9)			
Group influence	—	—	—	0.02
				(1.0)
Collective benefits	—	—	0.24***	0.16***
			(8.2)	(5.6)
Costs	—	—	−0.02	−0.01
			(1.1)	(0.4)
Outcome incentives	—	—	0.38***	0.38***
			(13.6)	(14.0)
Process incentives	—	—	0.29***	0.21***
			(9.1)	(7.7)
Ideology	—	—	−0.01	−0.12***
			(0.3)	(5.2)
Expected benefits	—	0.54***	—	—
		(26.4)		
Social norms	—	−0.18***	—	—
		(2.6)		
Expressive incentives	—	0.27***	—	0.27***
		(14.2)		(26.0)
R^2	0.11	0.48	0.36	0.42
χ^2	32.9***(5 df)	303.5(2 df)	206.4***(6 df)	—

*$p < 0.10$; **$p < 0.05$; ***$p < 0.01$

significantly more important for explaining Conservative high-intensity participation than they are for Labour.

Once again we can see that the general incentives model encompasses the rational choice model. But none of the other models encompasses each other, suggesting that some hybrid model is best for explaining high-intensity participation in the Conservative party. The goodness of fit of the civic voluntarism model is slightly smaller for the Conservatives than it is for Labour, largely because only educational attainment and personal influence are significant predictors. It appears that social class, income, time, and the mode of recruitment to the party are irrelevant as factors that explain Conservative participation. These findings suggests that the civic voluntarism model is a rather weak explanation of participation, although the chi-square test indicates that the other models do not encompass it. The results also indicate that the mobilization model is not relevant for explaining high-intensity participation among Conservatives.

Discussion

We have seen that the models are rather similar for both parties, although there are important differences between them, particularly in relation to the civic voluntarism model. It is also the case that some of the rival models encompass others; the mobilization model is encompassed by the civic voluntarism model, and the rational choice model is encompassed by the general incentives model. However, there is no clear optimal model that encompasses all the others, so it appears that different variables from the civic voluntarism, social psychological, and general incentives models are needed to define such an optimal model.

These results show that, when data confront theory in empirical tests that do not privilege one theory at the expense of others, no clear winner is found. One could only prefer a rational choice account of participation by ignoring empirical evidence that supports social psychological accounts. By the same token one could only prefer social psychological models by ignoring the evidence that rational calculations play an important role in influencing participation. A similar point can be made about the civic voluntarism model, which is incomplete on its own, but it nonetheless contains important insights into participation that are not adequately captured by its rivals. Having said this, it is important to rec-

ognize that the general incentives theory receives stronger empirical support than do its rivals, even if it does not wholly encompass them.

   If the testing up to this point does not identify a clear winner, what is
the next step? In the earlier discussion of encompassing methodology we
pointed out the importance of carrying out exogeneity tests to identify an
optimal model. This issue has not been addressed up to this point because
such tests cannot be effectively carried out with cross-sectional data.
Clearly, before trying to identify an overall optimal model it is important
to examine the issue of causal sequence using the panel surveys of Labour
and Conservative party members. This issue is addressed in chapter 4.

Chapter 4

The Dynamics of High-Intensity Participation in Britain

◦✦◦

IN CHAPTER 3 WE DISCOVERED THAT NONE of the models examined could be described as optimal in relation to either low-intensity or high-intensity participation. This suggests that a hybrid model is likely to be best for explaining participation among the grass roots members of British political parties. In this chapter we examine the question of exogeneity as a criterion for identifying the optimal model, which takes us into an examination of the dynamics of participation in the grass roots parties over time. From now on we focus primarily on high-intensity participation, since the low-intensity and high-intensity participation scales can be modeled in a rather similar way and since high-cost participation is our main focus of interest.

A recurrent theme in much of the contemporary literature is that political parties are increasingly being marginalized in the political process (Flanagan and Dalton 1984; Lawson and Merkl 1988). Hence the study of party dynamics is an important question in its own right, apart from the light it throws on questions of the nature of political participation. The idea that parties are becoming increasingly irrelevant in politics is based on several lines of reasoning. First, the growth of the media, particularly the electronic media, has marginalized the parties in the processes of communication between elites and the electorate. The suggestion is that party members are no longer needed as "ambassadors to the community" (Scarrow 1990, 1996) or as channels of communication between the mass and elites, since the leadership can communicate more effectively with the voters directly rather than via the party members. An important aspect of this is the growth of direct mail, which enables parties to bypass the members in fund-raising and campaigning.

Another feature of the declining importance of grass roots parties is the growing reliance of parties on experts for policy advice; party leaderships will consult outside experts, think tanks, and research organizations when formulating policies, but they will rarely consult their own party members, whose advice they may regard as amateurish or extremist. A third development that promotes this view of the role of parties relates to the growing state subsidies to political parties in many democratic systems, which threatens to co-opt or capture them, ultimately transforming them into agents of the state. The cartel party thesis discussed in chapter 1 (Katz and Mair 1995) argues that parties are increasingly becoming, in effect, state organizations that do not need voluntary contributions and an active grass roots to maintain an effective organization. All these arguments weaken the incentives to participate and imply that there is likely to be a decline in high-intensity participation over time.

Against these arguments is the point that parties are crucially important for aggregating political interests, thereby helping to avoid the well-known problems of indeterminacy in social choice (Aldrich 1995). This is particularly important in the British political system, with its uncodified constitution and ill-defined institutional responsibilities. As we point out in chapter 1, the executive could not be recruited and sustained in the House of Commons without party discipline. If parties were as weak in Parliament as they are, for example, in the United States Congress, Britain would face a severe problem of ungovernability. In the United States, it has been argued that there are 535 members of Congress and 535 parties (Arnold 1990), and the weakness of party cohesion is one of the causes of policy gridlock, or the inability of the system to deal with major political problems (see Cox and Kernell 1991). In Britain, where the executive is not elected independently of the legislature, it would make government difficult, if not impossible. On the other hand this is an aggregate-level argument for maintaining a strong party system, which is a different question from the issue of sustaining incentives to participate at the individual level.

The analysis in this chapter is divided into four sections. We begin by examining the evidence on trends in party activism in both parties, discussing in an informal way some of the short-term and long-term factors that might explain these trends. This leads into a section in which the dynamic model of activism is specified and the strategy for testing the causal status of the predictor variables is discussed. The third section examines estimates of the models and identifies the optimal model. Finally, we discuss the implications of the findings in a concluding section.

Trends in Party Activism over Time

Trends in political participation in the Labour and Conservative parties are examined by means of panel surveys conducted over a four-year period.[1] The Labour panel covered the period 1989–90 to 1992, and the Conservative panel covered 1992 to 1994. Table 4.1 contains information about how the number of hours worked for the party by the members changed over time between the two waves of the panel surveys. It can be seen in table 4.1 that the number of hours worked for the party in the average month declined for both parties over time. The mean number of hours worked in the case of Labour fell from 1.96 to 1.89, and the mean number of hours for the Conservatives fell from 1.44 to 1.40. Both these changes, though modest, are statistically significant, indicating that the panel evidence suggests that both parties are becoming de-energized over time. However, the decline was nearly twice as large for Labour (–0.07) as it was for the Conservatives (–0.04).

In fact Labour started from a more active base than the Conservatives, since just under 50 percent of Labour respondents spent at least some time on party activities in the average month in 1992, compared with only 25 percent of Conservatives; this approximate two-to-one ratio of active Labour members to active Conservatives appears to be reproduced at

TABLE 4.1.   Hours Worked by Labour and Conservative Party Members in the Average Month, 1990 to 1994 (in percentages)

Hours Worked	Labour		Conservatives	
	1990	1992	1992	1994
None	47	51	75	77
Up to 5 hours	33	30	16	15
From 5 up to 10 hours	9	9	5	5
From 10 up to 20 hours	7	5	2	2
More than 20 hours	5	5	2	2
Mean hours	1.96	1.89	1.44	1.40

Note: Labour panel 1990 to 1992, N = 2,935; Conservative panel 1992 to 1994, N = 1,604. Difference of means test statistically significant for Labour (t = 3.74) and Conservatives (t = 2.75).

every level of activism, from the very active, who devote more than twenty hours to party activity, to the totally inactive. Overall, Labour was still more active than the Conservatives, even after these changes took place.

Another interesting feature of table 4.1 is that for the Conservatives the decline in activism came exclusively from members in the relatively inactive category of those who devote up to five hours in the average month. By contrast, for Labour some of the really high-intensity participants who devoted between ten and twenty hours to party activity in the average month in 1990 also became de-energized.

Table 4.2 contains information about changes in the number of hours devoted to party activity in the average month, expressed in the form of the percentage of party members who became more or less active over time. Looking at the data in this way reveals that the percentage of party members whose activities declined was nearly twice as great for Labour as it was for the Conservatives. But again, the percentage of Labour party members whose activities increased was also twice that of the Conservatives, so the net difference between the more active and the less active in each party is small. However, there was clearly more volatility in activism for Labour compared with the Conservatives.

The overall activism measure in tables 4.1 and 4.2 is interesting, but it gives little insight into which activities increased and which decreased over time. This information is provided in table 4.3, which contains data on the eight specific aspects of participation introduced in chapter 3, which vary from the low-intensity activities like displaying an election poster in a window to the high-intensity activities like standing for elective office in a local or national election. The first section in table 4.3 contains information about Labour party members, and it can be seen that in their case all types of political activities, with the exception of

TABLE 4.2. Changes in the Percentages of Hours Worked by Labour and Conservative Party Members, 1990 to 1994

	Labour	Conservatives
Percentage of party members who		
(a) worked less	21	12
(b) worked the same	63	81
(c) worked more	16	8
(a) – (c)	5	4

TABLE 4.3. Labour and Conservative Party Members' Activities, 1990 to 1994 (in percentages)

	Not at all		Rarely		Occasionally		Frequently	
	1990	1992	1990	1992	1990	1992	1990	1992
Labour party members								
Displayed an election poster in a window	9	9	3	3	20	18	69	70
Signed a petition supported by the party	5	9	4	9	31	37	60	45
Donated money to party funds	16	10	15	12	35	39	35	40
Delivered party leaflets in an election	15	17	5	6	20	22	60	56
Attended a party meeting	16	21	14	17	25	24	44	38
Canvassed voters on behalf of the party	32	36	9	11	22	20	37	33
Stood for office in the party	69	70	5	6	11	10	15	14
Stood for office in a local or national election	83	83	3	2	4	5	10	10
Conservative party members								
Displayed an election poster in a window	47	43	9	9	24	27	20	21
Signed a petition supported by the party	49	43	14	14	27	34	10	10
Donated money to party funds	13	10	10	10	46	49	32	31
Delivered party leaflets in an election	57	55	4	6	14	15	25	24
Attended a party meeting	48	49	14	14	19	22	18	16
Canvassed voters on behalf of the party	73	76	6	4	11	9	11	11
Stood for office in the party	87	88	2	2	5	5	6	5
Stood for office in a local or national election	93	94	1	1	3	2	3	3

donating money to party funds, declined over time. The decline was most marked in relatively high-intensity activities such as attending meetings, delivering leaflets, canvassing, and standing for office in the party organization.

The largest decline for Labour relates to attending meetings, which is the yardstick often used by many to measure whether a party member is an activist. Thus some 6 percent fewer Labour members frequently attended meetings in 1992 compared with 1990, and at the other end of the scale the number of members who never attended meetings at all increased by 5 percent. A similar point can be made about canvassing and delivering leaflets during elections; some 4 percent fewer reported canvassing frequently for the party, the same percentage decline as among those who frequently delivered leaflets.

These election-related activities are particularly significant, since the first wave of the survey took place before the 1992 general election and the second after that election. Thus respondents are largely reporting on the 1987 election in the first wave and on the 1992 election in the second wave. It appears that Labour's election campaign at the grass roots was less effective in the latter election compared with the former, at least among individuals who were party members at the time of both elections.

The second section in table 4.3 on Conservative party members is rather different from the Labour section. Looking at the "frequently" column, it can be seen that declines in activity are recorded for some items, but they are much smaller than they are for Labour. Thus 2 percent fewer Conservatives frequently attended meetings in 1994 compared with in 1992, and at the other end of the scale only 1 percent more members never attended meetings at the time of the second wave in comparison with the first wave. Election-related activities show small declines for the Conservatives. As with Labour, the first wave of the survey took place before the 1992 general election, so respondents in this wave are principally describing their election-related activities in 1987. Thus it appears that the Conservative grass roots campaign in 1992 was only slightly less effective than the 1987 campaign, again with respect to members who stayed in the party between the two waves of the survey.

The evidence from these two-year panels is interesting, but since it measures changes over a relatively short period of time the reduction in the rates of activism observed are necessarily rather modest. To get a fuller picture of these trends we need to examine changes in activism over a longer period. This is done in table 4.4, which compares the 1990 survey of Labour party members with the most recent survey conducted in 1999, which is examined in more detail in later chapters. The evidence in table 4.4 shows a striking reduction in the number of hours of work done for the party by the average member over time.

The proportion of the members who did no work at all for the party increased from about one-half to nearly two-thirds over this ten-year period. There were similar reductions in rates of activism of members who did up to twenty hours of work for the party in the average month. The sole exception to this pattern were the most active members, who did more than twenty hours a month. Many of these were elected representatives involved in official meetings and other business commitments of various kinds arising from their status as elected officials, so for them activism could only be reduced by stepping down from elected office altogether.

Clearly, the key issue is to explain why these trends in activism have occurred. The theoretical models discussed in chapter 2 and estimated in chapter 3 suggest that three classes of variables are at work. The first class of variables is demographics, which as we have seen are the main factors accounting for participation in the civic voluntarism model. The second class is social psychological variables such as social norms and expressive attachments to the party; finally, the third class involves cognitive calculations of the costs and benefits of participation.

Since the demographic variables change very little over a period of two years, we focus primarily on the affective and cognitive variables in the discussion, although demographics have an important indirect influence, which we point out later. Thus selective and collective incentives, perceptions of individual and group efficacy, evaluations of the effectiveness of different types of political activities, expressive attachments, and social

TABLE 4.4.   Trends in Party Activism in the Labour Party, 1990 to 1999 (hours spent on party activities in the average month, in percentages)

	1990	1999
None	51	65
Up to 5 hours	30	22
From 5 up to 10 hours	10	7
From 10 up to 20 hours	6	3
More than 20 hours	4	4

norms might all play a role in explaining the decline of activism. We consider these, together with demographic variables in an informal way,
before modeling the relationships more formally later.

While demographic variables change relatively slowly over time, there
is a way they can nonetheless influence participation in the grass roots
parties. This works indirectly through the influence of the demographic
profiles of the existing party members. Such profiles are skewed in comparison with party supporters in the wider electorate. Thus in 1990 some
61 percent of Labour party members were male, 49 percent were professionals or members of the salariat, and only 22 percent were under the age
of thirty-five. The profile of Labour voters at the time of the surveys was
rather different: 52 percent were female, 32 percent were under the age of
thirty-five, and only 16 percent were white-collar professionals (Seyd and
Whiteley 1995: 470). Conservatives faced a similar problem particularly
in relation to age; only 5 percent of their members were under the age of
thirty-five, and 55 percent were members of the salariat in 1992. In contrast 29 percent of Conservative voters were under the age of thirty-five,
and only 38 percent of them were members of the salariat (Seyd and
Whiteley 1995: 470).

It seems likely that in the case of Labour many working-class people,
and in the case of the Conservatives many young people, thought of the
parties as organizations not for them. Thus potential working-class
Labour party members may have been put off by the middle-class character of the party organization; similarly, potential young Conservatives
may have seen the party as essentially a retired person's club. So the
demographic profiles of the membership may have inhibited potential
new members from joining the party and existing members from being
active, and if this became more important over time it might account for
some of the observed trends.

Turning to the cognitive variables that appear in rational choice models, we have seen that selective incentives can be subdivided into process,
outcome, and ideological incentives for political action. With regard to
process incentives, or the incentive to be involved in politics for its own
sake, there are many political and nonpolitical alternatives to party activity that an individual can pursue. The leisure industry has grown in
importance over time, which includes everything from sports and home
improvement to watching television, and so the growth of attractive nonpolitical alternatives to party activity is one possible explanation for
declining activism.

In the political arena, there are a number of competing organizations that provide process incentives for participation, particularly interest groups and the new social movements. The latter includes the green movement, the women's movement, and the peace movement. These are attractive alternatives for an individual who enjoys being involved in politics for its own sake. Conservatives are more likely to be involved in environmental groups than they are in peace or women's movements (Whiteley, Seyd, and Richardson 1994: 255–56), as can be seen by the fact that some 27 percent of Conservatives were also members of the National Trust.[2] In contrast Labour party members were more likely to be involved in the peace movement (Seyd and Whiteley 1992: 232). Clearly, if many party members are attracted by conservation groups or the peace movement, it seems plausible that many members will find them to be an attractive alternative to party membership. In this sense membership of interest groups is a substitute for membership of party groups. There is evidence that some of these interest groups have substantially grown in size in recent years (Moloney and Jordan 1997), which could explain some of the observed changes in party activity.

Selective outcome incentives relate to private incentives for participating in politics, such as the desire to achieve elected office in local government or the goal of developing a full-time career in party politics. Since the late 1970s there has been a dramatic decline in the powers and prestige of local government (Jones and Stewart 1983; Stewart and Stoker 1989). As King points out:

> since 1979 there have been almost 50 separate Parliamentary Acts affecting local authorities. The aim of these reforms is to marginalise local government as a political institution by creating alternative local agencies to deliver policy and by denuding its representative role. (1993: 194)

If the importance and prestige of local government have declined, this will reduce selective outcome incentives for participation in local politics and also in the party system. Individuals who might otherwise have valued a career in local government, for example, as a local councillor, will increasingly conclude that it is not worth getting involved, which in turn will inhibit their participation in local party politics.

There is another factor at work influencing outcome incentives that should inhibit participation in the Labour party in comparison with the

Conservatives. This is the fact that Labour lost four general elections in a row from 1979 until the 1997 Labour landslide. A few studies examine the effects of elections on political variables, such as voters' sense of political efficacy and their attitudes toward issues. These studies show that such variables are all significantly influenced by election outcomes (Finkel 1985, 1987; Clarke and Kornberg 1992). Therefore election defeat is likely to have an effect on participation.

From the point of view of the individual party member hoping to build a political career, to have his or her party in office is a big advantage. Winning an election brings two benefits with regard to outcome incentives at the local level; first, it makes it more likely that an activist seeking a parliamentary career will get elected; the probability of being elected in 1992 was 0.521 for Conservative candidates and 0.427 for Labour candidates, a modest but significant difference.[3] But it also allows the party in government to promote policies that favor the local authorities they control, thus providing additional incentives to participate at the local level in those authorities. The redistribution of central government revenue away from Labour-controlled authorities to Conservative-controlled ones in the 1980s is a clear example of this development (Travers 1986). Clearly, the effect of the election defeat of 1992 would have been to reduce the incentives to participate for Labour party members in comparison with Conservatives.

The third type of selective incentives is ideological incentives. We noted earlier that the general incentives model suggests that Labour members to the left of the ideological spectrum and Conservative members to the right should, according to the curvilinear disparity thesis, be rather more active than members who are in the center of the ideological spectrum. The evidence in chapter 3 suggests that this idea appears to apply to Labour but was less true for Conservatives. In the latter case ideology did not appear to influence high-intensity participation, although it did affect low-intensity participation. Clearly it is important to investigate the links between ideology and participation over time.

The Labour party has shifted significantly to the right over the last two decades, starting with Neil Kinnock in the early 1980s and culminating with Tony Blair in the 1990s (Shaw 1994). This is discussed more fully in chapter 5. These changes do have implications for activism, since left-wingers appear to be more active than right-wingers. The shift to the right will therefore tend to produce a decline in activism over time as left-wingers become discouraged. Even if the effect is modest it will very likely show up over a two-year period.

Up to this point we have focused on the effects of changes in selective incentives on participation by party members. But the general incentives model suggests that collective incentives, associated with policy goals, also play a role in influencing the commitment of grass roots party members. In the case of the Conservatives, earlier research shows that many grass roots members are "One Nation," or progressive Tories (Whiteley, Seyd, and Richardson 1994: 137). Thus supporters of welfare and poverty programs, advocates of the traditional NHS, and sympathizers with the idea of generous unemployment benefits would have found themselves increasingly at odds with the party during the Thatcher era. Many of them would have remembered the Macmillan years, when "One Nation" Toryism was at its height, and the changes in party programs since that time would have discouraged them.

Labour faced a rather different problem from the Conservatives in relation to collective incentives. Since it lost four elections in a row, it was not in a position to supply collective benefits to its supporters prior to 1997. Again, repeated electoral defeats would have inhibited the incentives for participation associated with achieving policy goals, and this would have served to reduce participation in the party.

In relation to social psychological variables, a decline in expressive or emotional attachments to a party can be an additional factor that explains declining activism. A long-term decline has taken place in the strength of partisanship in the British electorate over time (Crewe, Sarlvik, and Alt 1977; Sarlvik and Crewe 1983; Heath et al. 1991). Clearly, this is very likely to have affected recruitment to the political parties, since, if party identification has weakened, the pool of individuals who are potential recruits is going to shrink. Fewer people will be motivated to join or to become active if they do join. In addition, if this trend also influenced existing party members this would reduce the rates of activism over time. While this is a long-term phenomenon, its effects should be discernible over a two-year period.

This process of partisan dealignment has been linked to changes in the social structure, particularly the decline of class voting (Sarlvik and Crewe 1983). But as we suggest in chapter 7, party identification is significantly influenced by policy outcomes, particularly those relating to the economy (Fiorina 1981; Clarke, Stewart, and Whiteley 1995). Applying this idea to the expressive attachments of party members, such attachments may have declined because of the failure of the Conservative government to achieve policy success, particularly in relation to the management of the economy.

Yet another factor in the decline of party membership and activism is linked to the influence of social norms on political participation. Integrated, stable communities with a strong tradition of Conservative or Labour party support will sustain the party over time by a set of social norms that promote party membership. Rural villages in the south of England in the case of the Conservatives and mining villages in the north of England in the case of Labour come to mind as clear examples of the relationship between community and party allegiance. However, social and geographical mobility over the years, the gentrification of rural communities, and the collapse of the mining industry in Britain have changed this picture.

There is a residual Conservative and Labour vote in such areas as the rural Home Counties and the former Yorkshire and South Wales coalfields. Such places will remain fairly fixed in their voting behavior, but they will be less likely to sustain an active local party. Affluent, educated, middle-class professionals have too many other leisure pursuits or activities to occupy their time to become involved in the routine tasks of running the local Conservative party. Similarly, chronically unemployed members of the underclass have such a low sense of political efficacy that they are unlikely to participate in Labour party politics. A general weakening of social and community ties and a decline of social capital (Putnam 1993, 1995) will tend to undermine local parties for reasons quite separate from policy concerns or expressive attachments to the party. These are relatively slow, long-term processes and are not directly related to policy concerns or short-term political developments. Such changes are slow to take place and for that reason may not be observable in our panel samples.

Finally, we have suggested that participation is influenced by a sense of group efficacy, or a belief that the party to which the individual belongs is effective in achieving its political goals. This is an aspect of the "civic culture" that motivates individuals to become involved in politics. In their classic study, Almond and Verba define the civic culture in terms of a set of "attitudes towards the political system and its various parts, and attitudes to the role of the self in the system" (1963:13). In their discussion of the role of parties in promoting civic attitudes they suggest that:

> political parties . . . are analogous to the veins and arteries of a circulatory system. Unless they are connected effectively with the primary structure of community—family, friendship, neighborhood, religious

groups, work groups and the like—there can be no effective flow of individual impulses, needs, demands, and preferences from the individual and his primary groups into the political system. (Almond and Verba 1963: 105)

Since we know that a sharp decline in the individual membership of both the Labour and Conservative parties has occurred since 1959, when the Almond and Verba survey in Britain was carried out, the links between parties and the community have also attenuated.[4] This may have produced a spiral of decline, with the party membership itself becoming a source of further decline, as the grass roots activists become thin on the ground and unrepresentative of the communities in which they live (see Whiteley and Seyd 1998).

To summarize the discussion up to this point, a number of cultural and sociological factors are at work that have produced a long-term decline in the membership and in levels of political activism within the Labour and Conservative parties through their effects on the incentives to participate. Our panel surveys may not have identified all of the long-term cultural and sociological factors in explaining the decline of activism, since they bridge only a relatively short period of time. But some effects will appear, and changes relating to the cognitive and affective variables should be apparent. Clearly, before focusing on which of the variables matter in explaining the decline, we need to identify the optimal model of activism.

Identifying the Optimal Model of Party Activism

The analysis in chapter 3 suggests that none of the rival models was uniquely identified as the optimal model, although some models encompass others. The advantage of panel data is that we can address directly the question of exogeneity in these models and use this as a criterion for searching out the optimal model.

Finkel and Muller (1998) address the question of evaluating alternative models of unorthodox participation with panel data from West Germany. They make the point that

decisive tests of rational choice theories cannot be conducted with cross-sectional data using individuals' reports of past behavior. Most obviously, an individual's expected utility from participation, by definition, refers to some future state, rendering reports of past participation irrelevant from the point of view of rational choice theory. (37)

Their approach to this problem was to utilize panel samples. With panels, independent variables measured at time one can be used to model the behavior of a dependent variable at time two, an exercise that has two distinct advantages. First, it makes the independent variables unambiguously exogenous, since activism at time two cannot influence the predictor variables in the equation at time one. Second, it addresses Finkel and Muller's point that rational choice models, or in our case a model that contains rational choice variables, should contain prospective and not retrospective variables in the specification. In other words the attitudes that are thought to influence participation should be measured before, not after, the behavior takes place. Finkel and Muller use incentive variables measured in 1987 to predict reported participation in 1989 and then go on to examine reciprocal linkages in the model by predicting incentives in 1989 from both participation and incentives in 1987. In this way they are able to identify causal links.

A more general approach to that used by Finkel and Muller, adapted from recent work in applied econometrics, is to test models of political participation for evidence of strong exogeneity, or Granger causality (Granger 1988). In econometrics, the concept of Granger causality plays a very important role in identifying causal relationships in time-series variables. It can be formulated as "x is a Granger cause of y, if present y can be predicted with better accuracy by using past values of x rather than by not doing so, other information being identical" (Charezma and Deadman 1997: 165).

In the econometric literature Granger causality testing takes place in the context of vector autoregressive (VAR) time-series modeling (Sims 1980) in which the causal relationships between a system of variables is identified without making unwarranted assumptions about the exogenous or endogenous status of the variables in the system. This approach can be applied to the task of identifying the optimal model of participation using panel data by employing the following specification:

$$A_{i2} = a_{11} + b_{11}A_{i1} + b_{12}P_{i1} + b_{13}B_{j1} - b_{14}C_{i1} + b_{15}O_{i1} + b_{16}P_{i1} + b_{17}\mathrm{ID}_{i1}$$
$$+ b_{18}G_{i1} + b_{19}E_{i1} + b_{110}\mathrm{EB}_{i1} + b_{111}\mathrm{N}_{i1} + g_{11}R_{i1} + g_{12}\mathrm{ED}_{i1}$$
$$+ g_{13}\mathrm{SC}_{i1} + g_{14}\mathrm{INC}_{i1} + g_{15}\mathrm{FT}_{i1} + u_{i1}.$$

From the discussion of the previous chapter this will be recognized as the global model of participation, containing all the variables in the models examined earlier. A_{i2} refers to activism measured in the second wave of the panel survey, and A_{i1} refers to activism measured in the first wave; the b_{ji} are the coefficients of variables that may or may not be exogenous in a cross section but that are clearly exogenous in a panel specification where variables from wave one are used to predict a variable from wave two; finally, the g_{ji} are coefficients of variables that are obviously exogenous in both a cross section and panel specification. The latter refer to the demographic variables in the civic voluntarism model.

This specification is of the type used to identify Granger causality adapted to panel rather than to time-series data, since it examines the effects of the predictor variables in wave one on activism in wave two, controlling for activism in wave one. In other words it estimates whether the incentive and demographic variables have a significant influence on future activism over and above current values of activism. If one or more of the predictor variables are caused by activism rather than being causes of activism, they will not pass such an exogeneity test.

This last point can be illustrated by an example. Assume that current activism causes current perceptions of political efficacy rather than the other way around, as the specification of the global model implies. In this situation a control for current activism in the model should make the influence of current political efficacy on future activism nonsignificant. In other words the link between current political efficacy and future activism would be revealed as spurious once current activism is taken into account. This approach makes it possible to identify spurious effects caused by reciprocal causation.

The Granger causality test does not end at this point, however, since a further investigation of reciprocal links in the model is possible. To apply Finkel and Muller's (1998) approach to our example, they would investigate the reciprocal effects of activism on political efficacy with the following equation:

$$P_{i2} = a_{21} + b_{21}A_{i1} + b_{22}P_{i1} + u_{i2}.$$

In this specification, if b_{21} is statistically significant, it means that wave one activism influences wave two efficacy, suggesting that inferences about the influence of efficacy on activism in a cross-sectional model are problematic because of this feedback process.

However, Finkel and Muller's approach is unduly restrictive, since it fails to take into account other variables in the system that might produce a spurious relationship between political efficacy and activism. A more general specification that allows us to test for Granger causality involves incorporating those variables that are statistically significant in the global model into the reciprocal model. For example, if all of the variables in the global model were significant predictors of activism, the correct specification of the reciprocal effects model would be:

$$P_{i2} = a_{21} + b_{21}A_{i1} + b_{22}P_{i1} + b_{23}B_{j1} - b_{24}C_{i1} + b_{25}O_{i1} + b_{26}P_{i1} + b_{27}ID_{i1}$$
$$+ b_{28}G_{i1} + b_{29}E_{i1} + b_{210}EB_{i1} + b_{211}N_{i1} + g_{21}R_{i1} + g_{22}ED_{i1} + g_{23}SC_{i1}$$
$$+ g_{24}INC_{i1} + g_{25}FT_{i1} + u_{i2}.$$

If this specification revealed a significant relationship between activism at time one and political efficacy at time two, it would mean that efficacy does not Granger-cause activism.

To sum up, if political efficacy Granger-causes activism, it should pass two tests. First, current political efficacy should be a statistically significant predictor of future activism controlling for current activism, and second, current activism should not be a significant predictor of future political efficacy, again controlling for the other predictors in the model. In our example the coefficient b_{12} in the global model should be significant, while the coefficient b_{21} in the equation above should be non-significant. A similar approach can be applied to all of the other predictor variables in the global model, apart from the demographic variables that we know to be exogenous in any case.

We turn to the exercise of estimating the optimal model next.

The Optimal Model of High-Intensity Participation

The estimation of a panel regression makes it possible to assume that all predictor variables in a model are exogenous, but it also changes the interpretation of the coefficients in comparison with chapter 3. In the previous chapter we examined the contemporaneous impact of the predictor variables on activism, but in table 4.5 we examine the lagged impact of these variables on high-intensity participation, given that prior participation has already been taken into account. In effect these models estimate the

effects of incentives at time one on the change in high-intensity participation between time one and time two. They mix up the contemporaneous effects predicted by theory with longitudinal effects that may work in
the opposite direction.[5] This is a complication in the interpretation of the
coefficients that offsets to some extent the advantage of this approach in
identifying Granger causality.

Table 4.5 contains estimates of the global models and the optimal
models of high-intensity participation for both parties. It can be seen that
some of the effects have changed sign in comparison with the effects
identified in chapter 3. In the cross-sectional model of chapter 3, for
example, process incentives have a positive impact on participation,
which is consistent with theory. In the Labour panel model of table 4.5,
process incentives are negative predictors of participation. The latter
effect means that members who are motivated by social interaction in
wave one of the survey became less active over time. Both types of effects
are possible because the coefficients in table 4.5 measure both contemporaneous and longitudinal effects at the same time.

This is an important point that can be illustrated with an example; if
the intervention of the general election that took place between the two
waves of the panel caused members to focus more on campaigning than
on socializing, this could serve to discourage members who are primarily
motivated to be active for social reasons. As a consequence members who
score high on the index of process incentives would become significantly
less active than would members motivated to be active for other reasons.
This would produce a negative relationship between lagged process
incentives and contemporaneous activism in the models of table 4.5.
More generally, changing circumstances might have the effect of overrid-
ing the contemporaneous positive relationship between process incentives and activism. Clearly the panel effects may differ from the cross-sectional effects.[6] However, the important thing from the point of view of
exogeneity testing is that the effects are statistically significant, which
serves to establish Granger causality.

The optimal models exclude nonsignificant variables in the global
model, with no loss of fit. In both cases the R^2 goodness-of-fit statistics are
very high. The chi-square (χ^2) statistics measure the deterioration in the
fit caused by deleting variables from the global models in order to estimate
the optimal models. Both of these statistics are nonsignificant, which
implies that the optimal model encompasses the global model in each
case.

TABLE 4.5. Optimal Models of High-Intensity Participation for Labour and Conservative Party Members Using Panel Data—Dependent Variables (wave two)

Predictor Variables (wave one)	Labour Activism	Labour Activism	Conservative Activism	Conservative Activism
Activism	0.88***	0.86***	0.90***	0.91***
	(31.2)	(38.3)	(36.0)	(38.1)
Personal influence	0.07	—	−0.02	—
	(1.0)		(0.5)	
Group influence	0.02	0.30***	0.03***	0.03***
	(1.4)	(3.6)	(2.7)	(2.7)
Collective benefits	−0.06***	−0.05***	−0.03	−0.04*
	(3.9)	(3.6)	(1.5)	(1.9)
Costs	−0.06	—	−0.01	—
	(1.5)		(1.2)	
Outcome incentives	0.06***	0.07***	0.03*	0.02*
	(4.2)	(5.9)	(1.7)	(1.6)
Process incentives	−0.18*	−0.09***	−0.01	—
	(1.9)	(2.6)	(0.3)	
Ideology	−0.03**	−0.02**	0.05***	0.05***
	(2.3)	(2.3)	(2.9)	(2.7)
Expressive incentives	−0.02**	−0.02**	−0.07***	−0.07***
	(2.2)	(2.1)	(5.1)	(5.3)
Expected benefits	0.09***	0.08***	0.07**	0.05*
	(3.2)	(3.3)	(2.1)	(1.8)
Social norms	−0.03**	−0.02***	−0.02*	−0.02*
	(2.8)	(2.7)	(1.8)	(1.7)
Full-time employment	0.01	—	−0.00	—
	(0.8)		(0.2)	
Household income	−0.02	—	0.03**	0.03***
	(1.4)		(2.4)	(2.8)
Social class	0.03**	0.03***	−0.04***	−0.04***
	(2.4)	(3.2)	(2.8)	(3.3)
Educational attainment	−0.00	—	−0.10***	−0.11***
	(0.1)		(7.2)	(8.1)
Recruitment to party	0.02	0.02*	−0.02	−0.02*
	(2.1)	(1.9)	(1.6)	(1.9)
R^2	0.84	0.84	0.89	0.89
χ^2	—	5.92	—	3.37
		(5 df)		(4 df)

*$p < 0.10$; **$p < 0.05$; ***$p < 0.01$

To examine the Labour models in table 4.5 first, high-intensity participation in wave one, not surprisingly, was a strong predictor of such participation in wave two, although the coefficient of 0.88 is significantly different from 1.0, indicating that the effect of past participation decays over time.[7] The optimal model contains variables from three of the models discussed earlier, but in a number of cases the signs of the variables have changed in comparison with the cross-sectional models in chapter 3.

One example of this is expressive incentives, which is a positive predictor of high-intensity participation in the cross-sectional models but is negative over the two-year period of the panel. Again, this implies that participation among individuals with strong attachments to the party in 1990 declined more than did participation among individuals with weak attachments at that time. Thus once prior participation is taken into account, which theory predicts is positively related to expressive attachments, strong expressive feelings reduced participation over time, and this is one of the sources of the decline in Labour activism. We are observing a kind of burnout in which the strongly attached became less active.

Elements from each of the three rival models are found in the optimal Labour high-intensity participation model. From the civic voluntarism model, social class and recruitment are significant predictors of participation, although again the effects are reversed in sign in comparison with the cross-sectional models. Thus the participation rates of middle-class party members declined more than those of working-class members, once the direct relationship between class and high-intensity participation is taken into account. Similarly, party members recruited by friends and family became less involved over time, compared with those recruited by other means.

With respect to the social psychological model, both social norms and expected benefits influenced high-intensity participation over time. In this case the signs of the effects are the same as in the cross-sectional models; members who thought that the various activities benefited the party were more likely to be active over time, in comparison with members who thought the opposite. Thus expected benefits positively influence participation both in the cross-sectional and dynamic specifications. A similar point can be made about social norms.

With regard to the general incentives model, it is noteworthy that a number of the variables did not have an impact on participation over time. This is true of personal influence and perceptions of costs. While these variables clearly impact high-intensity participation in the short run, they do not appear to Granger-cause such participation as measured in this specification.[8] It is more promising that selective incentives relating to outcome, process, and ideological incentives are all significant predictors of high-intensity participation over time, and all have the same signs as in the cross-sectional models, with the exception of process incentives. So five of the eight predictor variables in the optimal model are from the general incentives model, suggesting that the general incentives model dominates the others, even if it does not formally encompass them.

The Conservative participation models are very similar to the Labour models. Thus personal influence, perceptions of cost, and full-time employment do not appear to have an influence on high-intensity participation over time. In contrast selective incentives, with the exception of process incentives, appear to be important, as do expected benefits and social norms. The major difference between the Labour and Conservative models relates to the civic voluntarism variables; unlike Labour both household income and education appear to influence participation. High-income individuals became more active than low-income individuals, and middle-class Conservatives became more active than working-class Conservatives. The sole exception to this pattern relates to education, since graduates were less likely to remain active than were nongraduates.

As mentioned earlier, the models in table 4.5 provide only half of the test for Granger causality, since we have yet to examine reciprocal effects. This is done in table 4.6, which includes the coefficients measuring the influence of current participation on the future values of the predictor variables, controlling for all other significant variables in the models.

There is no evidence of significant reciprocal effects between high-intensity participation and the predictor variables in table 4.6, with the exception of expressive incentives. It appears that the latter are influenced by prior participation for both Conservatives and Labour party members. This means that, when expressive attachments are included in cross-sectional models as contemporaneous predictors of participation, the reciprocal effects may lead to distorted estimates. Accordingly, in response to this finding when the optimal model is used in later panel estimates it always incorporates wave one measures of expressive incentives rather than wave two measures to avoid this problem.

Overall, the estimates in tables 4.5 and 4.6 taken together indicate that, with the exception of expressive incentives, the predictor variables in the optimal model all Granger-cause high-intensity participation. This is fairly conclusive evidence that participation is explained by incentive and social psychological variables of various kinds, and these measures are not just by-products of activism explained by something else.

The optimal model is clearly a hybrid model, but it is nonetheless dominated by the general incentives model. The prominent role of the selective incentives indicates the importance of cost-benefit calculations in explaining why some party members become highly active when others do not. However, the results also indicate that a narrowly defined rational choice account of participation is not consistent with the evidence, since expressive incentives, group incentives, and social norms are all important influences on participation in the optimal model. None of these variables is compatible with a narrow rational choice account that focuses purely on a calculus of the costs and benefits of participation. Clearly, social norms, emotional attachments, and feelings of group solidarity are all crucial to understanding high-intensity participation.

From the perspective of the optimal model, the weakest of the theoretical explanations of participation is provided by the civic voluntarism model. None of the resource variables in that model Granger-causes Labour participation, with the exception of social class. But even in the

TABLE 4.6.   The Influence of Current High-Intensity Participation on Future Values of the Predictor Variables Controlling for Other Predictors in the Models

	Labor	Conservatives
The influence of prior activism on:		
Group influence	−0.03	−0.04
	(1.5)	(1.0)
Collective benefits	0.01	−0.03
	(0.3)	(0.9)
Outcome incentives	0.02	0.03
	(1.5)	(0.7)
Process incentives	0.02	—
	(0.8)	
Ideology	0.01	0.01
	(0.6)	(0.3)
Expressive incentives	−0.03*	0.10***
	(1.9)	(3.0)
Expected benefits	0.02	0.02
	(1.1)	(0.7)
Social norms	0.02	0.01
	(1.1)	(0.1)

$*p < 0.10$; $**p < 0.05$; $***p < 0.01$

case of class, the sign of the coefficient is the opposite of that predicted by the civic voluntarism model, although to be fair this model makes no predictions about participation over time. However, the finding that middle-class activists became less active over time in comparison with working-class activists does not fit well with a theory that suggests that the middle class have more resources than the working class and as a consequence are more likely to participate.

The Conservative model is different in that education and income play a role in explaining changes in participation, which at first sight supports the civic voluntarism model. However, once again some of the effects are inconsistent with this model; as the rich and the middle class became more active in comparison with the poor and the working class, graduates became less active. This finding is quite inconsistent with the civic voluntarism model, which, as the earlier discussion shows, regards education as a good indicator of resources.

Overall, a modified version of the general incentives model, which includes additional social psychological variables, appears to explain high-intensity participation. Demographic variables play a residual role in explaining the dynamics of participation, but not in a way that is fully consistent with the civic voluntarism model. These results establish that all the variables in the optimal models of table 4.5 Granger-cause participation, with the exception of expressive attachments.

We mentioned earlier that the signs of the estimates are not easily interpreted since they are a mixture of contemporaneous and longitudinal effects. It is possible to correct this problem by estimating the optimal model with contemporaneous rather than lagged predictor variables, in other words by modeling high-intensity participation in wave two using the wave two predictors in the optimal model. This approach cannot of course be used to establish Granger causality, which requires lags to identify the causal processes. But once Granger causality is established by other means, it can be used to estimate contemporaneous effects free of longitudinal influences. This specification includes a control for past activism, which implies modeling the effect of contemporaneous predictors on the change in activism over time. Put another way, if, for example, process incentives cause activism, then such incentives should also cause a change in activism, and this is what the version of the model seeks to establish.

Table 4.7 contains the contemporaneous estimates of the optimal models. To examine the Labour model first, it can be seen that the strongest predictor of high-intensity participation is outcome incentives. This suggests that political ambition, a selective incentive for involvement, is the most important variable in explaining why some individuals are more active than others at the high end of the scale. It is also true that the other measures of selective incentives—process and ideological incentives—are important predictors of participation as well, and all of these effects have the expected signs. Thus individuals who enjoy meeting other like-minded people are more likely to participate for that reason, and individuals on the left of the ideological spectrum are more active than those on the right.

Clearly, once longitudinal effects have been cleaned from the models the relationships appear to be consistent with theory. The results suggest that selective incentives outweigh any other type of incentive when it

TABLE 4.7. The Optimal Models—
Contemporaneous Effects with Exogenous Variables
(all wave two variables)

Predictor	Labour	Conservatives
Group influence	0.03***	0.04
	(2.4)	(0.3)
Collective benefits	0.05**	0.15***
	(2.1)	(2.9)
Outcome incentives	0.37***	0.28***
	(16.6)	(6.3)
Process incentives	0.12***	—
	(3.3)	
Ideology	−0.04*	−0.05
	(1.8)	(0.4)
Expected benefits	0.13***	0.82***
	(4.7)	(6.4)
Social norms	−0.04***	−0.18**
	(2.7)	(2.4)
Expressive incentives	0.13***	0.29***
(wave one)	(8.9)	(6.3)
Social class	−0.06***	−0.16***
	(3.6)	(3.7)
Educational attainment	—	0.12***
		(3.6)
Recruitment to party	−0.02	0.08**
	(1.7)	(2.5)
R^2	0.37	0.52

$*p < 0.10$; $**p < 0.05$; $***p < 0.01$

comes to explaining variations in high-intensity participation in the Labour party.

The expected benefits measure is also an important predictor of participation in the Labour model, again with the correct sign; individuals who see immediate payoffs to the party from different types of political activity are more active for that reason. Expressive incentives are also important in having a positive impact on participation, although in this case we are using the wave one measure of expressive attachments because this variable did not pass the Granger causality test. It is clear though that members who strongly identify with the party are more likely to participate than are those with weak attachments.

Additional variables in the Labour model that are important predictors of activism include the group influence variable, collective benefits, social norms, and social class, which all have signs consistent with theory and with the results in chapter 3. Thus party members who have a strong sense that the Labour party is an effective organization at achieving its goals are more likely to participate as a consequence. Similarly, members who have policy goals that are congruent with those of the Labour party are more likely to participate, and individuals who believe that party members have a favorable image in society are also more active. Finally, the middle-class members are more likely to participate than are the working-class members.

Turning to the Conservative models, again the results are very similar to the Labour models and are also consistent with theory. Outcome incentives are clearly prominent predictors of high-intensity participation, although in this case their impact is eclipsed by the importance of expected benefits. Clearly, for Conservatives the perception that particular types of participation are very effective in achieving the party's goals is very important. Again, in common with the Labour model, expressive incentives are an important factor in explaining participation, as are social norms and collective benefits.

The main difference between the Conservative and Labour models relates to the role of social background variables.[9] In the case of Conservatives both education and social class are important predictors of participation, whereas for Labour there is only a class effect. The estimates show that highly educated, middle-class Conservatives were more likely to participate than were less educated, working-class Conservatives. Finally, the recruitment variable is important for Conservatives, such that members recruited by friends and family were more active participants than were those who joined the party by other means.

Discussion

The results of this modeling exercise suggest that, while some differences exist between the parties and some variables are statistically significant in some models and not in others, there is nonetheless a core set of variables that are robust predictors of high-intensity participation that make up the optimal model. The variables common to both parties are collective benefits, outcome incentives, expected benefits, expressive incentives, social norms, and social class. In addition there is evidence that ideology plays an important role for Labour and that education and recruitment play a role for the Conservatives. Taken as a whole, the optimal models provide a close insight into the underlying determinants of high-intensity participation of the type we have been examining in this study.

The results lead to a number of conclusions about the nature of political participation and the relevance of different theoretical approaches to an understanding of participation in politics, a topic we return to in chapter 8. But for the moment the major conclusion from this modeling exercise is that the general incentives theory clearly dominates the rest. By contrast, the civic voluntarism model makes a rather modest contribution to understanding high-intensity participation, and some findings are clearly inconsistent with it. Clearly, high-intensity participation is largely the product of cognitive and affective variables found in both rational actor and social psychological theoretical accounts.

This chapter has focused on the dynamics of high-intensity participation among both Labour and Conservative party members. The evidence up to this point has suggested that grass roots participation in the British party system has been in decline, which is true for a number of reasons. But between 1994 and 1997 the Labour party increased in size by about 40 percent, as the leadership embarked on a conscious effort to recruit new members. This striking reversal of long-term trends in the grass roots Labour party suggests that declining participation is not inevitable but can be reversed if the parties themselves take concerted action. We examine this intriguing episode in the next chapter.

Chapter 5

New Labour:
Reversing the Decline?

∾◈∾

IN THIS CHAPTER WE CHANGE THE FOCUS of attention from the dynamics of activism to the question of why individuals join a party in the first place, relating this to the optimal model of participation. Up to this point we have suggested that weakening partisanship and declining activism have characterized the British party system in the postwar years. However, New Labour achieved a remarkable electoral victory in May 1997, giving it a parliamentary majority larger than the entire parliamentary Conservative party. This victory was the culmination of the modernization process that was nearly fifteen years in the making (see Shaw 1994, 1996; Jones 1996; Mandelson and Liddle 1996).

As we pointed out in chapter 1, part of this modernization process involved a conscious effort by the leadership to rejuvenate the grass roots party by recruiting new members and giving existing members new incentives to participate. Thus we focus on whether this change of strategy, which can be dated from Blair's accession to the leadership in 1994, has fundamentally changed the character of the grass roots party. The wider issue raised in this chapter is whether political parties can reverse decline and rebuild themselves, even after years of neglect of their grass roots organization.

Labour's modernization strategy had a number of elements involving changes to the party constitution, policy changes, a new media strategy, and also a thorough overhaul of the party organization. One aspect of the latter was a new recognition of the importance of individual party members in sustaining an effective party organization. The party leadership had paid lip service to the importance of recruiting members for many years but in practice had done little to reverse the long-run decline in the membership that had been taking place since the early 1950s (Seyd and Whiteley 1992: 16). However, after Blair became party leader in 1994 this situation radically changed, such that by the time of the general election of 1997 individual party membership had increased by about 40 percent (Labour Party 1998). As shown in table 1.1, there was a remarkable renaissance in Labour's individual membership after 1994.

This raises the intriguing question of whether the decline in grass roots activism discussed earlier has been reversed in the light of this remarkable achievement. A similar point can be made about the Conservative party. Following their election defeat in 1997, the new leader, William Hague, set in train a modernization process whose purpose was "to organize and motivate voluntary membership, which we aim to double to well over 600,000 members" (Conservative Party 1997: 10). Thus the Conservatives followed in the footsteps of the Labour strategy with the same aim of revitalizing the grass roots party.

Because Labour pioneered this modernization process, the focus in this chapter is on the Labour strategy, with the aim of assessing whether it has successfully reversed the decline of grass roots party activism. The key to this development was a change in the recruitment and retention strategy from that of a traditional passive/responsive mode to that of an active/mobilization mode. For the first time the party developed a well-resourced national campaign aimed at recruiting members instead of relying on the traditional method of merely responding to individuals who approached the party or relying on haphazard local recruitment campaigns.

The change in recruitment strategy occurred in a fairly clearly defined period, so it is possible to examine the effects with something that approximates a quasi-experimental research design (Cook and Campbell 1979). This change makes it possible to evaluate the effects on participation of a shift to a mobilization model of recruitment. Essentially we show that the shift to the new recruitment strategy significantly altered the incentives for participation in the grass roots party, which in turn led to the recruitment of a new type of relatively inactive member. These findings suggest that while Labour has clearly reversed the decline in membership it has also stimulated the decline in activism, even though this is measured from a higher base of total membership.

The basic findings of this chapter conclude that, while the absolute level of participation in the grass roots party increased as a result of the new recruitment strategy, the relative decline in participation continued.

Put another way, although the party had more members and hence the total amount of activity in the grass roots party increased between 1994 and 1997, the average amount of activity per member continued to decline. Furthermore, after Labour entered office in 1997, the absolute decline in activity resumed.

This chapter is divided into four parts. We begin with a review of Labour's modernization strategy, insofar as it related to the recruitment of party members. The effects of a change from a passive/responsive mode to an active/mobilization mode of recruitment on participation are then examined in the second section. The distinction between Old Labour and New Labour party members is examined at this point and is used to construct hypotheses about the effects of the changing membership recruitment strategy on participation. This leads into the third section, which examines whether the optimal model developed in chapter 4 explains the differences between Old and New party members in their rates of participation. The model is estimated with data from a second panel survey of Labour party members conducted in 1997–99, the methodological details of which are described in the appendix. The final section contains a discussion of the results and conclusions.

Labour's Membership Recruitment Strategy

As is well known, individual membership of the Labour party had been in decline from the early 1950s until 1994, when Tony Blair became party leader (Whiteley 1982; Seyd and Whiteley 1992:16). This was true despite the fact that the party leadership had sought to modernize the party and its recruitment strategy following the massive electoral defeat of 1983.[1] The new party leader, Neil Kinnock, who was elected after that defeat, set in motion a modernization strategy aimed at revitalizing the party organization, constitution, and policies. As part of that strategy, in 1987 he announced a commitment to double the party membership, and this and other reforms led to the creation of a national membership scheme in 1989.[2] Despite these efforts, the objective was not pursued with any vigor or organizational resources, and as a consequence it had little effect on membership recruitment in practice.

Part of the reason for this was a certain ambivalence on the part of the leadership concerning the role of individual members in the political process. On the one hand the leader's commitment to an increased membership suggested that he thought they were quite important. On the other hand the Shadow Communications agency, which coordinated campaign strategy, announced a declared aim to bring about "a shift in campaigning emphasis from 'grass roots' opinion forming, to influencing electoral opinion through the mass media" (Hughes and Wintour 1990: 52). So the objectives of the strategy were divided and unclear.

One student of Labour party politics observing this period argued that "the organizational transformation achieved under Kinnock resulted in the reinforcement of oligarchical tendencies inherent in all voluntary organizations" (Shaw 1994: 223). If so, part of the problem was that despite the rhetoric Kinnock may not have accepted the need to give grass roots members greater incentives to participate.

However, following the election defeat of 1992, Labour strategists began to see the political and electoral advantages of a revitalized grass roots party. These advantages are related to campaigning, fund-raising, and the legitimation provided by a mass membership among the wider electorate. Of these factors campaigning and fund-raising were undoubtedly the most important in the minds of the party leadership.

In relation to campaigning, a conventional wisdom had developed over time that local campaigns were largely irrelevant in influencing voting behavior and turnout (see Butler and Kavanagh 1992: 245). But new research had begun to show the importance of grass roots campaigning in winning elections at the local level (Johnston and Pattie 1995; Pattie, Johnston, and Fieldhouse 1995; Whiteley and Seyd 1992, 1994; Denver and Hands 1985, 1997). This alerted party strategists to the importance of developing a thriving grass roots party organization.

Speaking from the platform on behalf of the National Executive Committee at the 1992 Labour party conference, Clare Short announced:

> There is an important new book that I hope many comrades have looked at, by Patrick Seyd and Paul Whiteley, which is a study of Labour's grassroots and it shows very clearly that where we have a strong and active local party, we do better electorally. So the NEC intends, despite the financial difficulties that we face, to put a major effort into work that has been neglected in recent years to revitalise and strengthen our grassroots. (Labour Party 1992: 74–75)

Fund-raising had become more important as well. While legal restrictions on campaign advertising prevent the type of escalating campaign costs experienced in the United States, fund-raising has nonetheless become a growing problem for British political parties in the face of the rising costs of election campaigns (Pinto-Duschinsky 1983; Fisher 1994, 1995; Kavanagh 1995). Party strategists began to see the party members as a resource to be tapped for donations, particularly at election times.

The view that members legitimated the party in the wider community was strongly supported by John Smith, the leader who took over from Neil Kinnock after the 1992 general election defeat. He took membership very seriously and regarded party members as "ambassadors to the community" (Scarrow 1996: 43). In an article he wrote for *Labour Party News* he argued:

> It is vital that we increase our membership. Members are the lifeblood of the party. From them flow ideas, campaigns, activities and income. And through them we can campaign on our policies and build local support for the party. (Smith 1993)

Part of the impetus for the recruitment strategy was the assumption that new members would be much less opposed to changes in the party constitution and policies than would be the long-established members. So grass roots support for the leadership's modernization strategy itself became an additional reason for recruiting members (see Whiteley and Seyd 1998).

After the election defeat of 1992, the national party headquarters set up a project for revitalizing the grass roots called "Active Labour,"[3] which aimed to guide local parties in reviewing organizational problems, setting up recruitment drives, and motivating new members to join the party. Thus the change from a traditional passive/responsive mode of membership recruitment to an active/mobilization mode was chiefly a response to Labour's fourth election defeat in a row.

However, it took the election of Blair as the new party leader after the untimely death of John Smith in 1994 for the new approach to be fully implemented. Before he became leader Blair had worked to build a large membership in his own constituency of Sedgefield, and the new leader was anxious to create a new image for the Labour party, depicting it as a new and dynamic force in British politics. New members would serve to demonstrate that the party had shed its past identity and would help to undermine Conservative claims that Blair was a front for the politics of nationalization and centralization. Furthermore, rising membership depicted a reforming party as the forerunner of a reforming government, enabling him to claim that "Without a radical and vibrant party, there will be no radical and vibrant government" (Blair 1994: 19).

The new active membership recruitment strategy turned out to be very successful. Writing in 1996 Peter Mandelson and Roger Liddle were able to claim that "the British Labour Party has become the fastest growing political party in Europe. At over 363,000, the party has its highest level of membership since 1979" (219). By 1997 the membership had reached 405,238 (Labour Party 1998), a 40 percent increase over the 1994 figure. However, the change in recruitment strategy had implications for the type of member being recruited. In particular, the shift to an active/mobilization mode of recruitment changed the incentives for active participation in the party organization, an issue we examine next.

Old and New Labour Activism and Recruitment
· ❧ ·

The terms "Old Labour" and "New Labour" have acquired ideological meanings in popular discourse, with the former describing supporters who favor old-style policies of nationalization, state intervention, redistribution, and high taxes and the latter describing supporters who favor public-private partnerships, little redistribution, and limited taxation. In the present context, however, we will use the terms purely in a chronological sense: Old Labour will refer to party members who joined prior to Blair becoming the leader in 1994, and New Labour will refer to the members who joined between 1994 and 1997. The first wave of the panel survey showed that in 1997 the former group made up about 59 percent of the membership and the latter 41 percent. If we examine the differences between these two groups using the same indicators of activism that appeared in tables 4.1 and 4.3, clear distinctions between the two types of member appear.

Table 5.1 indicates that very significant differences existed between the Old and New Labour party members with respect to their rates of activism. While the Old Labour members were less active than their counterparts in 1989–90 (see table 4.1), they were considerably more active than the New Labour members; some 10 percent of the Old Labour members worked more than ten hours in the average month for the party in comparison with only 2 percent of the New Labour members. This suggests that the decline of activism noted in chapter 4 has continued among long-standing members, and it has accelerated when new recruits are taken into account as well.

Table 5.2 provides more detailed information about the rates of activism of the Old and New Labour members. In every case the former were more active than the latter; Old Labour members were more likely to display election posters, donate money to party funds, deliver leaflets, attend meetings, and canvass. The magnitude of these differences can best be gauged by looking at the right-hand columns of table 5.2, which provide information on the highly active party members. It can be seen that Old Labour members were roughly twice as likely to sign a petition, donate money, and deliver leaflets and were three times as likely to canvass voters than were their New Labour counterparts. Not surprisingly, when it came to standing for office within the party organization or in the wider society, the differences were even larger; Old Labour members were nine times more likely to run for office in a local or national election than were their New Labour colleagues.

There are two possible explanations of these findings; one might be described as a socialization hypothesis, which suggests that the New Labour members were less active because they had only recently joined the party and thus were not yet socialized into the norms and values of the party or fully integrated into the local party organization. As a result they were likely to be less active than Old Labour members, although the presumption would be that eventually they would become as active as party members in general. It is not clear how long this socialization process takes, but much of it should have taken place by the time of the second wave of the panel survey in 1999.

TABLE 5.1.   Hours Worked by Old and New Labour Party Members in the Average Month in 1997 (in percentages)

Hours Worked	Old Labour	New Labour
None	54	73
Up to 5 hours	28	21
From 5 up to 10 hours	8	4
From 10 up to 20 hours	5	1
More than 20 hours	5	1

Note: N = 5,761. Old Labour made up 59 percent of the membership, and New Labour made up 41 percent.

The second hypothesis can be described as the recruitment hypothesis. It suggests that New Labour members are a new type of member altogether who have been persuaded to join the party by the mobilization campaign but who in the absence of such an intensive campaign would not have joined at all. If this interpretation is correct the New Labour members are always going to be much less active than their traditional counterparts, with the gap between the two groups likely to continue into the future. This means that, if the party continues to recruit more new members of this type, as they become a larger proportion of the total membership, average rates of activism within the party organization are likely to decline further.

We can test these competing hypotheses using the panel data that tracks the rates of activism of the two types of member over time. If the socialization hypothesis is correct, then the difference in rates of activism between the Old and New Labour members should have narrowed or even been eliminated by 1999. On the other hand if the recruitment hypothesis is correct, this difference should have remained the same or even widened in the intervening period.

The evidence from table 5.3 is fairly unequivocal and shows that the recruitment hypothesis rather than the socialization hypothesis best fits the data. The first point is that by 1999 only 36 percent of the sample were New Labour members in comparison with 41 percent in 1997. Even

TABLE 5.2. Old and New Labour Members' Activities in 1997
(in percentages)

Activity	Not at All		Rarely		Occasionally		Frequently	
	Old	New	Old	New	Old	New	Old	New
Displayed an election poster in a window	11	26	4	7	20	28	66	39
Signed a petition supported by the party	18	32	11	13	37	36	34	18
Donated money to party funds	12	23	11	15	11	15	38	23
Delivered party leaflets in an election	23	55	5	6	20	17	52	23
Attended a party meeting	28	56	16	14	22	17	34	14
Canvassed voters on behalf of the party	49	81	8	5	17	7	26	8
Stood for office in the party	75	94	4	2	10	2	12	2
Stood for office in a local or national election	84	97	3	1	5	1	9	1

taking into account sampling error, this suggests that New Labour members were more likely to be nonrespondents in 1999 than were Old Labour members. The obvious inference is that they have dropped out of the party in greater numbers than have Old Labour members.[4]

But even setting aside the issue of differential response rates, the gap between Old and New Labour members in relation to hours worked in the average month widened over the two-year period. In 1997 some 54 percent of Old Labour members did no work at all for the party in the average month. By 1999 this had increased to 56 percent, suggesting that the decline of activism discussed earlier continues. However, in the case of New Labour members these figures went from 73 percent doing nothing in 1997 to 79 percent in 1999, an increase three times greater than for Old Labour members.

A similar picture emerges from table 5.4 in which the Old and New Labour members are compared in relation to specific political activities. There is no evidence in this table that the differences in overall activism rates between Old and New Labour members have declined during the two-year period. Indeed in a number of cases the gap between the two types of member actually increased. For example, the number of members who frequently donated money to the party fell by 4 percent for Old Labour members and by 6 percent for New Labour members. Similarly, the number of Old Labour members who frequently canvassed voters fell by 1 percent, whereas for New Labour members it fell by 2 percent. To be fair, there are examples in tables 5.2 and 5.4 of narrowing differences between the Old and New Labour members, but these are all in relation to low-intensity types of participation, such as displaying election posters and signing petitions.

TABLE 5.3. Hours Worked by Old and New Labour Members in the Average Month in 1999 (in percentages)

Hours Worked	Old Labour	New Labour
None	56	79
Up to 5 hours	26	15
From 5 up to 10 hours	9	4
From 10 up to 20 hours	3	2
More than 20 hours	6	1

Note: N = 1,325. Old Labour made up 64 percent of the membership, and New Labour made up 36 percent.

Clearly it is useful to get an overall measure of activism to examine whether the difference between Old and New Labour members widened or narrowed over time. The 1990 activism scale examined in table 4.3 measures the same election-related activities such as delivering leaflets, canvassing, and attending meetings as in tables 5.2 and 5.4. A previous analysis of this scale showed that the mean score for all party members at the time of the original survey was twenty-one.[5] In our book, *Labour's Grass Roots* (1992), we illustrate the activities of the average party member in the following terms:

> He or she is very likely to have displayed a poster at election times and signed a petition sponsored by the party; quite likely to have given money occasionally to Labour party funds, attended a party meeting or canvassed; and unlikely to have stood for office in the party or in a local election. (97)

If we calculate overall activity scores in the 1997 survey using the eight activities in table 5.2,[6] the mean activism score for the entire sample was sixteen, or about 76 percent of the mean score associated with the 1990 cohort of members. This confirms the point that rates of activism within the party have declined by about one-quarter for all types of members over this period. In addition, in the 1997 survey the mean activism score

TABLE 5.4. Old and New Labour Members' Activities in 1999 (in percentages)

Activity	Not at All		Rarely		Occasionally		Frequently	
	Old	New	Old	New	Old	New	Old	New
Displayed an election poster in a window	14	28	4	7	24	32	58	33
Signed a petition supported by the party	24	36	12	12	36	38	28	15
Donated money to party funds	14	23	14	18	39	41	34	17
Delivered party leaflets in an election	23	55	4	5	20	20	53	20
Attended a party meeting	27	55	16	15	22	17	35	13
Canvassed voters on behalf of the party	49	80	10	5	16	8	25	6
Stood for office in the party	74	92	4	1	10	4	12	3
Stood for office in a local or national election	83	95	3	1	5	2	9	1

for the New Labour members was thirteen, or about 72 percent of the mean score of eighteen for Old Labour members. Thus the New Labour members were about 28 percent less active in 1997 than members who joined the party earlier.

Interestingly, the mean scores for Old and New Labour members in 1999 were also eighteen and thirteen respectively, indicating that no change had occurred in the activism rates of these two types of member in the interim period. Thus it is fairly clear that socialization processes did not narrow the gap in activity rates between Old and New Labour party members.

These results strongly suggest that Labour has been recruiting a new type of member since the mobilization campaign began and that individual membership increased significantly after 1994. These new members are less active than their long-standing counterparts in all categories of activism, and this is particularly marked at the high-intensity point on the activism scales.

Obviously, the explanation for these differences should be found in the variables that make up the optimal model of participation identified in chapter 4. For example, if New Labour members had fewer outcome or ideological incentives to participate, or if their class and recruitment characteristics were different, this could explain why they were less active than Old Labour members. To investigate this issue we need to examine the predictor variables in the optimal model of high-intensity participation for Old and New Labour members. Accordingly, the optimal model identified in table 4.6 is reestimated with the 1997 data in table 5.5.[7]

The goodness of fit of the optimal model in table 5.5 is similar to that of its equivalent in table 4.6, and the signs of the variables are the same. However, in this version of the model it appears that group influence is not a statistically significant predictor of activism. On the other hand outcome and process incentives for participation are strong positive predictors of activism, as are expected benefits and expressive incentives. Similarly, social norms, social class, and the mode of recruitment to the party are significant negative predictors of participation in the same way as they were in the earlier version.

We can get a preliminary sense of whether the predictor variables in the optimal model fully account for differences in activism between Old and New Labour by incorporating a dummy variable into the optimal model. This variable scores one if the respondent is New Labour and zero if he or she is Old Labour, and it has a very significant negative impact on high-intensity participation in the second model in table 5.5, even in the presence of the other predictor variables. This clearly implies that additional factors are at work in explaining the differences in rates of activism between Old and New Labour members other than the variables in the optimal model. As the earlier discussion indicates, it seems likely that the party has recruited a new type of member since the mobilization strategy was introduced in the early 1990s.

Before exploring more fully the additional factors that explain differences between Old and New Labour members, it is interesting to examine differences in the predictor variables in the optimal model. In this way the contribution of the optimal model to explaining variations in participation can be assessed. This is done in table 5.6, which gives a breakdown

TABLE 5.5.   The Optimal Model of High-Intensity Participation in 1997

Predictor	Optimal Model	Optimal Model with New Labour Dummy
Group influence	–0.00	–0.00
	(0.0)	(0.1)
Collective benefits	0.01	0.04**
	(0.6)	(2.0)
Outcome incentives	0.32***	0.31***
	(20.4)	(22.0)
Process incentives	0.26***	0.19***
	(8.1)	(6.7)
Ideology	–0.02	–0.03**
	(1.3)	(2.3)
Expected benefits	0.20***	0.22***
	(7.9)	(10.0)
Social norms	–0.04***	–0.02**
	(4.0)	(2.2)
Expressive incentives	0.17***	0.10***
	(15.9)	(10.0)
Social class	–0.03***	–0.02**
	(3.2)	(2.2)
Recruitment to the party	–0.11***	–0.01
	(11.8)	(1.4)
New Labour dummy variable	—	–0.35***
		(36.0)
R^2	0.40	0.54

$*p < 0.10; **p < 0.05; ***p < 0.01$

TABLE 5.6. Differences between Old and New Labour in Predictors of the Optimal Model in 1997 (in percentages)

	Strongly Agree		Agree		Neither		Disagree		Strongly Disagree	
	Old	New	Old	New	Old	New	Old	New	Old	New
Outcome incentives										
Respondent could do a good job as a councillor	16	12	39	34	20	24	20	24	5	6
Labour would succeed if more people like respondent were MPs	8	6	21	21	39	36	27	31	5	6
Process incentives										
Being active is a good way to meet people	10	7	57	51	23	34	9	7	2	2
Being activist is the only way to be politically educated	8	4	33	28	12	15	40	45	8	8
Social norms										
Work by ordinary party members is unrecognized	21	15	59	57	11	18	8	9	1	1
Many people think activists are extremists	12	11	54	56	16	16	17	15	2	2

	Very Strong		Fairly Strong		Not Very Strong		Not at All Strong	
	Old	New	Old	New	Old	New	Old	New
Expressive incentives								
Strength of party identification	58	38	37	53	4	9	1	1

	Salariat		Routine Nonmanual		Petty Bourgeoise		Foreman & Technician		Working Class	
	Old	New	Old	New	Old	New	Old	New	Old	New
Social class	67	60	12	13	2	2	7	8	13	17

	Not at All Effective		Not Very Effective		Effective		Very Effective	
	Old	New	Old	New	Old	New	Old	New
Expected benefits								
Displaying an election poster	2	3	19	24	55	52	24	21
Donating money to election funds	1	1	7	6	51	53	41	41
Delivering party leaflets	2	2	14	17	55	58	29	23
Attending a party rally	12	9	48	43	32	39	8	9
Canvassing voters door to door	2	3	15	19	48	51	35	27

	Face-to-Face Contacts		Impersonal Contacts	
	Old	New	Old	New
Mode of recruitment to the party	80	55	20	45

of the observed variables in the optimal model for Old and New Labour members.

While some differences are not large it is clear that Old Labour members are more likely to be politically ambitious, more likely to respond to process incentives, and much more strongly attached to the party than are New Labour members. Thus 55 percent of Old Labour members agree or strongly agree with the idea that they could do a good job as a local councillor, compared with 46 percent of New Labour members. Again, some 67 percent of Old Labour members believe that activism is a good way to meet interesting people, compared with 58 percent of New Labour. Equally, 58 percent of Old Labour members are strong identifiers with the Labour party in comparison with only 38 percent of New Labour members.

A similar point can be made about social class; since the Old Labour members are slightly more middle class than the New Labour members, they are more active as a consequence. In relation to the expected benefits of participation, once again the Old Labour members are marginally more likely to think that various types of campaigning are effective in comparison with New Labour members. All of these effects mean that Old Labour members are likely to be more active than New Labour members, since they clearly have greater incentives to participation.

One intriguing finding in table 5.6 relates to the mode of recruitment of members to the party. It will be recalled that the civic voluntarism model predicted that individuals recruited into political activity by friends and family are more likely to be active than individuals recruited by other means. The data in table 5.6 suggest that there are large differences between the Old and New Labour members with respect to the mode of recruitment. This of course reflects the national change in the party's recruitment strategy discussed earlier. We shall argue that this finding is quite important in accounting for the unexplained differences in activism between Old and New Labour members. Accordingly, the issue is probed in more detail in table 5.7.

Table 5.7 contains data on the mechanisms that triggered an individual's decision to join the Labour party. It identifies the individual components of impersonal and face-to-face contacts identified in table 5.6. In the case of Old Labour members no less than 52 percent of them were recruited through friends and family in comparison with only 34 percent who were recruited in this way among the New Labour members. Social contacts were similarly more important among the Old Labour members compared with New Labour. In contrast the impersonal methods associated with the mobilization strategy of party political broadcasts and advertisements in national newspapers accounted for 48 percent of the New Labour recruits in comparison with only 11 percent of the Old Labour recruits.

Table 5.8 indicates that this lack of face-to-face contact in the process of recruitment continued even after the members had joined the party. It can be seen that 44 percent of New Labour members had met other activists either rarely or not at all during the previous year, whereas this was true for only 25 percent of the Old Labour members. In contrast, some 43 percent of Old Labour members frequently had contact with other active members in comparison with only 22 percent of New Labour members. In addition the second part of the table suggests a slight tendency for the New Labour members to be less satisfied with their levels of contact with the party in comparison with the Old Labour members.

In examining the role of face-to-face contact in influencing participation, it is important to distinguish between contact and activism. As we pointed out in chapter 1, contact and activism are not the same thing. In many localities inactive members are in regular contact with activists who deliver newsletters, ask them to sign petitions, call on them to vote during elections, and seek donations as well as collect their membership subscriptions and Tote funds (Seyd and Whiteley 1992: 86–117).[8] There are good reasons for thinking that a local party that maintains regular contact with the inactive members has a better chance of keeping them in the party in comparison with a local party that neglects its members.

TABLE 5.7. **Differences between Old and New Labour Party Members in Recruitment in 1997 (in percentages)**

"Thinking about the circumstances when you actually joined the party, what triggered your decision to join?"

	Old Labour	New Labour
Telephone or door-to-door canvasser	5	4
Party political broadcast	4	13
National party advertisement	7	25
Local newsletter	3	4
Trade union contacts	22	16
Family contacts	27	19
Social contacts	25	15
Work contacts	6	5

A good deal of recent evidence concerning the importance of face-to-face contact can be found in research on political learning and political communication. For example, in his two-step model of political communication Popkin (1994) argues that in political campaigns, "the campaign and the media only send the initial messages; until these messages have been checked with others and validated, their full effects are not felt" (46). Popkin argues that most commonly this validation process takes place in face-to-face communication between individuals and opinion leaders, such that personal contact plays a key role in validating political messages (47). Applying this idea to the recruitment of party members, recruits who know other party members are in a position to validate any television or newspaper advertisements that make claims about the party and its members. Individuals who lack such contacts cannot do this, and therefore they face great uncertainty in evaluating the costs and benefits of party activism, which in effect acts as an extra cost of participation.

Similar conclusions can be drawn from Huckfeldt and Sprague's work (1990, 1995) on politics and social communication. They make the point that "the face-to-face encounters that occur through routine patterns of social interaction have an especially high potential for political influence" (1990: 29). Their work stresses the importance of networks of communication between individuals as mechanisms for creating and reinforcing political support. Thus members recruited through social, work, or

TABLE 5.8. Differences between Old and New Labour Party Members in Contacts with the Party in 1997 (in percentages)

"Thinking back over the last year, how often have you had contact with people active in your local branch or constituency Labour party?"

	Old Labour	New Labour
Not at all	10	21
Rarely	15	23
Occasionally	32	33
Frequently	43	22

"Are you satisfied or dissatisfied with the level of contact from your local Labour party?"

Very satisfied	27	21
Satisfied	46	45
Neither satisfied nor dissatisfied	20	25
Dissatisfied	5	7
Very dissatisfied	2	2

family networks will have more knowledge and less uncertainty about political activism, and the affective relationships between actors in these settings will also tend to promote party activism. In addition Huckfeldt and Sprague point out that "social influence has the capacity to strengthen political boundaries between groups by bringing group members into line with the preferences that dominate within the group" (1995: 78–79). This implies that there is a socialization effect of face-to-face contact, which produces greater agreement on policy goals and develops group solidarity within the organization. Thus members linked to the social and political networks that make up the party organization are likely to have a greater knowledge of, and possibly are in greater agreement with, party policies as a whole. Again, this is likely to increase their incentives for activism.

With regard to the affective dimension of the incentives for participation, Sniderman, Brody, and Tetlock argue that "One way people can compensate for a lack of information about politics is to base their policy preferences on their likes and dislikes" (1991: 8). Again, face-to-face contact with other party members provides the setting for this "likeability" heuristic to operate (93–119). In fact it is difficult to conceive of how such a heuristic might motivate individuals to participate in the absence of face-to-face contact with other members. Thus expressive motives for participation will be reinforced by social links with other party members.

The literature on the formation of party identification, for example, supports the idea that interaction with other people is an important factor in explaining party attachments. Moreover, this is likely to be true whether the traditional mechanism of socialization in the family (Campbell et al. 1960) creates partisanship or, alternatively, whether more diffuse mechanisms of political and social communication are at work (Sniderman, Brody, and Tetlock 1991: 179–205; Huckfeldt and Sprague 1995: 81–99).

It is clear that the change in recruitment strategy in 1994 affected not only the recruitment processes but also the relationships among party members after they joined the party. As a consequence one of the additional factors that explain the differences in participation between Old and New Labour members is the level of contact with other party members. Accordingly, these measures are added to the optimal models in table 5.5.

A second factor that is relevant to differences in rates of activism between the two types of member relates to changes in Labour party policies and objectives that occurred during the reformist period of the 1990s. As is well known this period produced significant policy and organizational changes, as well as a shift away from traditional concerns with socialism and state intervention in the economy.

In an analysis of class differences in rates of activism within the Labour party in the early 1980s, Whiteley (1983: 57–64) introduces a distinction between "instrumental" and "expressive" motives for joining the Labour party. The former motives were linked to policy goals, such that individuals motivated to join by a desire to reduce unemployment or to increase welfare spending, for example, were classified as instrumental in their motives. In contrast, individuals who joined in order to "build socialism" or to "create a fairer society," that is, who had generalized ideals not related to specific policy goals, were classified as expressive in their motives.

Important differences existed between these two groups of members in their rates of participation at that time, with the expressive members being significantly more active than instrumental members. Survey evidence suggested that working-class party members were more instrumental and that middle-class party members were more expressive in their beliefs, and these differences explain the decline in working-class political activism that was evident at that time (see also Forrester 1976). The reason why expressive members were more active than instrumental members was explained in the following way:

> When [motives for joining] are instrumental and relate to the production of public goods they need nurturing or reinforcing by the successful implementation of those policies. Thus the individual who cited the fight against unemployment as the main reason for joining the party is much more vulnerable to defection than an individual who has diffused and generalized aims, at a time when the Labour government presided over increasing unemployment. (Whiteley 1983: 63)

Thus these differences were linked to the policy failures of Labour in office. Of course the political context was rather different in 1997, after the party had been out of office for some eighteen years. However, the mechanism may still be relevant, such that members who originally joined with an idealistic commitment to socialism may still be more active than members who are more instrumental in their motives for joining. If as a result of the modernization strategy few of the recent recruits are joining with expressive motives, this would make the new cohort of members less active than older cohorts. Table 5.9 classifies the motives for joining the party given by Old and New Labour members in the survey.

It is apparent in table 5.9 that Old Labour members are significantly more likely to cite expressive motives as reasons for joining the party in comparison with New Labour members; some 56 percent of the former cited such motives compared with only 36 percent of the latter. In contrast, 47 percent of New Labour members cited instrumental motives for joining in comparison with only 33 percent of Old Labour members. The instrumental motives in the table varied widely, ranging from those of a personal character, such as the desire to be better informed about politics, to those of a more collective character, such as the desire to help get

TABLE 5.9.　Differences between Old and New Labour Party Members in Reasons for Joining the Party in 1997 (in percentages)

"People join the Labour party for a variety of different reasons. How about you, what was your most important reason for joining the Labour party?"

	Old Labour	New Labour
New Labour motives		
Tony Blair's leadership	—	7
New Labour's policies	—	8
Instrumental motives		
To help get Labour into power	8	13
To oppose the Conservatives	9	13
To be politically active in the party	2	1
To help my local Labour council	1	1
To have an influence on the party	1	1
To be better informed about politics	0	1
To show my support for Labour	12	17
Expressive motives		
To make a commitment to socialism	17	6
To help create a more equal society	18	14
To help create a more just society	21	16
Neither instrumental nor expressive		
The influence of my family and friends	3	1
The influence of my trade union	4	1
Other reason	4	1

Labour into power. Thus the definition of instrumental is rather broad, but it is nonetheless clear that an important distinction exists between Old and New Labour members in their motives for joining the party. To examine the influence of these motives on activism, we included a dummy variable to capture this effect.[9]

Some motives cited in table 5.9 are much more likely to apply to the New Labour rather than the Old Labour members, simply because of chronology. For example, Old Labour members could not be motivated to join by New Labour policies if they joined the party before the modernization strategy began in the mid-1980s. But this raises the question of whether contemporary attitudes to New Labour policies and to Blair might influence rates of activism within the party. Once again, if there are differences between Old and New Labour members in their attitudes toward these issues, and if such attitudes influence activism, this could be a source of differences in activism between the two groups.

Two alternative interpretations of the influence of attitudes toward the leader and toward New Labour policies on activism are possible. The first is that Blair and the policy and organizational changes to the party have mobilized new types of individuals to be active. As was pointed out earlier, the modernization strategy promoted the idea of grass roots participation, for example, in policy forums and elections for the leadership. As a consequence, support for the modernization strategy and for the leader who promoted it might be associated with higher rates of activism.

The alternative view is that the modernization strategy has merely introduced a type of plebiscitary democracy into the party at the expense of a true participatory democracy. This means that, despite the formal emphasis on participation in the modernization strategy, in practice the role of party members in effective decision making is really very limited. Essentially, their role is to legitimize elite decisions after they have been made rather than to participate in agenda setting and policy-making. In this view the opportunities for genuine participation have declined rather than increased in the grass roots party organization. We investigate these alternatives by examining members' attitudes toward Blair as well as their attitudes toward the reforms of the decision-making process in the party. A third aspect is to investigate their attitudes toward the effects of these changes on the traditional values and principles of the party.

Table 5.10 contains responses to questions in the survey about attitudes to Blair. The evidence in the table suggests that the great majority of members felt that the Labour leader sticks to his principles, keeps his promises, and listens to reason. However, there is a small minority, which is notably larger for Old Labour members than for the New Labour members, who disagree with these descriptions. Roughly twice as many Old Labour members thought that Blair did not stick to his principles. Similarly, more than one-quarter of the Old Labour members agreed or strongly agreed that the Labour leader is too powerful, compared with only 12 percent of New Labour members. Obviously, if such attitudes influence participation, this might in part account for differences between the two types of member.

Table 5.11 examines attitudes toward the reform of the party decision-making process carried out in recent years. Traditionally, the annual party conference was the ultimate source of sovereignty in the party, although in practice it was often bypassed by the leadership (see Minkin 1978). However, members who agree that the conference should be the ultimate authority in the party are traditionalists, and Old Labour members are significantly more likely to be in this group than New Labour members. Another source of potential conflict between modernizers and traditionalists concerns the selection of parliamentary candidates. Traditionally, this selection was exclusively the prerogative of local parties, with only occasional interventions by the National Executive Committee. This implies that traditionalists are likely to disagree with the idea that the

TABLE 5.10. Differences between Old and New Labour Members in Their Attitudes toward Tony Blair in 1997 (in percentages)

	Old Labour	New Labour
Tony Blair is someone who		
Sticks to his principles	87	93
Does not stick to his principles	13	7
Keeps his promises	89	95
Breaks his promises	11	5
Listens to reason	89	96
Does not listen to reason	11	4

	Strongly Agree		Agree		Neither		Disagree		Strongly Disagree	
	Old	New	Old	New	Old	New	Old	New	Old	New
The leader is too powerful	8	3	18	9	21	19	43	56	11	14

National Executive Committee should have the final say in candidate selection.

Once again, the Old Labour members differ from the New Labour members, with a majority opposing the idea of centralizing the selection process in comparison with only about 40 percent of New Labour members. Finally, there are highly significant differences between the two types of member in their attitudes toward the methods of policy-making in the party. Some 53 percent of the New Labour members favor the plebiscitary model in comparison with only 39 percent of Old Labour.

Table 5.12 contains indicators of attitudes toward the effects of the modernization strategy on traditional party principles and values. Just over 40 percent of Old Labour members think that the party places more emphasis on its media image than it does on its principles, while the same is true for only about one-quarter of New Labour members. Similarly, the Old Labour members are more likely to believe that the party has abandoned socialist principles than are New Labour members, and finally, they are more likely to believe that the party has moved away from its traditional values and principles in comparison with their New Labour counterparts.

A number of differences between Old and New Labour members emerge from tables 5.8 through 5.12, but it is important to assess the

TABLE 5.11. Differences between Old and New Labour Members in Their Attitudes toward Reforms of the Party Decisionmaking in 1997 (in percentages)

	Strongly Agree		Agree		Neither		Disagree		Strongly Disagree	
	Old	New	Old	New	Old	New	Old	New	Old	New
Conference should be the ultimate authority	16	9	28	23	21	25	29	36	7	8
The NEC should have the final say in candidate selection	5	6	28	30	15	23	35	32	16	9

	Old Labour	New Labour
Policy should be formed by the party leadership and endorsed by the members in postal ballots	39	53
Policy should be formed at the annual conference or at policy forums by the members	61	47

extent to which they distinguish between the two types of member in a multivariate model in order to identify the importance of the different factors. This assessment is done in table 5.13, which is a logistic regression model estimating the effects of variables in the optimal model along with the additional variables in predicting the distinction between Old and New Labour members. In each case when multiple indicators are used, a measurement scale is constructed by means of a factor analysis of the underlying set of variables. This scale is then used to predict whether a respondent is New Labour or Old Labour.

The "contact with the party" scale is derived from a factor analysis of the measures in table 5.8, with a high score denoting frequent contact and satisfaction with those contacts.[10] The expressive motives scale is a dummy variable scoring one for those respondents in table 5.9 who cited expressive motives for joining the party in the first place. The "attitudes toward the party leader" scale is derived from a factor analysis of the measures in table 5.10, with a high score denoting favorable attitudes toward the Labour leader and disagreement with the proposition that the leader is too powerful.[11] The "attitudes toward party reforms" scale is derived from a factor analysis of the indicators in table 5.11, with a high score meaning that the respondent disapproves of the reforms, thinks that the conference should be the ultimate authority, and disagrees with National Executive Committee involvement in candidate selection.[12] Finally, an "attitudes toward party principles" scale is constructed from a factor analysis of the three indicators in table 5.12, with a high score denoting

TABLE 5.12. Differences between Old and New Labour Members in Attitudes to Labour Party Principles in 1997 (in percentages)

	Strongly Agree		Agree		Neither		Disagree		Strongly Disagree	
	Old	New	Old	New	Old	New	Old	New	Old	New
Party places more emphasis on media images than principles	13	5	30	21	20	23	31	42	7	10
Labour is no longer socialist after dropping public ownership	10	5	27	22	17	19	39	45	8	9
Party has not moved from its traditional values and principles	5	5	27	33	12	16	42	39	14	8

that the respondent thinks the party has not abandoned its principles or departed from its traditional values.[13]

Table 5.13 incorporates the additional variables into the optimal model of table 5.5 to predict the difference between Old and New Labour members.[14] It can be seen that in the optimal model there are statistically significant differences between Old and New Labour members on all of

TABLE 5.13.   Logistic Regression Model of New Labour Membership in 1997 and 1999

Predictor	Predictors in Optimal Model	Predictors in Extended Model
Collective benefits	−0.13***	−0.036
	(9.2)	(0.3)
Outcome incentives	−0.12***	−0.10**
	(8.6)	(3.7)
Process incentives	−0.16***	−0.08*
	(13.8)	(2.3)
Ideology	0.24***	0.05
	(25.9)	(0.8)
Expected benefits	0.00	0.00
	(0.0)	(0.0)
Social norms	0.05	0.02
	(1.2)	(0.1)
Expressive incentives	−0.63***	0.60***
	(85.9)	(56.9)
Social class	0.13***	0.10***
	(20.4)	(9.5)
Recruitment to the party	−0.87***	−0.82***
	(106.9)	(75.4)
Contact with the party	—	−0.36***
		(51.5)
Socialist motives for joining	—	−0.66***
		(49.0)
Attitudes toward party leader	—	0.17***
		(7.9)
Attitudes toward party reforms	—	−0.14***
		(7.0)
Attitudes toward party principles	—	0.20***
		(12.7)
Percentage of cases correctly classified	66.6	68.7
Improvement in loglikelihood	367.4***	476.3***

Note: Dependent variable = 1 if respondent New Labour, 0 otherwise.
*$p < 0.10$; **$p < 0.05$; ***$p < 0.01$

the variables, except expected benefits and social norms. The estimates can be examined in conjunction with those in table 5.5, and they show that all of the variables in the optimal model, with the exception of recruitment to the party, inhibit the participation of New Labour members in comparison with Old Labour members. Thus New Labour members have weaker outcome, process, and expressive incentives to participate than do their Old Labour counterparts. The effects of expressive incentives are particularly marked, with New Labour members being significantly less attached to the party and thus significantly less active as a consequence. Furthermore, that they are slightly more working class and less middle class than Old Labour members also serves to inhibit their activism. Only the recruitment to the party variable serves to stimulate their rates of activism in comparison with their Old Labour counterparts.

When the extra variables are added to the logistic regression model of table 5.13, they all have statistically significant effects. Thus New Labour members are less likely to have contact with other party members, less likely to cite socialist motives for joining, and less critical of party reforms than are Old Labour members. In addition they are more likely to think favorably of the Labour party leader and are less likely to think that the party has changed its principles.

Given that table 5.13 establishes that New Labour members differ from Old Labour members with regard to a number of attitudes, it is necessary to examine whether these attitudes inhibit or stimulate party activism. This subject is investigated in table 5.14, which is an expanded version of the optimal model of table 5.5 incorporating the extra variables into the high-intensity participation model. It can be seen that the expanded model has a considerably higher goodness of fit than the original, and all of the extra variables are significant predictors of participation. To gauge the effects of recruiting the New Labour members on high-intensity participation it is useful to examine table 5.14 in conjunction with table 5.13.

It is clear from table 5.14 that respondents who are in regular contact with other party members, who had socialist motives for joining, who are skeptical about Blair, and who are opposed to the reforms participate more than do respondents without these attitudes. Since New Labour members tend not to share these attitudes in comparison with their Old Labour counterparts, they participate less as a consequence.

It is worth noting that the most powerful factor influencing high-intensity participation in table 5.14 is the contact variable. Members who lack contact with the grass roots party and who are discontented about this are much less likely to participate than are other types of members. As table 5.8 shows contact is one of the key differences between the two types of member, a difference that follows logically from the mobilization strategy of recruitment.

This suggests that, while the mobilization strategy was successful in bringing new people into the party, it simultaneously inhibited the participation of these new recruits. Because New Labour members were typically recruited by impersonal means and subsequently had limited con-

TABLE 5.14. The Extended Optimal Model of High-Intensity Participation in 1997 and 1999

Predictor	Predictors in Extended Optimal Model
Collective benefits	0.05***
	(3.2)
Outcome incentives	0.22***
	(18.4)
Process incentives	0.23***
	(8.2)
Ideology	0.04***
	(2.9)
Expected benefits	0.10***
	(5.0)
Social norms	−0.03***
	(3.3)
Expressive incentives	0.12***
	(13.4)
Social class	−0.06***
	(6.7)
Recruitment to the party	−0.02**
	(2.4)
Contact with the party	0.45***
	(46.9)
Socialist motives for joining	0.05***
	(6.6)
Attitudes toward party leader	−0.26***
	(8.7)
Attitudes toward party reforms	0.10***
	(3.1)
Attitudes toward party principles	0.08*
	(1.8)
R^2	0.68

*$p < 0.10$; **$p < 0.05$; ***$p < 0.01$

tact with the rest of the grass roots party, they did not get drawn into party activity. Thus the change from the passive/responsive to the active/mobilization mode of recruitment has come with a price, even though it was successful in increasing the size of the membership.

Discussion

The findings from the 1997–99 panel survey of Labour party members suggest that the decline in rates of participation in the grass roots party has continued, even though the party has moved from opposition to government. In addition, the optimal model of activism, developed in chapter 4, provides a reasonably good explanatory model of activism in the later 1997 survey, even though there are some differences between the earlier and later versions of the model.

The switch from the passive/responsive mode of recruitment to the active/mobilization mode has certainly recruited many new members into the party, which for the time has reversed the decline in membership discussed earlier. But the evidence shows that this change of strategy has served to recruit a new type of relatively inactive member, which has served to reduce the average rates of participation in the grass roots party. While absolute levels of participation in the grass roots party may have increased because of these new members, relative rates of participation or the activism rates of the average member have continued to decline.

Part of the reason why the New Labour members are less active than their Old Labour counterparts is the lack of significant face-to-face contact between these new recruits and the rest of the grass roots party. There is a tendency for them to become "virtual" members who pay their dues but have little or no contact with the party organization. Furthermore, because this lack of contact inhibits socialization processes, these members are unlikely to become active in the future.

A further point is that the lack of face-to-face contact between many new recruits and the rest of the party also has a significant indirect effect on high-intensity participation, which operates via the other predictors in the optimal model. Such influences work through both cognitive and affective mechanisms. With regard to cognitive processes, the accuracy of the information the individual uses to decide whether to become politically active is greatly improved, and uncertainty is greatly reduced by face-to-face contact with other members. Many New Labour members are simply not sure what high-intensity participation involves and whether they would enjoy it. This "uncertainty premium" imposes extra costs in any kind of decision making about whether to become active, which in turn reduces rates of participation. A similar point can be made about the individual's perceptions of the expected benefits of participation; this is much easier to evaluate for someone with direct experience of working with other people in a political environment than it is for an outsider who lacks such experience.

In the optimal model, face-to-face contact itself operates as an important stimulus to participation. In the case of selective process and selective ideological incentives, for example, interaction with other like-minded people is itself an incentive for participation. In the case of selective outcome incentives, the process works somewhat more indirectly, but an ambitious individual can only build a political career by impressing their peers and by winning election to positions both within the party organization and outside it. Such incentives cannot operate if individuals have little or no interaction with other party members.

With regard to affective or expressive motives for participation, again recruits lacking any face-to-face contact with other members will only have abstract attachments to the party based largely on media images. In contrast, party members in regular contact with other members have a concrete experience of what the party stands for and what kind of people support it. As a consequence, they are much better able to ground their affective attachments to the party in personal experience.

This latter point is reinforced by the fact that the print media in Britain is relatively partisan and tends to distort the images of the party in line with its own political agenda (Newton 1992; Crewe and Gosschalk 1995). Thus it is harder for individuals to assess the party if they have to rely exclusively on media accounts of the organization as opposed to their personal experience.

The important general implication of these findings for studies of political participation in general is that rates of participation can be influenced by impersonal media-based mobilization campaigns but that the influence of these is ultimately rather limited. In the case of the Labour party, this type of campaign boosted party membership and reversed a long-term decline in the grass roots party that had been going on for decades. However, the campaign proved to be of limited value in recruiting high-intensity participants, whose involvement is particularly important in maintaining the party organization and in campaigning.

For potential activists the incentives that promote participation can only work properly through face-to-face contact with other like-minded individuals and through social networks. Since "virtual" members are not drawn into these networks they are unlikely to subsequently become active. Thus mobilization strategies of recruitment may work well for low-intensity participants, but they do not work well for recruiting high-intensity participants.

A second finding of importance for future participation in the grass roots party is that the moves to establish a plebiscitary type of participation are ultimately self-defeating if the aim is to sustain an active grass roots party. Simply giving members the occasional vote, in which they are invited to pass judgment on an issue that has already been effectively decided, is not going to promote widespread grass roots involvement. Insofar as the modernization strategy has promoted this kind of participation, it has not sustained high-intensity participation, since the members who approve of such a model are likely to be less active than those who disapprove.

The theoretical and empirical work up to this point has concentrated on understanding and modeling high-intensity participation. But if the basic story is one of decline, it is clearly important to understand why some people leave a party as opposed to why they become less active over time. The evidence suggests that the optimal model provides the best explanation of declining participation, but it is not clear whether the same model applies to individuals who go one step further and leave the party altogether. It is possible that a model that explains high-intensity participation does not explain exiting the party. In the next chapter we change the focus to address the question of whether the factors that explain why some people are less active also explain why others leave the party.

Chapter 6

Exitors and Loyalists:
Why Do Members Leave a Party?

⋘⊙⋙

OUR EVIDENCE UP TO THIS POINT SUGGESTS that the British party system is in decline both in membership and in the rates of activism of its remaining members. As the last chapter showed, the apparent exception to this decline is the recent experience of the Labour party in expanding its individual membership between 1994 and 1997. But earlier discussion showed that the decline in high-intensity participation has not been halted by this development because the great majority of the new recruits are low-intensity participants.

In this chapter we examine whether the optimal model of high-intensity participation can be reversed and applied to the task of understanding why some people leave the party altogether. The aim is to model exiting, with a view to examining which of the theoretical approaches to participation already discussed provides the best explanation for declining membership. To address this issue we use the same data utilized in the previous chapter, the 1997–99 panel survey of Labour party members. This survey contained a question that asked members to indicate whether they had left the party during the two-year period between the two waves. Unfortunately, there is no comparable data available for the Conservatives, so the focus of this chapter is on exiting from the Labour party.

It will be recalled from chapter 4 that the optimal model of high-intensity participation was a hybrid model, combining elements from rational choice theory, social psychology, and the civic voluntarism model. However, it was also apparent that the general incentives model dominated as an explanation of participation, even if it did not entirely encompass its rivals. In this chapter we adopt the same modeling strategy by examining a very general encompassing specification that combines all the different models of participation. However, we also take into account additional factors that might be expected to influence an individual's decision to quit the party. The general-to-specific modeling strategy makes it possible to derive an optimal model of exiting, which can then be compared with the optimal model of activism. If the optimal model developed in chapter 4 is robust, then it should apply equally well to the task of explaining exiting as it does to explaining activism.

In one sense decisions about leaving a party are fundamentally questions about whether to participate in politics, and in that sense they are similar to decisions about being politically active. However, there are important differences between these two types of decisions as well. Individuals may have joined a party in the first place without any ideas of becoming politically active. If, for example, their main motivation was to register strong partisanship by donating money to the party on a regular basis, but they lacked the time to get involved in meetings and campaigning, clearly their involvement is unlikely to be influenced by selective incentives such as meeting like-minded individuals or developing a political career. For them there would be little or no relationship between a decision to leave a party and selective incentives, because such incentives did not figure in their motivations in the first place.

Another individual may have joined the party with the explicit intention of becoming active, developing friendships with other members, and possibly building a political career. For them selective incentives would provide an important motivating factor for involvement, and consequently such incentives could well figure in any decision to subsequently leave the party. For such a person, declining selective incentives would be a key factor in his or her decision to leave the party.

These sorts of considerations mean that it would be useful to reexamine the global model introduced in chapter 4 and to evaluate the extent to which it provides a theoretical explanation of exiting as distinct from an explanation of declining activism.

Explaining Exiting

The pioneering theoretical work on decision making by individuals to end their participation in organizations they perceive to be failing was done by Hirschman. His classic book, *Exit, Voice, and Loyalty: Responses to Decline in Firms, Organizations, and States* (1970), examines the strategic alternatives open to consumers faced with a decline in the quality of the goods and services produced by private firms and organizations. In his book he also applies the theory to the task of understanding party competition (62–75). His basic thesis is that individuals can pursue three alternative strategies in response to a decline in the quality of products or services of an organization. In this situation, they can voice (protest), they can exit (stop buying), or they can remain loyal (put up with it). He writes:

> For competition [exit] to work as a mechanism of recuperation from performances lapses, it is generally best for a firm to have a mixture of *alert* and *inert* customers. The alert customers provide the firm with a feedback mechanism which starts the effort at recuperation, while the inert customers provide it with the time and dollar cushion needed for this effort to come to fruition. (24)

He was aware that quality, unlike price, means different things to different people, such that a decline in quality for one consumer may be an increase in quality for another (62). Faced with this possibility, he suggests, an organization will try to balance exit against voice; that is, it will avoid the profit-maximizing low-quality solution that might provoke massive exit while at the same time avoiding an equally costly solution that responds only to voice. This means that a firm will reduce quality to increase profits, but at the same time it will avoid reducing it to the point at which discontent among customers will provoke exit rather than voice.

Hirschman applied these ideas to the topic of electoral strategy in a two-party system. In his view this balancing of exit and voice explains why parties do not always adopt the policies preferred by the median voter in such a system. It may be recalled that the median voter theorem of Black (1958) and Downs (1957) predicts such policy convergence in a system in which voting preferences are aligned along a single left-right continuum and are single peaked.[1] In Hirschman's view this convergence does not occur because of voice. Thus supporters at the fringes of the left-right spectrum who oppose a move by their preferred party to the center ground of politics exercise voice, and this serves to inhibit the parties from moving too close to each other.

Hirschman's ideas can be applied to the task of explaining why some people exit from party politics, but the relevance of his model depends on the underlying theoretical model of participation being applied. Essentially, the ideas are relevant to theories based on incentives to participate, but they are much less relevant to other types of theory. Thus in the case of the civic voluntarism model, which as we pointed out earlier has little to say about incentives, these ideas do not really fit at all. By contrast, they are very relevant to both social psychological and rational choice models and hence by extension to the general incentives model of participation.

In incentive models of participation the relevance of Hirschman's ideas depends on the meaning of a decline in quality as it is applied to the task of understanding political participation. In this case it is the quality of the incentives to participate that counts. Thus individuals faced with declining collective or selective incentives to participate can either voice or exit. In the general incentives model, loyalty, in Hirschman's terminology, refers to the individual's strength of partisanship or his or her expressive incentives to participate. Such loyalty provides the ballast to the system and prevents changes in other types of incentives from having such a drastic and immediate impact on participation that the organization cannot recover from decline.

In the general incentives model weakening partisan attachments will influence the balance between the alternative strategies of voice and exit in the face of declining selective and collective incentives. It seems plausible that if expressive incentives are weak then party members are going to react to a decline in selective and collective incentives by exiting rather than by exercising voice. In an extreme case a party could lose most of its members if something occurs that seriously erodes members' incentives to participate in a situation where their attachments are quite weak.

For example, consider the effects of a massive electoral defeat on the incentives to participate. Such an event will create a rapid decline in selective outcome incentives, or in the probability that members can build a career in politics, because a party is unlikely to quickly recover from such a defeat. A party member who is primarily motivated by outcome incentives has the option of reacting to such a defeat by exercising voice and calling for a change of leadership and policies. But both options can take years to achieve, and even then electoral recovery is not guaranteed. This of course was the situation facing the Labour party in 1983 and more recently the Conservatives in 1997.

Party members interested in becoming elected representatives, particularly MPs, would recognize that recovery from a massive electoral defeat is a long and arduous process. If their partisan attachments were weak, they would be much more likely to exit than to exercise voice. In this situation changing incentives clearly point in the direction of abandoning political ambitions and dropping out of politics altogether rather than voicing concerns that might not have an effect for years into the future.

A similar point can be made about selective process incentives. If the social networks linked to local party activities atrophy and weaken, an activist who is primarily motivated by these incentives either has to undertake the herculean task of rebuilding the local party organization to restore such incentives or alternatively has to drop out altogether. Again, exit is a more attractive strategy than voice.

The same scenario is repeated in the case of ideological incentives, where the motivation for involvement centers around sharing political ideas with like-minded individuals. We observed a relationship between ideology and activism for Labour party members in chapter 4, with left-wingers being more active than right-wingers. Clearly, the shift to the right associated with New Labour may have encouraged some left-wingers to leave the party altogether by the late 1990s, even though the left tended to be more active than the right in the early 1990s.

In the case of collective incentives, as is well known, there is a difference between the policy goals of party members and those of the electorate as a whole.[2] Thus party members who are principally motivated by the idea of promoting equality and redistribution in the case of left parties, or tax cuts in the case of right parties, may create barriers to electoral success by pursuing these agendas. These members will resist a movement away from traditional policy goals in the search for electoral support. Again, if their party attachments are weak, they are likely to exit rather than to voice themselves if they are faced with large changes in policy goals.

Overall then, declining selective or collective incentives are likely to produce exit rather than voice, taking into account the influence of expressive incentives, if only because of the enormous difficulty of restoring such incentives when they have been lost. As a result these variables should be significant predictors of exiting from the party in the 1997–99 panel survey.

It is also important to consider other hypotheses that might explain exiting behavior but that do not follow directly from Hirschman's work. The global model examined in earlier chapters provides a framework for developing these hypotheses. Once again, we can use the global model to determine if one or more of the rival models of participation encompass each other as explanations of exiting from a party, within the framework of testing for Granger causality.[3]

The global model of exiting behavior in a dynamic context can be specified as follows:

$$EX_{i2} = a_{11} + b_{11}A_{i1} + b_{12}p_{i1} + b_{13}B_{j1} - b_{14}C_{i1} + b_{15}O_{i1} + b_{16}P_{i1} + b_{17}ID_{i1}$$
$$+ b_{18}G_{i1} + b_{19}E_{i1} + b_{110}EB_{i1} + b_{111}N_{i1} + g_{11}R_{i1} + g_{12}ED_{i1}$$
$$+ g_{13}SC_{i1} + g_{14}INC_{i1} + g_{15}FT_{i1} + u_{i1}$$

where

EX_{i2} measures if party member i had left the party at time 2.

A_{i1} is individual i's level of high-intensity participation in the party at time 1.

p_{i1} is individual i's sense of personal efficacy at time 1.

B_{j1} are the collective benefits resulting from the expected implementation of the party's program at time 1.

C_{i1} are the perceived costs of participation at time 1.

O_{i1} are selective outcome incentives from participation at time 1.

P_{i1} are selective process incentives from participation at time 1.

ID_{i1} are selective ideological incentives from participation at time 1.

G_{i1} is individual i's perceptions of group efficacy at time 1.

E_{i1} is individual i's expressive attachments to their party at time 1.

EB_{i1} is individuals i's perceptions of the expected benefits from participation at time 1.

N_{i1} is individual i's perceptions of social norms promoting participation at time 1.

R_{i1} measures if individual i was asked to join the party by friends, family, or work colleagues.

ED_{i1} is individual i's educational attainment.

SC_{i1} is individuals i's occupational status.

INC_{i1} is individual i's income.

FT_{i1} measures if individual i works full-time.

Once again, it is important to recall that the estimates from this specification of the model are a combination of contemporaneous and longitudinal effects, and we will examine the purely contemporaneous effects subsequently. In chapter 4 high-intensity participation at time one was included in the global model as a control variable, and it performs a similar function in this version of the model. However, in this context there are two rival theoretical explanations of the effects when applied to the task of explaining exiting. On the one hand it can be argued that active members are less likely to exit than inactive members, since so much of their time and energy is devoted to party matters. Since they have a stronger stake in the party organization than do the inactive members, we might expect to see a negative effect for the coefficient of activism (b_{11}) in the equation just listed.

An alternative interpretation of the effects of activism implies a positive relationship between high-intensity participation and exiting. This comes from the fact that active members are more vulnerable to burnout than are the inactive members. That is, devoting a lot of time and energy to party matters can eventually exhaust active members and make it more likely that they subsequently abandon party politics altogether. Obviously inactive members are much less vulnerable to this problem.

Turning next to personal efficacy, the most likely effect is that individuals with a strong sense of personal efficacy are less likely to leave the party than are individuals with a weak sense of efficacy. Again, this would produce a negative relationship between personal efficacy and exiting. On the other hand, it may be recalled that personal efficacy was not a significant predictor of high-intensity participation in the optimal model in chapter 4, so another possibility is that efficacy has little effect on exiting behavior once all the other factors have been taken into account. In any event it is important to examine this issue.

In addition to activism and personal efficacy, selective and collective incentives for participation are important predictors in the global model. With regard to the three indicators of selective incentives it seems likely that individuals who are strongly motivated by political ambitions, that is, who score high on the outcome incentives scale, would be less likely to leave the Labour party after the overwhelming victory of 1997. The opposite is likely to be true for the Conservatives, although we are unable to test this prediction in the absence of survey evidence for them over the same time period. Process incentives should sustain membership over time and offset exiting behavior, both with respect to the desire to meet like-minded people and also with respect to ideology.

The earlier discussion suggested that the effects of selective incentives are contingent on loyalty or expressive attachments. The important point here is that a control for prior participation is needed in the model to take account of the fact that selective incentives may not matter for members who joined without aiming to be active in the first place. If there are many of these members, a model that did not control for prior activism could fail to identify relationships because the links between selective incentives and exiting would be masked by prior participation. Fortunately, there is such a control in the specification of the global model.

A similar point can be made about collective incentives, which proved to be significant in the optimal model of activism in chapter 4. Since collective benefits refer to the congruence of the individual's policy preferences with those of his or her party, we might expect that such congruence promotes loyalty and prevents exiting. This would certainly be consistent with standard rational choice accounts of participation, which explain voting in terms of policy congruence.

On the other hand, to repeat an earlier point, collective benefits are subject to the free-rider problem. If the free-rider effect is important, it would eliminate a relationship between the individual's decision either to join or to leave a party and collective benefits. No matter how much policy congruence there is, if the individual decides to free ride, then policy concerns should be unrelated to participation. We observed a relationship between collective benefits and high-intensity participation in chapter 4, suggesting that free-rider effects are not so strong as to mask the effect. However, it is important to test the hypothesis that collective benefits have an independent influence on exiting, once other factors have been taken into account.

Free riding should not affect the relationship between exiting and social psychological variables such as perceptions of expected benefits, perceptions of group influence, or social norms. This is because free riding is not an issue that arises in social psychological models of participation. Since the earlier estimates show that these variables influence high-intensity participation, they should also be related to exiting. If members are encouraged to participate by the feeling that various forms of campaigning help the party, by the fact that the party is an effective organization, and by the perception that significant others look favorably on their participation in politics, then all of these factors should sustain individuals in their membership and should prevent them from leaving the party.

As well as effects associated with the general incentives and social psychological models of participation, it is possible that some of the variables in the civic voluntarism model also influence exiting, even if the mechanism for doing so is not the product of incentives to participate. Clearly, individual resources might well influence exiting, viewed from the supply side of the equation. If the individual works full-time, for example, the civic voluntarism model suggests that they will have less time to participate as a consequence. Actually, the idea was not supported by the evidence in the case of high-intensity participation, but it could nonetheless influence decisions to leave the party. In this case full-timers might decide to leave because of the pressures of work, which is similar to the activist burnout mentioned earlier. A similar point can be made about individuals with high socioeconomic status, high income, or advanced levels of education. The civic voluntarism model suggests that such people are more likely to participate than low-status individuals, again because of their resources. If so, this should make them less likely to leave the party.

The one remaining variable in the civic voluntarism model is mobilization, which in the activism model was operationalized by a measure of how party members were recruited. It will be recalled that if individuals were recruited by members of their immediate family, friends, or work colleagues the theory suggested that they should be more active as a consequence. There was some weak evidence to support this idea in the estimates of the optimal model of high-intensity participation, but it was not consistent across the samples of Labour and Conservative party members. Clearly, it is worthwhile to test whether the recruitment hypothesis applies to the case of exiting; if so, individuals who were recruited in this way should be less likely to leave the party.

There is a class of factors that have not been examined in the global model up to this point, and these relate to the effects of the party's moving from opposition to government. This transition could not be examined in chapter 4 using the 1990–94 Labour and Conservative panel surveys because there was no change in party incumbency during that period. However, the 1997–99 Labour panel survey does make it possible to test for these effects. Members surveyed in the first wave of the panel immediately after the general election of 1997 had not seen a Labour government for some eighteen years previously. By the time of the second wave of the survey in 1999, they had experienced almost two years of a Labour government. This makes it possible to assess the effects of a change from opposition to government on the participation of Labour party members.

This question is important because, arguably, incumbency could make some party members more enthusiastic supporters while at the same time disillusioning others. Since our concern is with exiting we focus on the latter. The working hypothesis is that party members who are dissatisfied with the performance of the Labour government or of the Labour leadership are more likely to leave the party than are members who are satisfied with that performance. This could well play an important role in explaining exiting behavior and is based on retrospective evaluations of party performance. Retrospective evaluations are well-known factors in influencing support for a government among the wider electorate (Fiorina 1981; Clarke and Stewart 1995, Clarke, Stewart, and Whiteley 1997), although they have not been used to explain wider forms of participation other than voting. It seems likely that they could influence the decisions of some party members to leave the party.

In the light of this discussion we specify the adapted global model of exiting as follows:

$$\begin{aligned}
EX_{i2} = a_{11} &+ b_{11}A_{i1} + b_{12}P_{i1} + b_{13}B_{j1} - b_{14}C_{i1} + b_{15}O_{i1} + b_{16}P_{i1} + b_{17}ID_{i1} \\
&+ b_{18}E_{i1} + b_{19}G_{i1} + b_{110}EB_{i1} + b_{111}N_{i1} + b_{112}PERF_{i2} \\
&+ b_{113}LEAD_{i2} + g_{11}R_{i1} + g_{12}ED_{i1} + g_{13}SC_{i1} + g_{14}INC_{i1} + g_{15}FT_{i1} + u_{i1}
\end{aligned}$$

where all the variables are defined in the same way as earlier and in addition:

$PERF_{i2}$ is an index of individual i's satisfaction with the performance of the Labour government at time 2.

$LEAD_{i2}$ is an index of individual i's satisfaction with the performance of the Labour leadership at time 2.

In the next section we review the measures used to operationalize this model in the 1997–99 New Labour panel survey.

Measures in the 1997–99 New Labour Panel Survey

The adapted global model of exiting involves replicating a number of the variables used in the 1990–92 Labour panel survey discussed in chapter 4, and in this section we examine the distribution of responses to the various measures required to do this.

The dependent variable in the exitors model appears in table 6.1, and it can be seen that during the period 1997–99 some 15 percent of party members indicated that they had left the party. Given that the membership in 1997 was around four hundred thousand people this implies an overall loss of about sixty thousand members during this period. Thus the number of exitors is not trivial, and given the fact that the recruitment of new members was much less of a priority for the party after the general election, the party began to decline in size again after 1997.[4]

Table 6.2 contains indicators of the resources and mobilization aspects of the civic voluntarism model. Obviously some of these variables repli-

TABLE 6.1. Exiting the Labour Party between 1997 and 1999 (in percentages)

"Do you consider yourself to still be a member of the Labour party?"

Yes	85
No	15

N = 1,325.

TABLE 6.2. Indicators of Resources and Mobilization in the Civic Voluntarism Model among Labour Members in 1997 (in percentages)

Full-time occupation	
Yes	45
No	55
Graduate status	
Yes	30
No	70
Occupational status	
Salariat	63
Routine Nonmanual	11
Petty bourgeois	2
Foreman & technician	8
Working class	16
Household income	
Under £5,000	8
£5000 to £10,000	19
£10,000 to £20,000	26
£20,000 to £30,000	20
£30,000 to £40,000	10
£40,000 to £50,000	7
£50,000 to £60,000	5
More than £60,000	5
Recruited by family, friends, or workmates	
Yes	38
No	62

cate the measures discussed in chapter 3, and modest changes occurred in the seven-year period between the two surveys. Thus compared with the 1989–90 survey slightly fewer Labour party members were in full-time employment and a fraction more were graduates in 1997. Between the two time points there was quite a significant change in occupational status, with 63 percent of the 1997 cohort categorized as members of the salariat compared with only 49 percent in 1989–90. As a result the later cohort has higher household incomes than does the earlier one.

Table 6.3 contains indicators of the variables that are used in the general incentives model of participation. Again, the distribution of attitudes are rather similar to those in chapter 3 for the 1989–90 survey. Thus most party members have a sense of personal efficacy while at the same time being conscious of the costs of participation. Many of them show signs of having political ambitions to serve either on the local council or in Parliament, and a large majority agree that participation is a good way to meet interesting people. As in the earlier survey, the distribution of opinions along the left-right ideological scale is skewed to the left, more so for Britain as a whole than for the Labour party. Also most members have attitudes that are congruent with party policies on the health service, private medicine, workers rights, and the alleviation of poverty. Finally, there is evidence of a slight weakening of partisan attachments in the later survey, with 53 percent of the sample being strong partisans compared with 55 percent in 1990.

Table 6.4 contains the indicators associated with the social psychological model of participation, which stresses perceptions of benefits to the party as a whole of different types of campaigning as well as social norms that can influence participation. Generally, party members think that various types of campaigning are fairly effective while at the same time they are conscious that the image of party members is not all that favorable and that members are often taken for granted.

Table 6.5 contains the additional indicators of performance that appear in the general model of exiting related to the performance of the government on the one hand and the performance of the leadership on the other. It is particularly interesting to note the gap between the evaluations of the party leadership and that of the government as a whole in these measures, which are taken from the second wave of the panel. Large majorities of the members were satisfied with the performances of Blair as leader, John Prescott as deputy leader, and Gordon Brown as chancellor.

TABLE 6.3. Indicators of the General Incentives Model among Labour Members in 1999 (in percentages)

	Strongly Agree	Agree	Neither	Disagree	Strongly Disagree
Personal efficacy					
People like me can have a real influence on politics	12	60	14	13	1
When party members work together they can really change Britain	34	56	7	2	1
Perception of costs					
Attending a party meeting can be pretty tiring after a day's work	11	61	16	11	1
Working for the party can be pretty boring at times	11	54	24	10	1
Outcome incentives					
A person like me could do a good job as a Labour councillor	13	37	20	24	6
The party would be more successful with people like me in Parliament	6	20	38	30	6
Process incentives					
Being active is a good way to meet interesting people	9	57	26	7	1
The only way to be educated about politics is to be a party activist	7	33	13	40	7
Group efficacy					
The leadership does not pay much attention to ordinary members	6	30	23	37	3
Parties are only interested in peoples' votes, not in their opinions	7	36	16	38	4
Ideological incentives	1 and 2	3 and 4	5 and 6	7 and 8	9
Left-right scale for party	15	41	32	9	3
Left-right scale for Britain	32	40	20	6	2

(continued)

TABLE 6.3.—Continued

Collective benefits	Definitely Should	Probably Should	Doesn't Matter	Probably Should Not	Definitely Should Not
Spend more money to get rid of poverty	61	33	2	3	1
Put more money into the National Health Service	76	23	1	1	0
Give workers more say in the workplace	48	43	6	2	1
Encourage the growth of private medicine	2	5	7	29	57

Expressive incentives	Very Strong	Fairly Strong	Not Very Strong	Not at All Strong
Strength of partisanship	53	41	5	1

TABLE 6.4. Indicators of the Social Psychological Model among Labour Members in 1999 (in percentages)

Expected Benefits	Very Effective	Effective	Not Very Effective	Not at All Effective
Displaying an election poster	22	54	21	2
Donating money to party election funds	40	53	5	2
Delivering party leaflets	28	55	15	2
Attending a party rally	8	35	48	9
Canvassing voters door to door	34	48	16	2

Social norms	Strongly Agree	Agree	Neither	Disagree	Strongly Disagree
Many people think party activists are extremists	12	54	15	17	2
The amount of work done by party members is often unrecognized	19	58	14	9	1

The rating of Brown, who was often described as the "iron chancellor" in the media because of his fiscal conservatism, is particularly striking.

On the other hand respondent evaluations of the government's overall performance and also its performance in tackling what they believed to be the most important problem facing the country were not so impressive. Nearly one-third of party members disapproved of the government's record to date, and three-quarters of them rated its performance on the

TABLE 6.5. Retrospective Evaluations of the Labour Government's Performance among Labour Members in 1999 (in percentages)

Evaluation of government's performance		Approve	Disapprove	Don't Know
Do you approve or disapprove of the government's record to date?		62	29	9

	Excellent	Good	Fair	Poor	Don't Know
How would you rate the government's performance on the most urgent problem facing the country?	5	21	39	33	1

Evaluation of the leadership's performance	Satisfied	Dissatisfied	Don't Know
Are you satisfied or dissatisfied with Mr. Blair as prime minister?	71	23	7
Are you satisfied or dissatisfied with the way Gordon Brown is doing his job of chancellor?	83	10	7
Are you satisfied or dissatisfied with the way John Prescott is doing his job as deputy prime minister?	76	14	10

most important problem as poor or fair. Clearly there was a difference between members' evaluations of the leadership and their evaluations of the government's policy performance. Obviously the working hypothesis is that members who are dissatisfied with the government's record and/or with the performance of the Labour leadership will be more likely to leave the party than will those who are satisfied. We examine estimates of the exitors model next.

Results

The estimates of the global model of exiting appear in table 6.6, which includes both the full version and the most parsimonious version of the model. Since the dependent variable is a dichotomous dummy variable the model is estimated by means of logistic regression,[5] with the test statistics in the table being Wald statistics. Model A in this table estimates the global model without the performance variables, and Model B includes the latter in the estimation.

TABLE 6.6. Estimates of the Global Model of 'Exiting' (logistic regression model)

Indicator	A	B	C	D
Activism	−0.41***	−0.44***	−0.43***	—
	(5.5)	(5.6)	(10.2)	
Personal influence	−0.11	−0.09	—	—
	(0.5)	(0.4)		
Collective benefits	−0.02	−0.14		—
	(0.0)	(0.8)		
Perception of costs	0.06	0.08	—	—
	(0.2)	(0.3)		
Outcome incentives	−0.20	−0.22		
	(1.5)	(1.7)		
Process incentives	−0.20	−0.23	−0.20**	−0.51***
	(1.7)	(2.1)	(3.0)	(24.7)
Ideological incentives	−0.37**	−0.25	—	—
	(5.3)	(2.2)		
Expected benefits	−0.06	−0.08	—	—
	(0.2)	(0.2)		
Social norms	−0.07	−0.09	—	—
	(0.2)	(0.3)		
Expressive attachments	−0.68***	−0.60***	−0.66***	−1.22***
	(9.9)	(7.1)	(17.0)	(95.7)
Group efficacy	−0.29**	−0.13	—	—
	(3.7)	(0.6)		
Full-time employment	−0.27	−0.26	—	—
	(0.8)	(0.8)		
Household income	−0.06	−0.07	—	—
	(0.5)	(0.5)		
Social class	0.15*	0.15	0.12**	0.11*
	(2.5)	(2.2)	(3.2)	(2.9)
Graduate status	0.14	0.16		—
	(0.2)	(0.2)		
Performance of the party	—	−0.74***	−0.93***	−0.64***
		(17.3)	(49.6)	(30.9)
Performance of the leadership	—	−0.13	—	—
		(0.8)		
Percentage of cases correctly classified	86.5	86.6	85.5	89.3
Improvement in log likelihood statistic	51.9***	79.0***	128.4***	255.2***
	(16 *df*)	(18 *df*)	(6 *df*)	(5 *df*)

$*p < 0.10$; $**p < 0.05$; $***p < 0.01$

Model A indicates that a modified version of the general incentives model provides the best explanation of exiting behavior. The modification involves incorporating a resource variable, namely social class, from the civic voluntarism model. Apart from social class all of the statistically significant variables in the global model come from the general incentives model. Thus it is apparent that this model encompasses the rational choice and social psychological models of participation when it is applied to the task of explaining exiting. The picture is rather similar though not identical to that of chapter 4, where the general incentives model dominated its rivals even though it did not formally encompass them.

To examine each variable in model A in turn, lagged high-intensity participation clearly influences exiting behavior, with high levels of activism inhibiting exiting. Clearly, of the two different interpretations discussed earlier, high-intensity participation inhibits subsequent exiting rather than promotes it. Thus there is no evidence of burnout, and it is the inactive members who are more likely to leave the party rather than the activists.

In the cases of personal influence, collective benefits, and perceptions of costs the relationships are not statistically significant, although in each case the signs are consistent with expectations. Thus the earlier point that the general incentives model provides the best account of exiting should be modified to recognize that a number of important variables in that model do not appear to influence exiting. On the other hand it is apparent that selective incentives are very important factors in influencing exiting. The most important effect is associated with ideology, with left-wingers being more likely to exit the party than right-wingers. The coefficients in the case of outcome and process incentives, while not being significant at the usual levels, are close to being so,[6] and the negative signs are consistent with expectations. They imply that members with strong outcome or process incentives are less likely to leave the party than are members with weak incentives of this type.

The other key variable in the general incentives model is expressive attachments to the party, which as we pointed out earlier is consistent with the loyalty variable in Hirschman's account of actor responses to declining performance. The highly significant effect associated with expressive incentives shows that strongly attached members are much less likely to leave the party than are weakly attached members. This highlights the importance of loyalty in preserving the membership of the party over time. If this effect were not so strong then changes in performance incentives, which can quickly react to government decision making and to events, would make party membership much more volatile over time. Expressive incentives clearly provide a ballast to the system that prevents this from occurring.

The effect of social class on exiting is not strong, but it does suggest that members in working-class occupations were more likely to leave the party compared with their middle-class counterparts. The thesis on the decline of working-class politics has been a theme associated with Labour party politics for many years (see Hindess 1971), and these estimates confirm its importance. The effect is consistent with a supply-side resources interpretation of participation, such that individuals having high levels of resources, that is, occupational status, are more likely to remain party members than are individuals who lack such resources. This is the mirror image of the argument from the civic voluntarism model that high-resource individuals are more likely to participate in politics than are low-resource individuals.

Turning finally to the performance variables that have been added to the equation in model B, it is readily apparent that the performance of the party in general had an enormous influence on exiting behavior. Individuals who were dissatisfied with the performance of the government in general or with a particular aspect of policy were much more likely to exit the party than were individuals who were satisfied with this performance. Interestingly, this effect did not extend to satisfaction or dissatisfaction with the party leadership. Members who were dissatisfied with the three party leaders were no more likely to leave the party than were those who were satisfied. Thus the focus of concern for party members is the performance of the government in policy terms, not that of the leadership.

This distinction may be partly the result of the much higher levels of discontent with policy performance than with the leadership, which we observed in table 6.5. But in any event it reinforces the earlier point about the importance of loyalty in sustaining membership through periods of adversity. If loyalty were not such an important factor in preventing exiting, it seems likely that many more party members would have left the party during this period in view of the relatively high levels of discontent with policy performance. Another effect of including the performance measures in the model is that it has made the group efficacy variable nonsignificant. This is a plausible outcome, however, for it implies that actual government performance is a better measure than perceptions of group efficacy when it comes to influencing members' calculations about whether to leave the party.

Model C in table 6.5 is the most parsimonious version of the exiting model, with all nonsignificant variables omitted. Clearly, once prior participation has been controlled exiting is the product of perceived policy failure, weakening selective incentives, and declining rates of loyalty. There is also a residual class effect at work as well, which has had the effect of making the party more middle class over time.

Finally, model D in the table estimates contemporaneous effects using the optimal specification identified in model C. It will be recalled that model C combines contemporaneous and longitudinal effects that might give a misleading picture, but the estimates in model D avoid this problem. It can be seen that model D is essentially the same as model C, except the effects are stronger for process incentives and expressive attachments. The size of the effect for social class is roughly the same as model C, and the effect of performance is rather weaker but still highly significant.

Discussion

Exiting behavior is not simply the mirror image of high-intensity participation, and yet the estimates from the global model show that these two phenomena can be understood with rather similar models. The optimal model of high-intensity participation identified in chapter 4 showed that the variables associated with the general incentives model dominated in explaining high-cost political participation. It is readily apparent that these factors also play an important role in explaining why some people give up party politics altogether and drop out. A general weakening of the incentives to participate has the effect of making some members less active and encouraging others to leave the party altogether.

It is also important to recognize that resources variables of the type that play a prominent role in the civic voluntarism model are also important in explaining exiting as well. But the results indicate that, if we modify the general incentives model to incorporate an indicator of resources, the resulting model encompasses its rivals in providing an account of exiting behavior. In this respect the findings from this chapter are similar to those of chapter 4.

One very important difference between the high-intensity participation and exiting models relates to the role of governmental performance. The strength of the effects associated with exiting suggests that performance is another key dimension to be considered in models of participation. The distinction between collective benefits and governmental performance can be interpreted as a distinction between prospective and retrospective evaluations, and clearly the latter are much more important than the former when it comes to explaining exiting.

As the review of the participation literature in chapter 2 makes clear, retrospective measures of macrolevel performance do not figure as causal mechanisms in models of participation, although such measures are important in the literature on electoral behavior. However, even in that literature they are used to explain party choice rather than voting turnout or participation. The findings from this chapter suggest that governmental and system performance may be an important missing dimension to the literature on participation.

The link between governmental performance and participation in this chapter is fairly direct, whereas in the wider literature on citizen participation, such as the analysis of electoral turnout, the links are much less clear-cut. In our case party members who are discontented with their own leadership and government have a clear incentive to leave the party, whereas it is not clear that discontent among citizens with the government of the day will provoke electoral abstention as opposed to a vote for another party. Thus the extent to which performance influences wider citizen participation is a topic for more intensive theoretical and empirical work. But this is clearly a relatively neglected issue in theoretical models of citizen participation.

As we pointed out in chapter 1, high-intensity participation takes place within an institutional context. The findings up to this point show that low-intensity participation, high-intensity participation, and exiting can all be explained by a rather similar model. This raises the intriguing possibility that the modified general incentives model might also provide an explanation of participation outside the context of an institution like a political party. The most obvious example of this is voting. Accordingly, in the next chapter we turn to the task of modeling party support in the electorate.

Chapter 7

Partisanship, Participation, and the Electorate

❧❦❧

SIGNIFICANT CHANGES HAVE OCCURRED IN VOTING behavior and in partisan attachments in the British electorate over time. Such changes have had far-reaching implications for the British political system in general and for party politics in particular. The aim of this chapter is to examine what light our model of political participation throws on the task of explaining voting behavior. Voting is not, of course, an example of high-intensity participation, but that it is the baseline activity in a continuum of participation makes it interesting in its own right. If the modified general incentives model performs well in explaining voting behavior as well as the high-intensity types of participation involved with party activism, the validity of the model is greatly strengthened.

The literature on electoral behavior is large, but it can be classified into distinct research traditions, each of which has an underlying theoretical model of electoral choice. There are many similarities between these models, making it possible to define a standard model that incorporates the key variables that have figured in most models of electoral choice. It turns out that this standard model has many similarities with the modified general incentives model, though the latter is more general and encompassing than the former. Thus the modified general incentives model provides an excellent theoretical framework for explaining the dynamics of party support among the electorate.

We begin this chapter by reviewing different research traditions in the analysis of electoral behavior in Britain, which leads in to a discussion of the standard model of voting behavior. We then examine the relationship between the modified general incentives model and the standard model of voting behavior. In a subsequent section we specify a vote function based on this model, which links time-series observations of voting intentions to a set of predictor variables derived from the modified general incentives model. This is followed by a section that discusses methodological issues involved in estimating the vote function for the Labour and Conservative parties, and subsequently we examine some estimates of these models. The final section discusses the findings and draws some conclusions about the determinants of party support in Britain.

Models of Electoral Dynamics in Britain

The modern literature on the dynamics of electoral support originates with Butler and Stokes's (1974) classic discussion of electoral change in Britain. As is well known, their model relies heavily on the Michigan school of electoral research, which focuses chiefly on social psychological variables as determinants of electoral choice (Campbell et al. 1960). As Butler and Stokes point out, political parties play a key role in this model: "Individual electors accept the parties as the leading actors on the political stage and see in partisan terms the meaning of the choices which the universal franchise puts before them" (1974: 20).

Thus partisanship, or the fact that "most electors think of themselves as supporters of a given party in a lasting sense" (Butler and Stokes 1974: 39), is the key mechanism by which voters can make sense of electoral politics. Party identification is seen as a long-term psychological attachment by voters to one or another of the major political parties, and it is the most enduring feature of their political attitudes and beliefs. Parties represent certain values and policy goals in the public's mind and also are perceived as being capable of affecting the world in ways that matter, such that they organize the voter's choice at election times. The existence of partisanship allows voters to hold the government of the day accountable for public policies, since that government must inevitably be a party government. In addition, partisanship creates a process of selective perception that acts as a filter and selects information that tends to reinforce party attachments over time.

Partisanship plays such a dominant role in the model that it is thought to be self-reinforcing over time, such that an individual who supports a party at a given election is more likely to do so at a subsequent election.

This implies that young people are more likely to be volatile in their voting behavior than are older people, because they have not yet fully acquired partisan attachments. Butler and Stokes supported the latter inference by showing that, while only 23 percent of people between the ages of eighteen and twenty-four in their 1970 survey had very strong partisan attachments, 63 percent of the those between the ages of sixty-one and seventy were in this category (1974: 58).

In their model partisanship is the product of enduring social cleavages, principally social class, and it is transmitted across the generations by means of socialization processes within the family. Thus the political environment within which the individual lives creates and reinforces partisan attachments along class lines. Butler and Stokes's surveys showed that in 1963 some 86 percent of respondents in the British Election Study with a higher managerial occupation were Conservative identifiers and 75 percent of unskilled manual workers were Labour identifiers (1974: 77). In addition, 86 percent of Conservative identifiers had a Conservative voting preference in that year, and 91 percent of Labour identifiers had a Labour voting preference (46). Thus their basic model is very simple: social class measured by occupational status largely determines partisanship, and in turn partisanship largely determines voting behavior. Clearly, this is a relatively static model, given that the occupational structure of society and the socialization process associated with the acquisition of partisanship change rather slowly.

This simple but powerful model had much appeal, but it did face a number of problems, particularly in relation to the task of explaining electoral change. Moreover, these problems became more apparent over time. One problem was that Butler and Stokes themselves did an extensive and pioneering series of panel surveys in the 1960s to analyze political change, and paradoxically in view of their basic model these showed great instabilities in both partisanship and voting behavior. When they tracked changes in voting behavior during that decade, they were obliged to conclude that "in the five intervals of change that we have examined in the 1960s, there were never as much as two-thirds of the public positively supporting the same party at two successive points of time" (Butler and Stokes 1974: 268).

Clearly such volatility poses problems for a model that emphasizes the central importance of stable partisanship in explaining electoral choice. Butler and Stokes never really dealt with this inconsistency, although they did attempt to discuss other variables that might explain the changes in voting patterns but for a variety of reasons tended to discount them. They examined three types of variable: voters' ideological beliefs, their evaluations of party leaders, and their issue perceptions.

In the case of ideology Butler and Stokes quickly discounted it as a relevant factor in influencing voting for all but "a tiny minority" (337), because the surveys appeared to show that the great majority of voters did not have stable ideological beliefs. In relation to party leaders, they conceded that public attitudes to leadership might play a role in explaining voting behavior but argued that the effects were rather weak in comparison with partisanship (364). Finally, in relation to issue perceptions, they were skeptical about the influence of attitudes to such issues as nationalization, immigration, and social welfare because of the great instabilities in opinions over time.

Such instabilities suggested that opinions on these issues were really nonattitudes, that is, unreflective responses to survey questions that shifted more or less at random over time (see Converse 1964). Furthermore, the surveys also showed that many voters did not appear to differentiate between the parties on these issues. As a consequence, Butler and Stokes concluded that issues play a rather residual short-term role in influencing voting behavior and that they are only really significant for individuals whose partisanship is weak.

Overall, the panel surveys demonstrated that significant instabilities in voting intentions and partisanship existed over time, and Butler and Stokes were rather skeptical about the importance of the variables that might have accounted for these, except in the case of individuals who had weak partisan attachments. The paradox was, however, that their own data suggested that only a relatively small minority of voters had nonexistent or weak partisan attachments, thus the weakness or absence of partisanship clearly could not explain electoral volatility.

Butler and Stokes did examine the circumstances in which a voter's party identification was likely to be weak, arguing that this can happen, for example, if an individual's parents have divided or weak party loyalties, which serves to inhibit the intergenerational transmission of partisanship. Alternatively, it might happen as a consequence of social mobility, when a voter moves out of the social environment in which his or her partisanship was developed and sustained. They added a third, rather ad hoc, reason for weak partisanship: when a major economic or political upheaval such as a war or serious economic depression occurs, causing a disruption in normal party loyalties. In this situation enough people might change their party attachments in the short run so as to precipitate a major realignment of the party system. This line of argument was developed to explain the realignment of the party system after World War I, but it fits very uneasily with the rest of their model.

Having largely discounted other factors, Butler and Stokes concluded that the main factor explaining long-term changes in partisanship, and thus voting behavior, is generational replacement. They argue that "demographic change is sufficient to yield a 10 percent turnover of the electorate within a five-year Parliament" (1974: 211). However, it is fairly clear that generational replacement provides an inadequate explanation of the observed instability of partisanship, since the instability is just too large. The strains these inconsistencies set up in their theoretical argument are apparent when at the end of the book they write: "We have shunned the adoption of any single model of change, trying instead to distinguish in the system we are studying some persistent processes that give partial clues to change" (406). This theoretical agnosticism sits rather uneasily alongside the clearly defined model developed earlier.

Despite this, Butler and Stokes's book was clearly a landmark study, and other writers tended to reflect and react to the theoretical framework Butler and Stokes developed. Crewe and his associates, for example, produced a comprehensive critique of the model, as the instabilities in voting behavior and partisanship became more apparent over time (Crewe, Sarlvik, and Alt 1977; Sarlvik and Crewe 1983). Crewe pointed out that in the 1951 general election the Conservative and Labour parties combined received the support of 79.9 percent of the electorate (i.e., voters and nonvoters). However, by the time of the October 1974 general election, the two parties received the support of only 54.7 percent of the electorate, a dramatic change in just over twenty years. This development was due principally to the rise in the Liberal and Nationalist votes, neither of which were predicted by a model that emphasized the self-reinforcing character and long-run stability of partisanship.

Since Butler and Stokes's pioneering work, a number of different theoretical approaches to the study of partisanship and electoral behavior in Britain have been developed. One such approach, associated with Dunleavy and Husbands (1985), adopted the idea of production and consumption sectors as significant determinants of voting behavior, an idea that was originally developed in the Marxist literature (see Habermas 1976). These sectors are vertical divisions in society that crosscut social class and relate to the different ways in which production and consumption is organized in society.

Dunleavy and Husbands argue that voters' sectoral status has an influence on their partisanship and voting behavior, independently of that of social class. Production sectors are usually measured in terms of the voter's employment status in the public or private sectors, and consumption sectors relate chiefly to different types of housing tenure. Their evidence suggests that council tenants and public sector workers were more likely to be Labour voters and that owner-occupiers and private sector workers were more likely to be Conservatives, with both effects working independently of social class (Dunleavy 1980a, 1980b).

This idea provided a more promising rationale for electoral change than did the slow processes of generational replacement, since they pointed out that large changes had occurred in both production and consumption sectors in Britain over time, with a significant decline occurring in trade union membership and a rise occurring in state dependency (Dunleavy and Husbands 1985: 129–46). Clearly if sectoral status influences voting behavior, and there have been large-scale changes in production and consumption sectors over time, this fact, along with the processes of generational replacement referred to earlier, might possibly explain the observed instabilities in partisanship and voting behavior.

However, Dunleavy and Husbands's work subsequently faced criticisms on both methodological and substantive grounds. The measurement of the sectoral model was criticized on methodological grounds for failing to control for other relevant variables (Harrop 1980). When controls for family background, socioeconomic status, political values, and leader images were included, sectoral status appeared to have a very weak influence on the vote (Rose and McAllister 1990: 148–49).

Another line of criticism of Butler and Stokes's model called into question the status of partisanship as a variable that is conceptually and methodologically independent of voting behavior. The concept was originally developed in the United States, where split-ticket voting for candidates from different parties has long been commonplace and has grown over time (Nie, Verba, and Petrocik 1976: 47–73). Clearly in the United States voting behavior and partisanship are not the same thing, but things may be different in Britain, where the institutional opportunities for split-ticket voting are rare. As a result it has been argued that party identification is merely another name for voting intentions (Budge, Crewe, and Farlie 1976; LeDuc 1980). Rose and McAllister articulated this view most strongly when they argued, "Demonstrating a high correlation between party identification and party vote supports the hypothesis that these are but two names for the same thing" (1986: 132).

However, this argument is problematic, since it implies that a strong relationship between two or more variables necessarily implies that they are indistinguishable from one another. Taken to its logical conclusion it implies that a valid causal link between variables can only exist if the relationship between them is, perversely, not too strong. While it is true that one interpretation of a very high correlation between variables is that they are both observable indicators of some underlying common latent measure, another equally valid interpretation is that these are different variables linked by a strong causal relationship. We will return to this issue later.

Rose and McAllister developed an alternative ideologies model of electoral choice, which challenges the relevance of partisanship (1990: 148–56). They argue that once broad underlying values, or ideologies, of the electorate are taken into account partisanship has a very weak influence on voting behavior. They define ideologies as "the expression of the values of a social group, such as the working class or churchgoing Catholics" (90; see also Scarborough 1984; Evans 1999). These values are measured by means of a factor analysis of a large number of issue indicators in the British Election Study and thus are essentially composite measures of broad issue perceptions. In this analysis, the electorate votes on the basis of broad perceptions of the policy goals and performance of the parties as well as economic evaluations play a central role in defining these goals.

However, Rose and McAllister's inference that party identification has a relatively trivial influence on voting once ideological values are taken into account is not well grounded. To test the rival impact of ideologies on the one hand and partisanship on the other, it is necessary to examine the impact of these variables on voting behavior in a properly specified multivariate model. Instead, Rose and McAllister merely assume that values are causally prior to partisanship and enter them into a vote function prior to partisanship, using a stepwise regression technique. Thus they are not testing rival theories so much as estimating the residual influence of partisanship after the values measure has been imposed on the model.

The methodological weakness of this approach can be seen by considering what would happen if this procedure had been reversed and partisanship entered into the model first. In this case it would have appeared that ideology had a vestigial influence on voting behavior once partisanship had been taken into account. Clearly, a much more reliable procedure would be to estimate the influence of ideology and partisanship on the vote simultaneously to see which one encompasses the other rather than imposing a causal sequence on the model.

Another development in the literature relates to the role of leadership evaluations in influencing voting intentions. As mentioned earlier, Butler and Stokes argue that images of the party leaders had an influence on voting behavior independent of partisanship but that the effects were rather weak (1974: 362–68). Subsequent research has shown that voter images of the party leaders, particularly that of the prime minister, play an important independent role in influencing voting intentions and that the effects are quite strong (Rose and McAllister 1990: 134–42; Clarke and Stewart 1995). Clearly, any model of voting intentions that omitted leadership evaluations would be misspecified.

It also appears clear from subsequent research that issue evaluations play a more important role in influencing voting intentions than Butler and Stokes recognized. Issue perceptions have played a prominent role in the literature on voting behavior arising from the rational choice tradition, which is a rather different theoretical approach to that of Butler and Stokes and the Michigan school.

As the discussion in chapter 2 indicates, rational choice theories of voting became prominent after the publication of Anthony Downs well-known book *An Economic Theory of Democracy* (1957). As mentioned earlier, in the Downsian model, voting behavior is driven exclusively by the "utility incomes" generated from the issue positions adopted by parties. Downs explains, "Each citizen in our model votes for the party he believes will provide him with a higher utility income than any other party during the coming election period" (38).

A voter judges these utility incomes on the basis of the past performance of both the incumbent and opposition parties and also on the promises that the parties make about the future. In the face of uncertainty, Downs argues, some voters will choose on the basis of "ideological competency, not on specific issues" (99), since uncertainty makes it difficult to evaluate all the issues that might be relevant to defining the voter's utility income. According to Downs, ideology is "a verbal image of the good society and of the chief means of constructing such a society" (96), and in Downs's model voters use ideology to reduce information-processing costs.

Downs's work is purely theoretical, but it has influenced much subsequent empirical work on electoral behavior in Britain. In the consumer voting model introduced by Himmelweit and her colleagues (1981), for example, voters choose between parties on the basis of the benefits they bring. She writes that "the individual, with his personal set of attitudes and beliefs, looks for the best match, or the least mismatch between these and his or her perception of the platforms and the records of the parties" (11). In this model demographic variables influence the goals and values of voters, which in turn explain their attitudes to issues and their perceptions of the parties. These attitudes and perceptions in turn determine their voting behavior, although normative pressures from other individuals and reference groups in the electorate also influence voters, something that is not true of the original Downsian model.

Similarly, in the prospective model developed by Sanders (1991, 1993), the key causal variable is voter's expectations of the effects of government policies on the economic welfare of their families in the future, or egocentric economic evaluations. The model is not wholly Downsian, but it is influenced by the idea that voters weigh up issues and link these issue evaluations to political parties when they are deciding how to vote.

Another model, the retrospective sociotropic economic evaluations model (Fiorina 1981; Whiteley 1983), is again derived from the Downsian tradition, but in this case the key causal variable is past evaluations of the economic performances of the parties in managing the national economy. This is not to be confused with the voter's egocentric evaluations of the effects of government policies on their own family incomes in the future.

Fiorina introduced a rational choice interpretation of party identification that radically differs from the concept discussed by Butler and Stokes. He defines partisanship as a running tally of retrospective evaluations of the parties, which are based on the performance of the parties in delivering benefits to the voter over time (Fiorina 1981: 90). In this model partisanship is no longer anchored in socialization processes that take place in early life, so it has the advantage of explaining the instabilities in partisanship that Butler and Stokes observed but were unable to explain in their theoretical model. Clearly, if economic management (or mismanagement) can influence partisanship, it is likely to be much more volatile than is true in a model where changes in partisanship depend on generational replacement.

A further model that was influenced by the rational choice tradition is the saliency model of Budge and Farlie (1983). In this model, issues take center stage in influencing the vote, but they influence it via processes of party mobilization. Thus the parties campaign on those issues they feel to be their strongest vote winners and ignore issues raised by their opponents on which they are perceived to be weak. Thus issue perceptions determine the vote in this model but only insofar as parties succeed in raising the saliency of their own preferred issues positions in comparison with those of their opponents.

In the light of this discussion, there is enough of a consensus in the literature to discern a standard model of voting behavior in Britain, even though there are disagreements about which variables are the most important. Such a model incorporates variables that most researchers would acknowledge to be essential components of a vote function if it is to be properly specified.

This standard model suggests that voting behavior in Britain is directly influenced by three classes of variables: party identification, issue perceptions, and leadership evaluations. These variables directly influence the vote and are in turn influenced themselves by other factors, notably demographic variables such as social class, age, sex, and the like. At the same time it is known that the direct influence of such demographic variables on voting behavior is very weak, once the effects of partisanship, issues, and leadership evaluations are taken into account (Whiteley 1986).

The standard model is not so well defined that there is universal agreement about which issues should be included in the specification or precisely how leadership evaluations should be measured. Thus in the popularity function literature, which uses time-series analysis of poll data, the focus has been exclusively on economic issues (Goodhart and Bhansali 1970; Whiteley 1986; Norpoth 1992; Clarke and Stewart 1995). In contrast, in the values and ideologies literature referred to earlier (Scarborough 1984; Rose and McAllister 1986, 1990), issues such as attitudes toward social welfare and nationalization are thought to play an important role as well as are evaluations of the economy. Equally, while there is a broad consensus about the measurement of partisanship, as we have seen there are significant differences over the conceptual meaning of this measure. In the light of this discussion it is interesting to examine the links between this standard theory of voting and the general incentives theory introduced earlier.

Modified General Incentives Theory and the Vote Function

It may be recalled that the general incentives theory is grounded in the assumption that participation occurs in response to different kinds of incentives and that five classes of incentives are relevant: selective, collective, group, expressive, and social. The basic theory was subsequently modified to take into account the individual's socioeconomic status, which influences his or her participation through the resources that high status bestows. It is interesting to examine how these different types of incentive relate to the standard model of voting behavior.

The first point is that leadership evaluations and issue perceptions are clearly examples of collective incentives for participation. The issue position adopted by political parties and the competence and effectiveness of the party leaders are both examples of collective goods. Thus the effects of the positions adopted by the parties, particularly in relation to the economy, cannot be confined only to those electors who vote for the governing party. Clearly opposition supporters, and more to the point nonvoters, share in the policy effects along with government supporters, and this creates incentives to free ride on the efforts of others.

A similar point can be made about the performance of party leaders. Voters who strongly support a party leader have nonetheless an incentive to free ride on the efforts of others and not to vote for that party, because their vote makes no difference to the outcome of an election, and in any case they will receive the benefits of leadership if that party leader is subsequently elected. This means that if voters were rational in the classical sense, and they only took into account issues and leadership evaluations in determining their vote, they would not vote. However, it will be recalled that the general incentives theory is not purely a rational choice account of political participation, even though it has its origins in the rational choice tradition. Thus it is important to take into account such collective incentives in the model.

However, applying the model to voting behavior does have implications for selective incentives, since they are not relevant to this type of participation. Turning up at the ballot box to vote clearly produces little or no social interaction with other people, and so process incentives appear absent. A similar point can be made about outcome incentives, since there is no possibility for advancing a political career by voting in an election. Ideological incentives are absent too, since in the general incentives theory they are relevant to participation only insofar as they are shared by other people who interact with the individual, something ruled out by the secret ballot. Thus selective incentives are irrelevant in the standard model.

As we mentioned in chapter 2, rational choice theorists have sought to inject selective incentives into the vote function as a means of avoiding the paradox of participation (e.g., Riker and Ordeshook 1973: 63). But these attempts have not been very successful, since they create as many problems as they seek to solve; if civic duty is a selective incentive that explains voting, it is not clear why it should vary across constituencies, or in the same constituencies over time, or among local, national, and European elections (Green and Shapiro 1994: 52). Moreover, there is also a collective action problem in explaining why civic duty motivates participation. Thus invoking such a concept does not solve the problem but merely relabels it. Overall, the conclusion must be that selective incentives cannot be used to explain voting behavior in national elections, and thus purely rational choice accounts of voting fail for this reason.

A second point relates to political efficacy, which figures in the modified general incentives theory. It will be recalled from the discussion in chapter 2 that political efficacy is important in high-intensity participation because a few individuals can be influential in changing political outcomes. However, the same cannot be said about political efficacy in relation to voting. In a vote function, the probability that the individual can influence outcomes is effectively zero, so it makes little sense to incorporate it into the specification of the model.[1] For this reason, we omit measures of efficacy from the vote function. A similar point can be made about the costs of political action, which can be substantial in the case of political activism but are negligible in relation to voting.

A key variable in the modified general incentives theory that it shares with the standard voting model is party identification. In the general incentives model party identification is interpreted as an expressive motive for participation and is not based on purely cognitive calculations of costs and benefits, as is the case in Fiorina's model (1981). Equally it is not based on socialization processes within the family, as in Butler and Stokes's (1974) analysis. Rather party identification is interpreted as a heuristic device adopted by voters that enables them to judge the political parties with only a modest expenditure of effort and low information-processing costs.

The role of heuristics in political decision making has been explored in recent work by political psychologists. The work of Sniderman and his collaborators was referred to in chapter 6. They write:

Citizens frequently can compensate for their limited information about politics by taking advantage of judgmental heuristics. Heuristics are judgmental shortcuts, efficient ways to organize and simplify political choices, efficient in the double sense of requiring relatively little information to execute, yet yielding dependable answers even to complex problems of choice. (Sniderman, Brody, and Tetlock 1991: 19)

Thus partisanship can be interpreted in terms of the likeability heuristic referred to in chapter 6 (see Sniderman, Brody, and Tetlock 1991: 93–119), although for voters it is more likely to be influenced by impersonal mechanisms such as the media than by face-to-face mechanisms associated with party activists.

A similar point can be made about group incentives for participation. It will be recalled that in the general incentives model citizens are motivated to participate if they think that the group to which they belong is competent and effective. Thus group incentives can be interpreted in terms of a competency heuristic; citizens make a rough judgment of the competency of a political party using indicators such as levels of unity or disunity and the coherence of the message it is trying to get across. This is a much easier task than monitoring the details of policy formation and implementation across the whole range of governmental activities, and it allows the citizen to make such judgments without incurring large costs of information processing.

The fifth and final variable in the general incentives model is social incentives for participation based on social norms. In our earlier work, indicators of such incentives have not always been statistically significant predictors of activism (see Seyd and Whiteley 1992: 112; Whiteley, Seyd, and Richardson 1994: 119). However, in the context of electoral behavior social norms may influence voting behavior in two ways. First, the influence operates via processes of political mobilization and campaigning of the type discussed in chapter 2. Second, social incentives operate through citizen perceptions of the relative popularity or unpopularity of the political parties in the electorate.

Mobilization processes operate at the national level via the media and at the local level through the activities of political parties and other organizations in campaigning, and they have not generally been incorporated into the standard model. In the case of media effects, this is because of the difficulty of identifying them in the presence of many other influences on voting behavior (Newton 1992). In the case of local campaigning, it is because of a prevailing attitude among many researchers that they are unimportant (see Butler and Kavanagh 1992: 245).

However, there is increasing evidence that voters are mobilized by national media campaigns during and prior to elections (Miller et al. 1990; Miller 1991; Newton 1992; Norris 1993). In addition evidence is growing that the local campaigning activities of political parties have a significant impact on both the vote and turnout (Seyd and Whiteley 1992; Whiteley and Seyd 1994; Pattie et al. 1994; Denver and Hands 1997). In this way pressure from other people, which is the basis of the social incentives effect, might well influence the vote.

The notion that voting behavior might be influenced by citizens' perceptions of the attitudes and opinions of their fellow citizens was originally introduced by Noelle-Neumann (1984). She suggested that there is a "spiral of silence" operating in relation to political issues, such that the perceived unpopularity of an issue position will make sympathizers reluctant to publicly support it and will encourage opponents to publicly oppose it. This sets up a dynamic that makes an unpopular issue even more unpopular, since waverers perceive that there is little support for it, which encourages them to oppose it. This dynamic process can effectively crowd out an issue from public debate and remove it from the political agenda.

This idea can be applied to the vote function, since it implies that public perceptions of the standing of the political parties in the polls will have a significant influence on support for those parties at any given point in time. In other words the desire to conform to majority opinion may make some individuals change their vote away from what is perceived to be an unpopular party to favor what is perceived to be a popular party. In this sense social norms might influence voting behavior.

Overall, this discussion implies that the standard voting model is a special case of the general incentives model. It shares collective incentives, expressive incentives, group incentives, and social incentives with the general incentives model but omits selective incentives. In the light of this discussion we will examine next the specification of the vote function to be estimated.

Specification of the Vote Functions for Labour and the Conservatives

The vote function, based on the general incentives theory, can be written as follows:

$$V_{ijk} = a_{jk} + b_{1jk}IP_{ijk} + b_{2jk}L_{ijk} + b_{3jk}PID_{ijk} + b_{4jk}G_{ijk} + b_{5jk}S_{ijk} + u_{ijk} \qquad (1)$$

where

V_{ijk} is the probability that individual i will vote for party j at time k.

IP_{ijk} is the probability that the issue preferences of individual i will favor party j at time k.

L_{ijk} is the probability that the evaluations of individual i of the political leaders will favor party j at time k.

PID_{ijk} is the strength of identification of individual i with party j at time k.

G_{ijk} is individual i's perceptions that party j is effective as an organization and deserves support at time k.

S_{ijk} is individual i's perceptions that party j is likely to win the next election at time k, and thus social norms favor voting for that party.

u_{ij} is an error term, where $E(u_{ijk}) = \sigma_{ujk}^2$ and $E(u_{ijk}u_{lmn}) = 0$, when $i \neq l; j \neq m; k \neq n$.

This is a very broad specification, and the indicators of the various variables need to be examined in detail. The model could be estimated using individual-level panel data, but it will be estimated using aggregate-level time-series data instead. This is because until 2001 adequate indicators of the variables are not available in the British Election Studies, which is the only source of individual-level panel data on electoral behavior in Britain.[2] The model contains indicators of collective, expressive, group, and social incentives but not indicators of selective incentives, political efficacy, or socioeconomic status. The first two are excluded on the theoretical grounds discussed earlier, since selective incentives are not relevant to voting and political efficacy is objectively zero in a national election. Socioeconomic status is excluded because the model is estimated using aggregate time-series data obtained from monthly Gallup surveys in Britain.[3] Clearly, an individual's socioeconomic status does not change sufficiently in a month to have any impact on the vote.

There are certain advantages to using aggregate time-series data; first, it is possible to track changes in the variables over many time periods, not just the limited number of time points available in a panel survey. Second, it is possible to estimate the impact of various recurring political events or exogenous political shocks to the system that might influence relationships between the variables in the vote model; again, the limited number of observations over time available from a panel survey makes this difficult. Third, it is possible to evaluate the effects of objective changes in the economy, such as increases in interest rates or unemployment on party popularity, alongside changes in voters' subjective perceptions of the economy, something that cannot be done with individual-level data (see Kramer 1983). Finally, aggregating the variables eliminates a lot of random noise that is present in individual-level data and gives a better insight into the forces that influence overall party success or failure in an election, as distinct from the influence of specific variables on the voting behavior of individuals.

Two vote function models are estimated, one predicting Labour vote intentions and the second predicting Conservative vote intentions. The predictor variables in these two vote functions include Labour and Conservative party identification; voter evaluations of the Labour and Conservative party leaders; objective and subjective economic issue evaluations; an indicator of group incentives; and an indicator of social norms. The details of the question wording and the variables appear in the appendix. The models are estimated using monthly observations from January 1992 to April 1997 and thus cover an entire Parliament from the general election of 1992 to the general election of 1997.[4]

The party identification and leadership evaluation variables are interpreted as indicators of a likeability heuristic toward the parties and the party leaders. As mentioned earlier in a purely rational choice account of voting, these variables would be subject to the paradox of participation and would not be significant predictors of voting for that reason. But in the present account they are indicators of affective feelings toward the parties, which in part are used to short-circuit the complicated calculations required to assess the costs and benefits of supporting one party rather than another.

The influence of issues or collective incentives concentrates on objective and subjective evaluations of the economy. In relation to the impact of the objective economy, this was measured using three different indicators: interest rates, the inflation rate, and unemployment. One interpretation of the effects of such variables on party support derives from the so-called reward-punishment model (Key 1966; Lewis-Beck 1988). According to this model the electorate rewards the incumbent party for a good economic performance and punishes it for a bad one. If the reward-punishment model applies, each of these variables would have a negative impact on support for the Conservatives, since increases in these measures represent public "bads." It would also imply a positive or a negligible impact on support for the Labour party, depending on whether Labour benefited from a bad economic performance by the incumbent Conservative government.

An alternative interpretation of these effects is provided by the issue-priority model (Budge and Farlie 1983; Clarke et al. 1992). This applies when parties are seen as having different policy priorities in relation to the management of the economy. If the Conservatives are seen as being particularly averse to inflation and Labour is seen as unreliable on this issue, an increase in inflation under a Conservative government might benefit rather than harm the Conservatives. This is because voters believe that the main alternative to the incumbent party would have a worse performance on inflation than would the government.

A similar point can be made about unemployment; if this is seen as a distinctive Labour issue, then a rise in unemployment under a Conservative government would help Labour and hurt the Conservatives. Equally, this would also be true if the incumbent party was Labour, again because voters perceive that the main alternative to the Labour party would have a worse performance on this issue. When the Conservatives are in office, this is the same outcome as the reward-punishment model. Thus it is only possible to distinguish between the two alternative models by focusing on the effects of inflation on party support during our estimation period.

With regard to the subjective economy or perceptions of the relationship between the economy and political support, Gallup surveys regularly ask a question about the most important issues facing the country, and economic issues consistently dominate the responses to this question. Accordingly, three indicators of the subjective economy are used in the vote function: the percentage of voters who perceive that inflation is the most serious issue facing the country; the percentage who feel the same way about unemployment, and the percentage of voters who think that Labour is the best party at managing the economy in the Labour vote function and the percentage who think this about the Conservatives in the Conservative vote function.[5]

The group incentives variable is measured by voter perceptions that the electorate has a favorable opinion of a party. If a party is thought to have a favorable image among voters this could act as an incentive for individuals to support it, particularly those voters who do not strongly identify with any party or think highly of the party leaders. This is what is meant by a group incentive to support a party. The percentage having a favorable opinion of Labour is used in the Labour vote function, and the percentage having a favorable image of the Conservatives is used in the Conservative vote function.

The social incentives indicator measures the percentage of respondents who think that Labour will win the general election in the case of the Labour vote function and the percentage of respondents who think that the Conservatives will win the general election in the case of the Conservative vote function. The idea behind this is that if individuals perceive that a party is likely to win the next general election, this might encourage them to support it, because they want to conform to a perceived social norm that favors that party.

The political "shocks" in the vote functions relate to political events that might influence the relationship between the predictor variables and party support. Some of these are recurring events such as the annual party conferences, which focus media attention on the parties, allowing them to present themselves in a favorable light. It seems plausible that political support for the parties will receive a temporary boost as a result of the annual conferences.

A second recurring, but in this case unpredictable, shock occurs when a party leader resigns, dies, or is challenged for the leadership. This focuses attention on that particular party for a short period of time, which may harm it in some circumstances and help it in others. For example, John Major resigned as leader of the Conservative party in June 1995 specifically to run again for the office as a way of asserting his authority over a quarrelsome parliamentary Conservative party. Arguably, this exercise harmed him in the eyes of the voters because it drew attention to his political weakness. In contrast, when the Labour leader, John Smith, died suddenly in May 1994 and Tony Blair was subsequently elected party leader, this may well have helped Labour because of the upsurge of public sympathy caused by Smith's untimely death. These possibilities are tested by means of dummy variables in the vote functions.

A third recurring but unpredictable shock is provided by by-elections. During the estimation period the Conservative government lost a series of by-elections to the opposition parties, which may have produced a temporary setback in their national standing in the polls. Labour won four of these by-elections, the most spectacular victory being in Wirral South in February 1997. Again, these by-election victories may have given a temporary boost to Labour in the polls.

The vote functions will be estimated in a form that allows us to examine both the short- run and long-run influences of the variables on political support. Thus before we examine estimates of the models, it is necessary to discuss some methodological issues explaining how this can be done in the context of time-series models of party support.

Modeling the Vote Function over Time
· ⑥· ·

As mentioned earlier, there are many studies of the aggregate dynamics of party support. A number of these studies have assumed that the time-series measures used to model party support are stationary processes, that is, that the variables fluctuate around a constant mean and have a constant variance over time.[6] This is a very important property for accurately modeling the relationship between time-series variables, since if it is violated and the series are nonstationary the researcher runs the risk of estimating "spurious regressions" (see Granger and Newbould 1974, 1986), which give entirely misleading results.

The problem of making spurious inferences with nonstationary data arises because many series that are totally unrelated to each other theoretically nonetheless grow in a rather similar way over time. Accordingly, if they are included in a regression model, statistically significant relationships can be found between them.[7] This problem can be dealt with by differencing the series, such that the researcher models the changes in one variable against the changes in another. This means that when the series are incorporated in differenced form into a model they should only be significantly related if they are causally linked in some way.

However, differencing a series produces its own problems, because it necessarily ignores possible long-run relationships between variables. For example, it seems plausible that there is a long-run equilibrium relationship between Labour voting intentions and Labour party identification, such that if Labour partisanship strengthens in the electorate this should increase Labour vote intentions at the same time, which should in turn stimulate partisanship, and so on. Such an equilibrium relationship will be hidden by differencing the series. In certain circumstances, it is possible to estimate both short-run and long-run relationships between variables of interest using what is known as an error-correction model. Such a model may be specified if nonstationary series are cointegrated.[8]

An error-correction model of the relationship between series implies that if one series is influenced by a short-term shock of some kind the

other series will subsequently respond in a similar way, such that diver-
gences between these series set up by the initial shock will eventually be
"corrected." In an error-correction model, the coefficient of the error-correction mechanism measures the speed and strength of the adjustment
resulting from the equilibrium relationship. Methodologically, it is important to test whether the variables in the vote function are stationary and,
if they are not, to model them in differenced form. If in addition an equilibrium relationship can be demonstrated between key variables in the
model, that is, if they cointegrate, it is possible to capture the long-run
relationship between the equilibrium variables in an error-correction
model.

One final requirement is to ensure that the predictor variables are
weakly exogenous to vote intentions. This relates to the question of
causality discussed earlier. Variable X_t is weakly exogenous to variable Y_t
if the latter does not contemporaneously affect the former. Weak exogeneity still holds if Y_{t-1} affects X_t, however, because there is no contemporaneous feedback in such a model resulting from the fact that Y_t is a
function of X_t and thus unbiased estimates of the coefficients can still be
obtained (Charezma and Deadman 1992: 251–69). If X_t is strongly exogenous to Y_t, then neither contemporaneous nor lagged values of Y_t affect
X_t, and this implies that Granger causality (Granger 1988) exists in the
relationship between the variables. Earlier research has shown that party
identification and leader evaluations are both weakly exogenous in time-
series models of Labour and Conservative vote intentions (Clarke, Stewart, and Whiteley 1997, 1998).

Estimating the Vote Functions

In the light of this discussion, we begin the analysis of the vote function
by testing whether the variables in the model are stationary. Figure 7.1
contains a plot of the Labour and Conservative voting intentions series
over the estimation period, and this plot certainly suggests that the series
are nonstationary. In figure 7.1 the Labour series increases continuously
from the start of 1992 and only gives the appearance of leveling out
toward the start of 1996. In contrast, there is a rapid loss of Conservative
support in late 1992 and early 1993, and the series reaches record low levels of support before recovering slightly in the run-up to the 1997 general

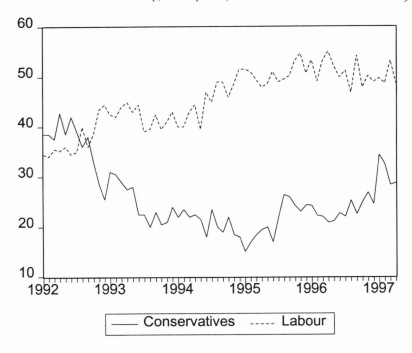

Fig. 7.1. Labour and Conservative voting intentions, 1992–97

election. Clearly neither series fluctuates around a constant mean. There is a formal statistical test of stationarity called the Dickey-Fuller test (Dickey and Fuller 1979), which is applied to all of the series in the two vote functions, with the results appearing in table 7.1.

The first column in table 7.1 tests whether the original series is stationary. In this test the null hypothesis is that the series has a unit root, or is nonstationary. This means that if the null hypothesis is accepted then the series trends upward or downward over time. On the other hand if the null hypothesis is rejected it means that the series is stationary and can be incorporated into an estimation equation without fear of spurious regression effects. It can be seen that all of the series apart from two, Labour party identification and public perceptions of the Conservative party, appear to be nonstationary, although these are close to being nonstationary as well. Clearly, differencing the series makes them all stationary, so the evidence in table 7.1 indicates that the variables in these models should be differenced if reliable estimates of the vote functions are to be obtained.

The second question in the analysis concerns long-term equilibrium relationships that might be present in the variables in the vote functions. Intuitively, there should be a theoretical reason for believing that variables are in equilibrium, and in addition they should closely track each other over time and not significantly deviate from one another if they are perturbed by a shock of some kind.

In figures 7.2 and 7.3 the relationship between voting intentions, party identification, and leader evaluations is plotted for Labour and the Conservatives respectively. It can be seen that in both figures the series tend to track each other fairly closely over time, the relationship being closer

TABLE 7.1.   Unit Root Tests for the Stationarity of
Variables in the Voting Intention Models, 1992M1 to 1997M4

Variable	Original Series	Differenced Series
Labour vote intentions	−2.49**	−13.30
Conservative vote intentions	−2.30**	−10.50
Labour party identification	−3.51	−12.20
Conservative party identification	−2.38**	−11.73
Labour leader evaluations	−2.59**	−12.12
Conservative leader evaluations	−2.10**	−7.38
Perceptions that Labour is best at managing the economy	−2.86**	−10.92
Perceptions that the Conservatives are best at managing the economy	−2.15**	−10.42
Interest rates (with trend)	−1.88**	−5.51
Inflation	−2.11**	−8.95
Unemployment	−2.87**	−6.15
Perceptions of inflation as most important problem	−2.50**	−10.94
Perceptions of unemployment as most important problem	−1.54**	−12.21
Perceptions that public has a favourable opinion of Labour	−1.77**	−8.24
Perceptions that public has a favourable opinion of Conservatives	−5.51	−6.82
Perceptions that Labour will win general election	−1.20**	−8.56
Perceptions that Conservatives will win general election	−1.80**	−8.99

** fails to reject null hypothesis of unit root, i.e., indicates that the series is non-stationary, $p < 0.05$ level.

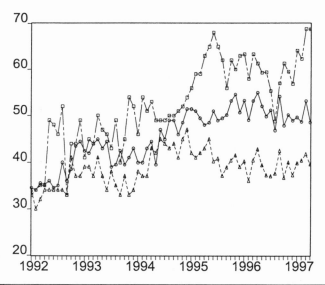

Fig. 7.2. Voting intentions, party identification, and leader evaluations for Labour, 1992–97

for the Conservatives than it is for Labour. In the case of Labour the variables appear to diverge a little at the start of 1995, but it is noticeable that fluctuations in each of the series are fairly in phase with each other throughout the entire period. The equilibrium relationship is particularly evident in the case of the Conservative series, where the variables track each other very closely.

To test whether these variables are in equilibrium or cointegrate, we employ the Engle-Granger (1987) two-step procedure. This involves regressing voting intentions on party identification and leadership evaluations, all without differencing, and then testing the residuals of this model for stationarity. Intuitively, if all three variables are in a long-term equilibrium relationship, partisanship and leadership evaluations should be significant predictors of party support and the residuals should be stationary. If the residuals of the model are not stationary and show evidence, for example, of a trend growth this means that the variables are not in equilibrium since they are drifting apart from each other.

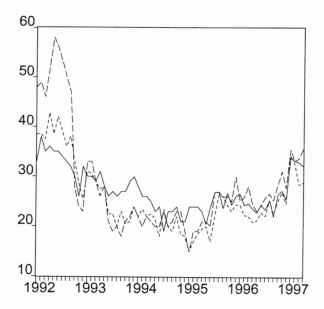

Fig. 7.3. Voting intentions, party identification, and leadership evaluations for Conservatives, 1992–97

From table 7.2, which includes the cointegrating regression models for the two parties, it is apparent that party identification and leadership evaluations are both significant predictors of voting intentions for both parties. There is a battery of diagnostic tests in table 7.2 designed to assess whether the model is well behaved.[9] The goodness of fit of the models is reasonable, but not surprisingly there is clear evidence of autocorrelation in the residuals produced, in part, by the fact that the variables are measured in undifferenced form. However, from the point of view of the cointegrating relationship it is evident that the augmented Dickey-Fuller test is statistically significant, indicating that we can accept the hypothesis that the model residuals are stationary. Thus these variables are in a long-term cointegrating or equilibrium relationship with each other.

Table 7.3 contains estimates of the vote function for Labour, the model being estimated in error-correction form. The first model contains all the variables discussed in the theoretical specification, and the second

TABLE 7.2. Cointegrating Regressions of Vote Intentions, Leader Approval, and Party Identification for the Labour and Conservative Parties, 1992M1 to 1997M4

Predictor Variables	Labour Vote Intentions	Conservative Vote Intentions
Constant	3.40	–0.43
	(0.8)	(0.22)
Party identification	0.52***	0.51***
	(4.3)	(5.0)
Leadership evaluations	0.42***	0.44***
	(8.4)	(10.2)
R^2	0.73	0.91
Standard error	3.06	2.07
Durbin-Watson test	1.06**	1.54**
RESET test	0.004	4.88***
Normality test	2.28	2.88
ARCH test	0.86	0.22
Heteroscedasticity test	0.001	0.08
Augmented Dickey-Fuller Unit root test of residuals	–4.65**	–6.25***

$*p < 0.10; **p < 0.05; ***p < 0.01$

TABLE 7.3. Error Correction Models of Labour Vote Intentions, 1992M2 to 1997M4

Predictor variables		
Constant term	0.04	–0.14
	(0.1)	(0.4)
Δ Labour leader evaluations (t)	0.24***	0.19***
	(3.3)	(3.2)
Δ Labour party identification (t)	0.27***	0.28***
	(2.7)	(2.9)
Δ Labour best party on the economy (t)	0.23**	0.30***
	(2.0)	(3.2)
Δ Inflation most important problem (t)	–0.17	—
	(1.0)	
Δ Unemployment most important problem (t)	0.07	—
	(1.0)	
Error correction mechanism $(t-1)$	–0.47***	–0.38***
	(4.3)	(4.0)
Δ Interest rates (t)	1.27	—
	(1.1)	
Δ Inflation (t)	–1.71*	–1.73**
	(1.8)	(2.0)
Δ Unemployment (t)	1.67	—
	(0.6)	

(*continued*)

TABLE 7.3.—*Continued*

Predictor variables		
Δ Percent thinking public has favourable opinion of Labour (*t*)	0.06 (0.6)	—
Δ Percent thinking Labour will win election (*t*)	−0.11** (1.8)	—
Labour party conferences (*t*)	3.16*** (2.8)	2.5** (2.3)
Smith becomes leader (*t*)	−2.20 (0.9)	—
Blair becomes leader (*t*)	0.15 (0.1)	—
Labour by-election wins (*t*)	1.26 (1.0)	—
R^2	0.55	0.50
Standard error	2.09	2.11
Durbin-Watson test	2.09	2.08
RESET F test	0.03	0.06
Normality test (χ^2)	2.52	2.32
Heteroscedasticity test	0.79	0.05
ARCH F test	0.36	0.73
Unit root test of residuals	−7.88***	−8.18***

Note: Dependent variable is Δ Labour vote intentions (Δ is the difference operator).
*$p < 0.10$; **$p < 0.05$; ***$p < 0.01$

model includes only those variables that are robust predictors of the vote. The estimates indicate that evaluations of the Labour leader, party identification, and perceptions that Labour is the best party in managing the economy are all statistically significant predictors of Labour voting intentions. The coefficients on all of these variables are rather similar, such that a 10 percent increase in voters' evaluations of the Labour leader translates into an increase of about 2.5 percent in voting intentions; the same change in party identification produces an increase in voting intentions of almost 3.0 percent; and for perceptions that Labour is the best party for managing the economy, the increase is just over 2.0 percent.

Clearly, perceptions of economic competence play an important role in influencing the Labour vote, although perceptions that inflation and unemployment are the most important problems facing the country do not significantly increase Labour support in this model. However, there is weak evidence of an issue-priority effect associated with inflation. It appears that an increase in inflation reduces Labour support, an effect no doubt associated with the legacy of high inflation during the last Labour government in the 1970s. The only other robust result in the model, apart from the error-correction mechanism, relates to Labour party conferences. Not surprisingly, these annual events appear to give a short-term boost to Labour support.

The error-correction mechanism measures the speed with which a deviation from the equilibrium relationship between voting intentions, partisanship, and leader evaluations is restored after it is perturbed by a political shock. The estimates show that some 47 percent of the effect of an exogenous shock on voting intentions is corrected by the equilibrium relationship within a month of it occurring. Thus the equilibrium relationship between these three variables is quite strong. The effect in the most parsimonious version of the model is rather weaker but still highly significant.

None of the other postulated effects appears to be statistically significant or robust predictors of Labour voting intentions. Thus perceptions that the party is viewed favorably by voters do not appear to influence voting intentions; nor does the indicator of social norms, the percentage of voters who think that the party is going to win the next general election. The latter variable appeared significant in the first model, but this result was not robust, as can be seen from the most parsimonious version. It is also the case that various political shocks associated with the appointment of a new leader, or victories in by-elections, do not appear to influence vote intentions independently of the other variables in the model.

The various diagnostic tests indicate that the model is statistically well behaved; there is no evidence of autocorrelation, heteroscedasticity, or nonnormality in the residuals, and the unit root test suggests that the residuals are stationary. The RESET test indicates that the functional form of the model is satisfactory. The most parsimonious model contains partisanship, leader evaluations, perceptions of managing the economy, inflation, and the Labour party conference dummy variable. The results indicate that the standard model encompasses the modified general incentives model, since the extra variables in the latter are not statistically significant.

The equivalent model for the Conservatives appears in table 7.4. Once again party identification, leader evaluations, and perceptions that the Conservatives are best at managing the economy all play a significant role in explaining variations in voting intentions, just as they did in the Labour model. However, it is also apparent in this model that changes in the objective economy, particularly in interest rates and unemployment, had a direct effect on voting intentions, in addition to changes in subjec-

TABLE 7.4. Error Correction Models of Conservative Vote Intentions, 1992M2 to 1997M4

Predictor Variables	A	B
Constant term	−0.68***	−0.29
	(2.9)	(1.5)
Δ Conservative leader evaluations $(t-1)$	0.15*	—
	(1.8)	
Δ Conservative party identification (t)	0.39***	0.37***
	(4.4)	(4.8)
Δ Conservatives best at managing the economy (t)	0.32***	0.47***
	(3.4)	(8.8)
Δ Inflation most important problem (t)	−0.13	—
	(1.2)	
Δ Unemployment most important problem (t)	−0.02	—
	(0.6)	
Error correction mechanism $(t-1)$	−0.60***	−0.64***
	(5.6)	(7.1)
Δ Interest rates	−2.54***	−2.11***
	(3.5)	(3.4)
Δ Inflation (t)	0.20	—
	(0.3)	
Δ Unemployment (t)	−4.06**	−2.51*
	(2.5)	(1.9)
Δ Percent thinking public has favorable opinion of Conservatives (t)	−0.05	—
	(0.6)	
Δ Percent thinking Conservatives will win election (t)	−0.05	—
	(1.3)	
John Major challenged for leadership $(t-1)$	4.45***	4.21**
	(3.1)	(3.0)
Conservative by-election losses $(t-1)$	−1.23**	−1.45**
	(2.1)	(2.7)
European & local elections 1994 $(t-1)$	6.25***	5.68***
	(4.2)	(3.7)
Conservative party conferences (t)	1.16*	—
	(1.8)	
R^2	0.82	0.81
Standard error	1.24	1.29
Durbin-Watson test	1.92	2.19
RESET test	7.66***	5.67***
Normality test	1.60	1.47
ARCH test	0.39	0.70
Heteroscedasticity test	0.16	0.89
Unit root test	−7.19***	−8.68***

Note: Dependent variable is Δ Conservative vote intentions.
*$p < 0.10$; **$p < 0.05$; ***$p < 0.01$

tive perceptions of economic competence. No doubt this is because the Conservatives were incumbent and therefore were held directly responsible for interest rate changes and unemployment by the electorate. An increase of 1 percent in interest rates translated into a decline in Conservative voting support of about 2 percent, and an increase of 1 percent in unemployment reduced voting intentions by about 2.5 percent.

As mentioned earlier a negative sign on unemployment in the Conservative vote model cannot distinguish between an issue priority and a reward-punishment model. But the same point does not apply to interest rates since there is no evidence that either party is regarded by the electorate as "owning," or being more competent on, the interest rate issue. Thus the interest rate effect is consistent with a reward-punishment model of economic effects. In any event, both the objective and subjective economies had an important influence on Conservative support.

The various political shocks associated with the party conference, the loss of by-elections, the leadership challenge to John Major, and the particularly disastrous European and local government elections of 1994 all appear to have influenced Conservative voting intentions in predictable directions. Moreover, the error-correction mechanism appears to have been slightly stronger in the Conservative vote function than it was for Labour, since 60 percent of the effects of a shock on voting intentions are restored by the cointegrating relationship within a month of it occurring. In the most parsimonious model the effect is even stronger.

Overall, the Conservative voting intention model has a better fit than its Labour equivalent, largely because the objective economy and the political events have a bigger impact on Conservative voting intentions than they do on Labour voting intentions. The signs of the objective economic variables in the model are consistent with a mixture of reward-punishment and issue priority models of the economic effects. Thus voters punished the Conservatives for interest rate rises and increases in unemployment, but they did not punish them for an increase in inflation. In contrast, Labour support is reduced by increased inflation. It seems likely that the Conservatives are insulated from the effects of rising inflation because they were identified as being strong supporters of anti-inflation policies in the minds of the voters. The diagnostics suggest that the Conservative models are statistically well behaved[10] and that the residuals are nonstationary, suggesting reliable inferences can be made from these estimates. Again, the standard model appears to encompass the modified general incentives model, since the extra variables in the latter are not statistically significant.

Conclusions: General Incentives and Voting Intentions

The evidence from the estimates of the vote functions suggests that electors will vote for a political party as a result of their party identification and their evaluations of the leader of that party. Issue preferences are also an important factor in explaining the vote, particularly the perception that a party is the best at handling the economy. In addition there is evidence that the objective economy influences voting intentions alongside subjective perceptions of economic competence, particularly in the case of the governing party. The Conservative incumbents were damaged by increases in interest rates and unemployment during this period, although interestingly there was no evidence that Labour was particularly helped by changes in these variables.

In terms of our earlier discussion it is clear that heuristics are important for guiding voting behavior. In the absence of detailed knowledge about how the economy works, or the complex causal chains that operate to link governmental action and policy outcomes, voters appear to use two related heuristics. One is a likeability heuristic and the other a managerial heuristic.

Party identification in particular involves a likeability heuristic, a mechanism for reducing complex calculations to a simple and economical form. If voters like a party and begin to identify with it, this directly influences the likelihood that they will vote for it. As the cointegration evidence suggests, this likeability heuristic is also closely associated with perceptions of managerial competence, and in turn this is linked to the objective performance of the economy in the case of the governing party.

The managerial heuristic is apparent in relation to perceptions of economic competence and also in relation to evaluations of the party leaders. If the economy is in difficulty, voters blame the managers, both in the form of the parties and also of the party leaders. The logic of this process is much like that of football supporters' calling for the resignation of the team manager when their team is doing badly. Football supporters do not have to work out the precise tactical or strategic problems facing their favorite club and how these should be solved if it is to win again.[11] Rather, they can simply blame the manager and call for his replacement. Such a heuristic makes it possible to pass judgment on complex policy issues and thereby exercise democratic accountability without having specialist knowledge or insight into the causal processes at work.

These findings attest to the continuing importance of social psychological processes in influencing the vote. The earlier skepticism about rational choice accounts of voting is reinforced by the findings of this chapter. Few, if any, of the variables that are important determinants of the vote can be derived easily from a classic rational choice account of decision making. But this is hardly surprising, since the paradox of participation inhibits a theoretically coherent rational choice account of voting behavior in any case. The variables that appear to be the most important influences on voting intentions are grounded in social psychological processes and do not fit at all well into a narrow cost-benefit model of political action.

Also, the standard model encompasses the modified general incentives model in both cases. This is because the indicators of group incentives and the measures of social norms are not significant predictors of vote intentions when both figure in the theoretical specification of the modified general incentives model. Perhaps not surprisingly the best model of a low-intensity activity like voting is different, although not radically different, from the best model of high-intensity participation.

Having started out with a discussion of high-intensity participation in the earlier chapters, our analysis has come full circle in this chapter to examine voting behavior. For theoretical reasons the model of voting behavior is not the same as the model of party activism. However, we can observe great similarities in these models. In the final chapter we bring the threads of the discussion together to try to assess the implications that follow from the findings of this book.

Chapter 8

Parties and High-Intensity
Participation in the Future

❧◉❧

THE RESULTS OF THIS ANALYSIS OF TRENDS in party activism over a decade of British politics are fairly clear. High-intensity participation is in decline, despite valiant attempts by New Labour to reverse these trends in the 1990s. The Labour party provides the best indicator of this development since our data for the party cover the period 1989 to 1999. A single measure encapsulates the trend. In the 1989–90 survey just over 50 percent of party members devoted no time at all to party activities in the average month (Seyd and Whiteley 1992: 228). By 1999 this figure had grown to 65 percent of the membership. In the earlier survey nearly 10 percent of members devoted more than ten hours to party activities, but by 1999 this figure had become 6 percent. If comparable data were available for the Conservatives it would be unlikely to show a different picture.

What are the implications of this development for the British political system? To use a cliché, is the party over? These are the topics for discussion in this final chapter. We begin by examining a literature that challenges party dominance, both from normative and empirical points of view, to see what light it throws on these developments. This leads into a section in which we discuss the implications of the trends for the Westminster system of government as well as for party structures in advanced industrial democracies more generally. Next we look at some scenarios for the future, considering what different models of party organization are available and what models are likely to be adopted in the future.

In the final section we turn attention to wider questions of the analysis of political participation. What are the implications of these findings for theories of participation? In particular what are the implications for controversies over rational actor and social psychological models of political behavior? In this section we return to the wider concerns that motivated the analysis of this book in the first place.

Challenges to Party Dominance
· ☞ ·

Declining confidence in parties is not unique to Britain: criticism of parties as representative institutions has become so extensive in liberal democracies that the phrase "party crisis" has become commonplace. Hans Daalder (1992) detected four distinct strands in the phrase's usage: first, a denial of party, in the sense that parties are seen as a threat to the good society; second, a selective rejection of certain types of party, such as the mass party organization; third, the rejection of certain types of party system, such as the two-party or multiparty system; and, fourth, the notion of the redundancy of parties, as other actors and institutions take over the roles hitherto performed by parties.

Antiparty sentiment of the type that fits Daalder's first three categories has never been strong in Britain (Scarrow and Poguntke 1996). The emergence and growth of parties in the late nineteenth and early twentieth centuries did not occur, however, without opposition. From the earliest days there were critics who were concerned that factional or party interest would replace the national interest and that as a consequence individual, rational judgment would be replaced by collective, irrational judgment.

John Stuart Mill (1861), for example, argued the need for political institutions and procedures that would enable the individual representative to arrive at political decisions unaffected by particular interests. Other writers such as Sir Henry Maine (1885), A. V. Dicey (1885), Moisie Ostrogorski (1902), and J. A. Hobson (1907) warned of the dangers of the party system and, in particular, of the powers of the party caucus (Birch 1964: 75–81; Meadowcroft and Taylor 1990). Criticism of the party system from a liberal point of view continued to be expressed in the twentieth century, with both Hollis (1949) and Mayhew (1969) arguing that Parliament's powers had been subordinated to the parties. However, this particular liberal critique was submerged by the development of collectivist politics starting in the 1920s, which was well documented by Samuel Beer (1965) in his classic study of the British party system.

In addition to this liberal critique of collectivist organizations, other criticisms of the institutions of party have emerged in the twentieth century. First, there is the managerialist critique, which argues that particular areas of policy-making, such as economic planning, defense, education, and budgeting, are too complex and specialized to be left to party politicians and should, therefore, be kept out of politics (see, for example, Shonfield 1965). The Labour government's decision in 1997 to make the Bank of England solely responsible for bank interest rates is one such example of this thinking and was the culmination of a campaign to remove this aspect of economic policy from the direct influence of party.

Another example was the Conservative government's belief in the 1980s and 1990s that local economic regeneration and service delivery should be removed from the influence of party-based local authorities and given to quangos, which are independent of party. Urban development corporations, training and enterprise councils, and single regeneration budget partnerships were institutional means of downgrading the impact of party in the locality.

The managerialist thesis may have validity, but it tends to ignore the problem of bureaucratic rent seeking (Tullock 1967; Mueller 1989: 229–46), a process by which managerial elites substitute their own private interests for the interests of the wider society. More generally, the call to make issues nonpolitical is open to the criticism that it is merely a device for removing legitimate points of view from the political agenda.

Second, there is the view that when government suffers from the periodic alternation of parties this results in abrupt changes of direction in policy outcomes. The adversary politics thesis, argued particularly by Finer in the 1970s, suggests that party government leads to bad government (Finer 1975; Gamble and Walkland 1984; Debnam 1994). However, work by Rose (1984) suggests that there was little support for this thesis in practice, since many of the key policy changes occurred within administrations rather than between them. This is true of such issues as the shift to monetarist macroeconomics by Labour in the 1970s and the drive to privatize state-owned industries developed by the Conservatives under Thatcher. Both are examples of policies that did not figure in the respective manifestoes of the parties when they took power or in the early years of their administrations but that later became key policies of these governments.

Third, there is the belief that parties have sought to maximize their control of civic society and have done so by appointing their placemen onto a wide range of public bodies. In today's quango state the opportunities to do this are considerable. The Committee on Standards in Public Life (HMSO 1995) heard expert witnesses who argued that ministers make ten thousand appointments each year, some two thousand of which are executive positions in the NHS, development agencies, and other quangos. These carry out executive functions on behalf of the government, and the vast majority of them operate at the local level (Weir and Beetham 1999). Some sixty-five thousand people occupy such appointed positions, very many of them placed there by parties (Marr 1996; Weir 1995). It is argued that such patronage provides opportunities for cronyism and corruption. On the other hand it is not clear whether any system of recruitment for such a large number of unelected positions could avoid this criticism.

Fourth, there is the argument that representation suffers because parties seek to control political debate and to capture all political issues, making discussion of issues impossible beyond the specific narrow parameters they have set down. Specifically, it is argued that debate does not extend beyond the white, middle-aged, male perspective of British party elites. The Equal Opportunities Commission published a report citing poll evidence that seven out of ten women felt political parties did not pay sufficient attention to issues of importance to them (*Guardian*, February 19, 1997), and the United Kingdom Action Committee on Islamic Affairs reported that the two million Muslims felt that issues such as state funding for Muslim schools, a ban on religious discrimination, and the outlawing of incitement to hatred against Muslims were being ignored by party politicians (*Guardian*, February 21, 1997).

On the other hand in the new Russia there is a women's party, and in many countries there are prominent Islamic parties. While it may be true that parties neglect the interest of minorities such as British Muslims or even majorities such as British women, the option is always open to political entrepreneurs to form a new party, or a faction within an existing party, to move those interests up the political agenda.

It is perhaps Daalder's fourth category—the redundancy of party—that has most relevance to contemporary debate in Britain. As the discussion in chapter 4 indicates, economic, social, and cultural changes in British society have served to weaken traditional political attachments. The decline in manufacturing industries and the growth in the professional and service sectors of the economy, the breakup of traditional working-class communities, the expansion of numbers in higher education, and the growth of the mass media have all affected individuals' political identification. Both the Conservative and Labour parties owe their origins, development, organization, and electoral support to Britain's class-based, industrial society.

As Lipset and Rokkan (1967) argue, Britain's party system in the 1960s, along with that of the rest of western Europe, reflected the cleavage structures of the 1920s. However, as voters' political attachments become weaker and as party identification declines, voters in aggregate are becoming increasingly volatile. Thus opinion polls reveal rapid shifts in party support, and at by-elections voters behave in a less predictable manner than was true twenty years ago (Butler and Butler 1994: 234).

It is also claimed that individuals now look increasingly to interest groups and the new social movements rather than to political parties as more effective mechanisms for conducting a dialogue with their rulers. According to Richardson, changes have occurred in the market for participation, and "citizens now have an active marketplace for participation in which to shop" (1994: 17). Group formation is on the increase, and a more specialized and customized market exists in which "parties are now somewhat *passe* amongst an increasing majority of citizens" (22). Other organizations than parties are now setting the political agenda, and Richardson concludes that "interest groups and social movements have come to present a major challenge to parties as channels of participation and for the resources which citizens are willing to donate" (26).[1]

Richardson's claim that there is an active market for participation in which interest groups and social movements vie with parties for adherents is certainly the case, but there is little empirical evidence for many of his other assertions. Although it is the case that certain groups, such as the National Trust, the World Wildlife Fund, Greenpeace, and Friends of the Earth, have much larger memberships than do parties, comparisons between these organizations have to be made with care. The barriers to entry have tended to be higher for those thinking of joining a party rather than a pressure group.[2] Richardson's claim that group formation is on the increase is difficult to verify when no comprehensive audit of groups has been carried out.[3] There are many examples of new groups being established, but less attention is devoted to the groups that disappear, so we have no accurate data with which to judge claims about the growth of groups. Richardson's claim that parties are "somewhat *passe* amongst an increasing majority of citizens" is not confirmed by recent British Election Study data referred to in chapter 1. Finally, his statement that parties as agenda-setting organizations have been replaced by interest groups requires extensive in-depth analysis of policy-making, little of which is available. Parties are just one of many agenda-setting organizations, but their role has not necessarily been subordinated to groups.

Thus some of the claims that interest groups are replacing parties as the major channels of representation may be exaggerated. Nevertheless, the development of organized public protest on issues such as the poll tax, the export of live animals, the building of motorways and airport runways, and protection of the countryside points to the fact that "the politically unaware are turning from a traditional, party-based model of activity, based upon a generality of policy, to a new policy-specific approach—one which lends itself to group rather than party activity" (Kelly 1999: 24).

We have already noted the relative weakness of antiparty sentiment in twentieth-century Britain; nevertheless the behavior of some politicians, ranging from lobbying activities in the mid-1990s to their behavior on the floor of the House of Commons, has contributed to a loss of confidence in politicians, which has been exploited by party critics to develop a more comprehensive case for bypassing, regulating, and weakening parties. Some of the proposals for citizen juries, deliberative polls, electronic town halls, and referendums are intended to do this (Demos 1994; Stewart, Kendall, Coote 1994; Bogdanor 1994). Similarly, after recent controversies over the funding of both Conservative and Labour parties, the view has been expressed that the state should fund parties but also should more strictly regulate them (Bogdanor 1997). Finally, some of the demands for the introduction of elected city mayors and for the adoption of a new electoral system have been made with the intention of weakening parties (Hodge, Leach, and Stoker 1997; Gallagher 1996–97).

Thus there are a number of strands to antiparty ideas in contemporary thought. But it is not clear whether any of these strands provide decisive support for the proposition that parties can be dispensed with in the future. Arguments against party all have their flaws, and as arenas for high-intensity participation it appears unlikely that they will disappear in the future. But as the earlier evidence indicates it is true that the British party system is characterized by declining rates of high-intensity participation. To assess the consequences of this decline it is necessary to return to the examination of the functions of parties we began in chapter 1.

The Consequences of Declining
Participation within Parties

That high-intensity participation is declining within British political parties means these organizations will perform their functions less effectively in the future. It might be useful to focus more specifically on the effects of declining activism for party organizations before returning to the more general issues of the role of parties in the political system. Parties recruit members for a number of different reasons, and party members have long possessed important powers. One such power is the selection of candidates, both to local government and also to the House of Commons (Ranney 1965; Rush 1969; Norris and Lovenduski 1995). Potential party leaders have had to impress local party members in order to be chosen as parliamentary candidates in the first place. In addition, party leaders are now elected by membership ballots in all three major parties, so members play the major role in determining the outcomes of these processes.

A decline of grass roots participation means that the mechanisms for selecting candidates will decay. In relation to the Westminster system local parties may show a tendency to select candidates whose opinions are increasingly unrepresentative and therefore unacceptable to a wider electorate. In this situation the center may very well step in to take away the right to select candidates from local parties, and indeed there are signs that this is already happening. However, this in turn will reduce the incentives to participate further.

In relation to local government the decline of high-intensity participation within parties means that fewer individuals will be willing to stand as candidates, and parties will not be able to fight effective election campaigns at the local government level for this reason. Alternatively, there is likely to be a lowering of the quality of candidates willing to come forward as party representatives in local politics. This in turn is likely to weaken the quality of local decision making and representation, adding a further twist to the spiral of decline.

A second problem linked to the issue of political recruitment relates to the socialization of individuals into political activity and as elected representatives. If high-intensity participation declines, the mechanisms for socializing candidates into politics will weaken. There will be fewer people around who know what high-intensity participation of various kinds actually means. Inactive parties will end up not merely recruiting candidates who have little or no experience in political activity, but they will prove weak arenas for socializing such candidates into the craft of politics, allowing them to learn how to be effective full-time elected representatives.

A third effect is linked to fund-raising. The point has already been made that British parties are voluntary organizations with only limited state financial assistance. Consequently, members provide significant sums of money to help the parties maintain day-to-day activities (TSO 1998a). This is likely to grow more important in the future as new legal restrictions on party finance are introduced that arise from recommendations of the Committee on Standards in Public Life (TSO 1998a). Parties will no longer be able to rely on a small number of anonymous rich donors to fund their activities but will have to raise funds from diverse sources, including large numbers of small donations from their individual members.

The surveys show that activists give more money to their respective parties than do the inactive members, and this is true for both the Labour and Conservative parties. In 1992 the median financial contribution to the party of inactive Conservative members in the previous year was 20 pounds, and for very active or fairly active members it was 50 pounds. Interestingly, exactly the same figures applied to inactive and active Labour party members in 1999. Thus active members give about two and a half times as much money to their respective parties as do inactive members. Clearly a decline in high-intensity participation is likely to reduce the amount of money that party members give to their respective organizations over time, which will create financial difficulties for the parties unless they are able to recruit many more inactive members to compensate for this reduction.

A fourth effect relates to election campaigning. Legal restrictions on constituency election campaign expenditures create a need for voluntary human resources as a substitute for hiring expensive campaign professionals. It is overwhelmingly members who provide this campaigning resource in both local and general elections. Making personal contact with electors, delivering party literature over and above the one free delivery provided by the state, and persuading electors to vote on election day are all activities that can only be maintained by parties if they have armies of volunteers in all constituencies (Denver and Hands 1997).

Recent research has shown that local election campaigns are increasingly important in influencing election outcomes in the context of an increasingly volatile electorate (Johnston and Pattie 1995; Pattie, Johnston, and Fieldhouse 1995; Denver and Hands 1985, 1997; Whiteley,

Seyd, and Richardson 1994; Whiteley and Seyd 1999). Obviously, a decline in high-intensity participation associated with election campaigning means that the parties will face increasing difficulties in getting their supporters to the polls. If the decline is uniform across parties this should not greatly influence the balance of campaigning on the ground, but if one party manages to counteract this trend while the others do not, this party will obtain a growing electoral advantage at its rivals expense. Arguably this is what happened in 1997, when Labour out-campaigned the Conservatives on the ground by a significant margin (Whiteley and Seyd 1999).

Finally, notwithstanding the steadily increasing centralization of the British state since 1945, local government possesses significant powers to provide services to people. Parties in local government have maintained an independence of their central headquarters, resulting in a variety and diversity of service provision and behavior (Gyford 1983). Local government by its very nature places greater emphasis upon grass roots activity. If this is not forthcoming the quality of representation and decision making at the local level will decline. This may in turn encourage central government to accelerate existing trends toward managerialism in local government, which in turn will reduce the incentives for participation.

Beyond these specific roles, party members have other more general roles. Scarrow (1996: 40–46) itemizes a number of these, including contributing to a party's legitimacy in the community, guaranteeing it a number of loyal and regular voters, providing it with some opinion leaders and links with voters, and finally offering it a source of innovatory ideas and personnel. If high-intensity participation continues to decline all these functions will suffer and the parties will become less able to support them.

These direct influences on the performance of parties in the British system of government caused by declining high-intensity participation are fairly clear. But there are indirect influences that are likely to undermine the ability of parties to perform the more general functions discussed in chapter 1. It will be recalled that these function related to aggregating preferences, expressing a collective will of the voters, in addition to selecting candidates and promoting political communication.

As the discussion in chapter 1 indicates the key function of parties in the Westminster system is to aggregate preferences and to provide reasonably stable government. If the ability of the system to do this declines, it will produce the kind of policy gridlock that has become a regular feature of the political landscape in the United States (Cox and Kernell

1991). Potentially, gridlock in the British system could be worse than it is in the United States because party cohesion is the linchpin that makes executive dominance of the legislature possible and makes the responsible party model work. If this weakens to the point that parties in the House of Commons begin to look like their nineteenth-century counterparts, strong, decisive government would become impossible. New coalitions of support would have to be constructed on every issue, and the system would begin to cycle between unstable majorities of short-lived coalitions in the manner predicted by the social choice theorists (see Schofield 1978; McKelvey 1986).

On the other hand the ability of the parties to adapt to new circumstances should not be underestimated. Over the past twenty-five years considerable changes have occurred in the prevailing political ideas in Britain, and the parameters of both Labour and Conservative party politics have shifted considerably. The Labour party came close to the electoral abyss in 1983, but in 1997 it was elected to government with its largest parliamentary majority ever. Its electoral success was the result of fundamental changes in both its program and structure over a ten-year period. A significant part of Labour's electoral appeal in 1997 was that New Labour had discarded old political baggage.

Similarly, adaptations to Conservatism have occurred. During its period under Thatcher, the Conservative party adopted a very distinctive ideology. However, in response to its worst electoral defeat since 1832 in 1997, it is now engaged in a process of transformation in which "new" Conservatism is also being asserted. First, William Hague, the former Conservative leader, and then his replacement, Iain Duncan Smith, have sought to follow in the footsteps of Blair by rebuilding his party from the ground up as a means of working toward a future electoral victory.

These developments show the resilience of parties in the face of considerable turbulence in the political landscape. Our focus has been on high-intensity participation among grass roots party members. But to what extent will membership parties remain important in the future? Would it be possible to retain the distinctive cohesive features of the responsible party model in the absence of an activist membership base? Are membership parties essentially nineteenth- and early-twentieth-century institutions, as has been claimed (*Demos* 1994; Mulgan 1994)?

Recently formed parties in Britain have attempted to either dispense with or downplay the role of activists in their organizational structures. The Social Democratic party, established in 1981, was founded by a splin-

ter group of the Labour leadership (Crewe and King 1995). Dissension in
the Labour party, particularly over the issue of European integration, was
the principle cause of their split with the party in the first place. The trau-
matic experience of being a minority frequently attacked by rank-and-file
Labour party members encouraged the new party leadership to want a top-
down organization capable of keeping a tight rein on members. The Referendum party, formed in 1995 by the millionaire businessman Sir James
Goldsmith, did away with members altogether and recruited only supporters. So in the new century are party members no longer necessary? We
set out to answer these questions by examining possible future models of
party structures.

Models for the Future of Parties
•⁄ʘ⁊•

There are perhaps four possible models for parties as political organizations in the future. First, there is the extinction model, in which parties
die out and are replaced by an ill-defined mixture of Internet democracy,
town meetings, and interest groups. The second is the leadership model,
which relies on a charismatic leader like Ross Perot or James Goldsmith
and has a heterogeneous group of supporters but little in the way of a permanent organization and no activist base of any great significance. The
third is the plebiscitary model, a structure in which there is an organization and a membership but in which power is concentrated heavily in the
leadership and the role of the members is merely to endorse fairly general
policy statements and to periodically legitimate the leadership in
plebiscites. Finally, there is the participatory model, which has an organizational structure characterized by genuine grass roots participation in
which members exercise influence over policy-making and the leadership.

The extinction model can be dismissed fairly easily. There are few
social science laws comparable to those in the natural sciences, but it is a
reliable proposition that no advanced industrial democracy can work
without parties. If parties did not exist, they would have to be invented
because of the functions they perform. We have reviewed these earlier,
but easily the most important functions are those of aggregating interests
and distributing costs so that parties combine many diverse interests into
broad programs that can be supported by large numbers of people and
share out the costs of these programs among the wider society.

Olson (1982) points out in an insightful analysis that special interest groups often seek benefits for themselves while aiming to distribute the costs associated with this among the wider society. Thus the strategy of interest groups is to concentrate benefits narrowly and to distribute costs widely. Such groups can afford to be irresponsible about the costs of their demands. In contrast, parties that seek to govern are in Olson's terminology encompassing organizations that have to consider both the costs and benefits of collective action when seeking to represent society as a whole.

Parties are different from interest groups in that they cannot hope to concentrate benefits on a minority group while distributing the costs among the wider society if they hope to win office, because winning power means obtaining the support of a majority of the voters. Thus collective action by parties is much more efficient and socially inclusive than is collective action by interest groups. This analysis implies that, if parties do not exist to perform these functions, democracy will become paralyzed by a cacophony of special interests, each of which seeks benefits from the state while simultaneously trying to ensure that someone else pays for these benefits.

More direct forms of democracy, such as Internet democracy, also face difficulties. The first is the problem of social exclusion; while Internet access is growing, there are large numbers of people in society who cannot get access, and they would be excluded from participation in any system of Internet democracy. A second difficulty relates to decision making on the Internet. While democratic debate can flourish on the Internet it is not clear how preferences will be aggregated into actual decisions by this means. Again the literature on social choice referred to earlier suggests that a system having many actors, each with differing policy agendas, will produce perverse problems of social choice (Mueller 1989: 63–65). Few stable decisions can be achieved in such a system, unless it is restricted in various arbitrary ways, and in effect becomes a type of plebiscitary democracy. Clearly, the Internet is going to play an increasingly important role in democracy in the future, but it is not without problems.

The leadership model has emerged in a number of different countries in recent years, and this is clearly a possible blueprint for the future. The essence of this model is that a charismatic leader establishes his or her own party with an organization mainly consisting of supporters rather than members or activists. These supporters generally play only a peripheral role in policy-making and are really there only to legitimize the leader and in some cases to provide finance rather than to participate in democratic decision making. The charismatic leader generally keeps a tight hold on power.

The track record of this type of party organization in winning elections and in governing is not good. Ross Perot's Reform party in the United States ran a very successful presidential election campaign in 1992 but was unable to capitalize on this success in the 1996 election and is now rather faction ridden and ineffective. The most successful example of such a party is Silvio Berlusconi's Forza Italia, which was modeled on a football supporters' club. It was in government in Italy in the mid-1990s and is now again in office. But its governmental performance on its first occasion in office was poor, and it suffered from factionalism and the defection of many of its parliamentary deputies.

The best example from Britain is Sir James Goldsmith's Referendum party, which was established with the explicit aim of obtaining a referendum on British membership of the European Monetary Union. Goldsmith took a strong anti-integration position on this issue, and he felt that voters would reject membership in a referendum. In the 1997 election the party contested 547 constituencies and claimed to have a fighting fund of twenty million pounds and two hundred thousand supporters (Butler and Kavanagh 1997: 149). On average its candidates secured 3.1 percent of the vote in these constituencies, and the party tended to do best in areas with large agricultural or elderly populations (306). The evidence suggests that it undermined the Conservatives to a certain extent, but as Butler and Kavanagh point out, "Our findings clearly suggest that, contrary to what has widely been claimed, only a handful of the Conservatives' losses of seats can by blamed on the intervention of the Referendum Party" (1997: 308). Goldsmith died shortly after the general election of 1997, and the party did not survive him.

Overall it appears that such parties usually fail electorally, and even when they succeed in winning a share of power, as Forza Italia did, their supporters find out that government is more difficult than they expected. This tends to produce faction fighting, a loss of objectives, and internal wrangling. The absence of a significant permanent organization, a cadre of activists, and a coherent set of values to sustain the party through hard times eventually counts against them.

The plebiscitary model appears to be the one that most readily applies to Britain at the present time. As the earlier discussion shows the modernization strategies adopted by the Labour and Conservative parties have shifted both of these parties in this direction. Plebiscitary politics is really designed to legitimize decisions already taken by the leadership and is not in any meaningful sense a deliberative process involving grass roots party members. In this kind of politics a small group of people around the leadership decide which issues will be put to the vote, and they decide the framing and the wording of the questions. There is no mechanism for an alternative group to frame different questions or to decide to have plebiscites on different issues. The model does not try to approximate a system of representative democracy in which members are represented in a smaller forum that actually makes the decisions. In this model the role of high-intensity participants is to react to initiatives taken by the center, not to initiate proposals of their own.

The fourth model is a participatory model in which members fully participate through representative institutions in policy-making and leadership selection. Historically, the Conservative party has never had this type of structure, since it originated with a top-down structure organized from within Parliament. In contrast, Labour was originally founded outside Parliament and organized around a participatory model in which the annual conference was the sovereign body making the final decisions (Pelling 1965). In practice the relationship between the parliamentary party and the annual conference was always complex, with a system of power sharing operating for most of the party's history (Minkin 1978). However, there has always been a strong participatory tradition within the party organization that has emphasized the importance of democratic decision making by the members.

In our 1999 survey of Labour party members, we asked members to express their preferences for alternative organizational structures, linking this to the question of who should make policy. The responses to this question appear in table 8.1.

TABLE 8.1.   Attitudes of Labour Party Members toward Alternative Organizational Structures in 1999 (in percentages)

"If you had to choose between one of the three methods for forming Labour party policy, which of the following would you favor?"

	All Members	Very Active Members	Inactive Members
Policy formed by the party leadership and endorsed by a postal vote of members	37	15	42
Policy formed by annual conference	25	35	22
Policy formed at regional and national policy forums	39	50	36

Note: N = 1,325.

The first option in the list is the plebiscitary model; the second option used to be the status quo until recent changes to the party constitution switched the model to a system of policy forums. Labour established these policy forums at the same time as it reformed the annual conference, with the aim of improving member participation in the policy-making process, and this system represents the third option. Interestingly, only about one-quarter of the members wanted to return to the position where the annual conference formally makes policy, and more than one-third opted for the plebiscitary model, in which members vote on proposals emerging from the leadership. The favorite option, however, was for policy to be made in the new national and regional policy forums, the participatory model.

There were interesting differences between active and inactive members with respect to their attitudes to these alternative models of decision making. About 50 percent of the very or fairly active members preferred the participatory model, compared with only 36 percent of the inactive members. The most preferred option among the latter group was the plebiscitary model, with 42 percent of them opting for this alternative.

These findings highlight the dilemma of the leadership in shaping the future of the party organization. If the leadership moves in the direction of the plebiscitary model it will not unduly worry the supporters, but it will antagonize the activists. The plebiscitary model appears ideal for a leadership party, but it creates real problems for a party seeking to establish a participatory style of decision making that motivates the high-intensity participants.

Given that the policy forums are the preferred model overall, and that Labour has pioneered this organizational form, why do we argue that the party has moved in the direction of the plebiscitary model? The answer to this question can be seen in the responses of those party members who had experience in the policy forum meetings. The 1999 survey showed that about 11 percent of party members had attended one of the policy forums, which translates into 35,000–40,000 people. When this group was asked about their experiences, their attitudes to the forums were very favorable. By large margins they found them interesting, friendly, efficient, and easy to understand.

The evidence for the plebiscitary model is that only 32 percent of participants with experience in a policy forum thought that the forums were influential (36 percent did not think so). More generally, some 53 percent of members agreed with the statement "The party leadership doesn't pay a lot of attention to ordinary party members," up from 35 percent who thought this in 1997. Labour's modernization strategy meant transforming itself into an electable, participatory party. The leadership could see the advantages of creating incentives to join the party and to be active. The current problem is that in the mind of many members it is becoming a plebiscitary party. As we can see in table 8.1 only 15 percent of the activists support such a development. The conclusion is that, if the party wholeheartedly embraces the plebiscitary model, this will demotivate the activists and further reduce high-intensity participation.

Some people might argue in private that this is an acceptable price to pay for a quiescent and manageable party. But there are two very likely consequences of a strategy that moves in this direction, as the earlier discussion indicates. One is that it will have a severe impact on finances, since the active members give more money than the inactive members. Second, it will weaken local election campaigns, which cannot be organized from party headquarters and which with an evermore volatile electorate are becoming more important as time goes by.

Peter Hain, a Labour politician with a long record of commitment to grass roots politics, argues:

> One-member-one-vote can't replace the feeling of being directly involved in the party in a collective way. It's all right to be involved in an individualistic way, which is what one-member-one-vote is all about, but being involved in a collective way is what being a member of the party should be all about. It shouldn't feel like being a member of the AA or RAC. (1999: 19)[4]

Thus the plebiscitary model will weaken members' powers unless they, rather than just the leadership, possess the right to initiate such ballots and have an influence on the question wording and the timing of votes.

Many years ago Duverger (1954) suggested that mass parties developed by a process of "contagion" (1954: 25) from the left such that the mass membership model overtook the cadre party model because it was more effective in a mass democracy. In Britain, there may be a new contagion from the left occurring in which the plebiscitary model becomes the norm and is characterized by a veneer of democracy overlaid by centralization and control. The problem with this scenario is that it is not clear whether a party bereft of high-intensity participants can provide a viable alternative model to the existing party organizations. If the party structure becomes hollowed out, then the functions of campaigning, recruiting, socializing, and fund-raising are not likely to be effectively carried out. If this happens, existing parties will become vulnerable to attack from more democratic forms of organization, in effect new parties that have retained the vigor and dynamism created by high-intensity participation.

If these situations are the implications of these findings for the future of the British party system, what are the implications for wider theoretical questions about the nature of political participation? We examine this issue in the final section.

Theories of Political Participation

The findings from this analysis of high-intensity participation in the British political system have implications for wider theories of participation and indeed for different paradigms in political science research. We referred earlier to an interesting if sometimes rancorous debate between rational choice theorists of participation (e.g., Tsebelis 1990; Aldrich 1993, Jackman 1993) and opponents of such theories (e.g., Hindess 1988; Lowi 1992; Eckstein 1992). What do these findings have to say about this debate?

The first point is that variables associated with a narrowly defined rational choice theory play an important but essentially limited role in explaining high-intensity participation. Their relevance is in relation to selective incentives, namely outcome, process, and possibly ideological incentives for participation. The political ambitions of individuals and their desire to work with other like-minded people are clearly important factors in explaining political participation of the high-cost type. But they are only a limited part of the story.

The second point is that in certain key respects the findings contradict the rational choice account of participation. They do so in relation to group incentives, since it appears that calculations of the costs and benefits of political action take place at the collective rather than at the individual level, something that makes no sense at all in a purely rational actor account. This finding is reinforced by the strong relationship demonstrated between expected benefits and participation. To reiterate a point made in chapter 2, that a particular activity is regarded as effective in achieving the goals of the party should not motivate a rational actor to participate, since it is only individualistic goals that matter in rational choice theory. Actors are not being rational if they ground their calculations of costs and benefits at the level of the group, since they have no control over group actions, and in any case they have an incentive to free ride on others. Only their own individual contribution to the benefits of collective action matters in this account. This point is further reinforced by the finding in the models in chapter 4 that, unlike group efficacy, personal efficacy is not a robust predictor of high-intensity participation, since it is not statistically significant in a number of specifications. In many ways these findings are quite subversive to rational choice explanations of political participation.

The third point is that political participation of this kind cannot be explained without reference to social psychological processes, which cannot be interpreted merely in cost-benefit terms. Affective variables that focus on the strength of actors' emotional attachment to their parties and the social norms that surround party activism are key factors in explaining high-intensity political participation. It is of course the case that social psychological variables were found to be important in the earliest research on voting behavior, which stressed the importance of psychological variables and the social contexts in which actors lived in explaining electoral participation (Berelson et al. 1954).

In this sense the finding that affective or emotional variables play an important role in explaining high-intensity participation is not surprising. As we pointed out earlier, such variables can provide a solution to the paradox of participation and the free-rider problem, which has been at the center of debates about the rationality of participation for many years. Frank is the best exponent of this point of view when he describes his commitment model in the following terms:

> I will use the term commitment model as a shorthand for the notion that seemingly irrational behavior is sometimes explained by emotional predispositions that help to solve commitment problems. . . . On purely theoretical grounds, the commitment model suggests that the moving force behind moral behavior lies not in rational analysis but in the emotions. (1988: 11–12)

His basic argument is that behavior based on emotional feelings is hardwired into human consciousness as a consequence of evolutionary processes that give such behavior a long-run survival advantage over more immediately self-interested courses of action. In this account apparently irrational acts, such as risking one's life to help a stranger or cooperating in the one-shot prisoner's dilemma game, have long-term survival value since they develop trust of others and help build an individual reputation for honesty. Such a reputation brings with it profitable opportunities that are not open to individuals with a reputation for being untrustworthy or selfish. Notice, however, that this account is not a rational actor account of the evolution of such norms, but rather it is a Darwinian account in which some types of behavior have survival value while other types do not.

In the present context emotional attachments associated with the party and the symbols and beliefs that it represents help to motivate participation and thereby overcome the free-rider problem. The emotional payoffs that individuals obtain from working for a cause they believe in are the driving force that overcomes the temptation to free ride on the work of others. This is manifest in both the strength of the individual's attachments to his or her party and also the social norms that surround participation in politics.

If these findings undermine simplistic rational choice accounts of participation, they also suggest that the civic voluntarism model gives a wholly inadequate account of high-intensity participation in politics. Few of the variables in that model are robust, statistically significant predictors of high-intensity participation, and those that are often have perverse signs from the point of view of theory. The findings suggest that the theoretical criticisms of this model set out in chapter 2 are supported by the empirical evidence.

It would be inaccurate to say that the civic voluntarism model is wrong, but it is clearly inadequate as an explanation for high-intensity participation. Arguably, the longevity of this model can be attributed to a research strategy that privileges its testing as the preferred theoretical model at the expense of possible rivals. Instead of comparing the model with alternatives, evidence is sought in favor of it, which is then used to support the model as the best theoretical explanation of participation.

The problems of the civic voluntarism model are exemplified by the role of educational attainment in predicting activism, which is a key variable in the U.S. versions of the model. Once cognitive and affective factors explained by other theories are taken into account education is not a robust predictor of participation. Thus it is not surprising that rising educational levels in most advanced industrial societies have not produced higher rates of participation or that many highly educated individuals do not participate in politics.

It seems plausible that the outcome of the 1992 general election played an important role in influencing the findings from the panel analysis, particularly the evidence that participation declined more for Labour than for the Conservatives. There are a number of ways in which winning or losing an election can stimulate or inhibit the incentives to participate. Activists in the winning party would tend to revise their evaluations of collective benefits, since the success of their party ensures that such benefits will continue to be provided at both the national and local levels.[5] Equally, group efficacy should also be boosted for the winning party and inhibited for the losing party. Outcome incentives should also become more important for the winning side, since being part of a winning team increases the probability that the individual can build a successful political career.

Activists in the losing party should have the reverse profile; for them the collective benefits should become less significant, because their party remains in opposition and unable to deliver collective goods. This is likely to be reinforced for the Labour party members by the fact that the party lost four successive elections in a row prior to the 1997 general election. Obviously, this will also be true of individual and group efficacy. Another effect of losing an election is to reduce the activist's chances of pursuing a successful political career, so outcome incentives to participate should be reduced in the case of the Labour party members. All these factors would reduce Labour activism more than Conservative activism.

These points have two important implications for electoral politics in general. First, they imply that prior elections can have an important influence on the ability of a party to campaign at the local level in a subsequent election. This suggests that there appears to be a dynamic process at work in electoral politics; if electoral failure can produce a decline in grass roots campaigning, which in turn reduces the effectiveness of subsequent electoral mobilization by a party, there is the potential for accelerating the electoral failure. Just as Noelle-Neumann (1984) argues that there is a spiral of silence at work in electoral politics in which issues perceived as unpopular are crowded out by issues that appear to be popular, a similar process may be at work in electoral behavior (Whiteley and Seyd 1998). There may be a spiral of mobilization at work in which electoral success stimulates campaign activity, which in turn helps to produce further electoral success. The corollary of this is of course that there may also be a spiral of demobilization arising from electoral failure.

It is important not to overstate this process, since Labour did after all go on to achieve the largest election victory in its history in 1997 and since there was little evidence of such a spiral in its case after 1992, although the process may well have influenced the result of the 1983 general election, which Labour lost by a landslide. On the other hand indirect evidence suggests that there may have been such a spiral in the case of the Conservatives in 1997. As Rallings and Thrasher point out in their analysis of trends in local elections in Britain, "No party before had seen its local electoral base destroyed in quite the way as the Conservatives during the 1990s" (1997: 125). Many of these defeated Conservative locally elected representatives became inactive as a result and failed to provide leadership or to campaign in the 1997 general election. As a consequence Labour significantly out-campaigned the Conservatives in that election (Denver, Hands, and Henig 1998).

The second implication for electoral politics is that regular elections serve to sustain and develop high-intensity participation. In other words there is a feedback process operating from the low-intensity participation of the many in elections to the high-intensity participation of the few in campaigning and running for office. The institutional framework of democratic politics sustains this type of participation, which in turn is crucial to the future of democratic politics.

In conclusion, high-intensity participation can be explained by a relatively small number of variables, some of which involve calculations of costs and benefits of the type familiar to rational choice theorists and others of which involve social norms and affective attachments of the kind that pervades social psychological accounts of political phenomena. The general incentive theory dominates the field of the rival theories tested in this book, although it does not eliminate them from consideration. With some caveats the general incentive theory appears to work as an explanation for high-intensity activism, for exiting behavior, and in a suitably modified form for electoral behavior as well. It is of course unlikely to be the last word in political science explorations of the key phenomenon of political participation. But measures of the type encompassed by this theory are likely to figure in any other accounts of high-intensity participation in political systems other than Britain.

Appendix

❧❀❧

THERE ARE A TOTAL OF SIX DIFFERENT SURVEYS used in this book, a two-wave panel survey of Conservative party members covering the period 1992 to 1994 and two different two-way panels of Labour party members. The first Labour panel covers the period 1989–90 to 1992, and the second covers the period 1997 to 1999. All these surveys used a two-stage systematic random sampling procedure to select the samples from party lists of members. In the case of Labour the sampling frame was the list of party members held in party headquarters. Further details of the questionnaire used in the first Labour panel can be seen in Seyd and Whiteley 1992.

For the Conservatives, membership lists were held at the constituency level at the time of the survey, so a 5 percent random sample of constituency parties was chosen at the first stage, stratified by region. Party agents were then approached in each of these constituencies with the permission of the Conservative central office, and the membership lists were obtained. A one-in-ten sample of individual members was then selected from these lists. Further details of the questionnaire used appear in Whiteley, Seyd, and Richardson 1994.

For the 1989–90 to 1992 Labour panel 480 constituencies were chosen at the first stage, stratified by Labour party regions, and a systematic random sample of one in thirty party members was selected at the second stage. The same procedure was used for the 1997 to 1999 panel, except a random sample of 200 constituencies stratified by region was selected at the first stage.

The surveys were conducted by mail. Initial mailings were sent to sensitize respondents about the survey, which were followed by up to four different mailings of questionnaires and reminders to maximize the response rate. The response rate for the first wave of the 1989–90 to 1992 Labour survey was 62.5 percent, resulting in 5,071 respondents after weighting for nonresponse. The response rate for the second wave survey was 58 percent, giving 2,955 usable questionnaires. In the case of the 1992 to 1994 Conservative panel the response rate for the first wave was 63 percent, giving 2,467 respondents after weighting for nonresponse. The response rate for the second wave of the survey was 65 percent, giving 1,602 usable questionnaires. The 1997 to 1999 Labour panel survey obtained a response rate of 63 percent in the first wave, yielding 5,761 respondents after weighting. One-third of these respondents were selected at random and surveyed in 1999, with a response rate of 69 percent, producing 1,325 usable questionnaires. This procedure was used in the second wave survey purely for cost reasons.

All the surveys were funded by grants from the Economic and Social Research Council, which is not responsible for any of the analysis in this book. The data are logged with the ESRC Data Archive at the University of Essex (www.data-archive.ac.uk).

Notes

Chapter 1

1. In 1999 the standard subscription paid by Labour party members was £17.50, or just under $30, per annum. The Conservatives did not have a standard subscription rate until recently, and donations were left to the discretion of individual members.

2. It should be noted, however, that in 1998 members of two government committees of inquiry—first the Committee on Standards in Public Life, examining the funding of political parties, and second the Independent Commission on the Voting System (the Jenkins Committee), examining electoral reform in the United Kingdom—stated that "political parties are essential to democracy," that "political parties perform an indispensable role in a democracy," and that "any Parliament endeavouring to function without any party organisation would be an inchoate mass, incapable not merely of giving effective sustenance to government . . . but even of organising its own business, from electing a speaker to deciding which issues should be debated on which day" (TSO 1998a: 24, 26; 1998c: 3).

3. Voter registration is an annual exercise conducted in the autumn, with a new register becoming operative in the following spring. The time from the cutoff date for voter registration to the end of the operative period of any register is sixteen months, and inevitably during this period of time mortality and mobility will diminish its accuracy. It has been estimated that over this sixteen-month period 1.5 percent of the adult population will die and a further 13 percent will move (Johnston, Pattie, and Rossiter 1996).

4. Epstein (1986: 36) writes that the APSA committee "did want American parties to be more like British parties." Beer (1965: 86–102) describes the modern British party system as one with cohesive, programmatic mass-membership organizations. See also Birch 1964, chap. 9.

5. The Liberal Democrat party was formed in 1988. We propose to use this

contemporary title throughout rather than the titles Liberal party (pre-1981) or Liberal Alliance party (1981–87).

6. Membership fell to 387,776 in 1998 (see table 1.1).

7. See the speech by Clare Short on behalf of the National Executive Committee (Labour Party 1992b: 74–75).

8. The Liberal Democrats in their short lifetime have never attracted large corporate donations and therefore have been more reliant upon their membership for money. The Committee on Standards in Public Life reports that between 1992 and 1997 almost one-half of the party's total annual income came from members' subscriptions (TSO 1998a: 31).

9. These figures vary slightly from those reported in the *Report of the Committee on Standards in Public Life* (TSO 1998a: 30).

10. The results of the membership ballots were (1) Endorsement of Hague's leadership, Yes 142,299 / No 34,092; (2) Endorsement of party reform, Yes 110,165 / No 5,970; (3) Ballot on the Euro, Yes 172,558 / No 31,492; (4) Leadership ballot, Iain Duncan Smith 155,933 / Ken Clarke 100,864.

11. For example, the announcement in January 1997 that a future Labour government would not increase the levels of personal income tax in the lifetime of a Parliament, a commitment of fundamental importance, was agreed by the two men with little consultation beyond their circle of advisers (Routledge 1998: 236, 277).

12. The joint policy committee is chaired by the prime minister and is composed of eight members each of the government and the National Executive Committee and three elected members from the national policy forum. The national policy forum is made up of 175 members who are elected for two years, representing constituency parties (54); regional parties (18); trade unions (30); the PLP (9); the EPLP (6); the government (8); local government (9); and socialist societies, the cooperative party, and black socialist societies (9). In addition, all 32 members of the National Executive Committee are automatically members. Eight policy commissions, composed of three representatives each from government, the National Executive Committee, and the national policy forum, have been established covering the following subjects: economic and social affairs; trade and industry; environment, transport, and the regions; health, education, and employment; crime and justice; democracy and citizenship; and finally Britain in the world.

13. The lack of power was demonstrated in a stark manner by the leadership's inability to force eight rebel MPs to modify their opposition to the European Union.

14. Examples of recent local by-election disasters include Bermondsey in 1983 and Greenwich in 1987 for the Labour party and Newbury in 1993 and Eastleigh in 1994 for the Conservatives.

15. One example is Liz Davies in Leeds North East (1997).

16. The Labour party's northwest regional director argues in a paper ("The New Labour Party: A Vision for Organisational Modernisation") that "New Labour politics should be matched by new Labour organisation" and goes on to suggest the replacement of fee-paying members with registered supporters and the abolition of the branch and constituency structure. Copy in the possession of the authors.

Chapter 2

1. Dr. Richard Taylor, an independent candidate, defeated the Labour and Conservative party candidates in the Wyre Forest constituency.

2. In their model of participation, the beta coefficient of the family income predictor variable is only 0.11 and is the weakest of seven predictors of participation used in this model (see Verba, Schlozman, and Brady 1995: 342).

3. Turnout in presidential elections has declined by more than one-fifth between the 1950s and 1980s (see Miller and Shanks 1996: 39–69).

4. Turnout in the 1979 election was 76 percent (see fig. 1.2). Participation in higher education has more than doubled from about 800,000 students in 1980–81 to more than 1,600,000 in 1996–97 (see *Times Higher Educational Supplement*, no. 1,299, September 26, 1997).

5. Putnam (1995) actually attributes the decline in civic voluntarism in the United States in part to the spread of television.

6. They can of course be jailed for refusing to pay taxes, which is the standard way the government ensures that the provision of collective goods in society is funded.

7. If actors know how many rounds of the game are going to be played, it is rational for them to defect on the last round, which implies that it is rational to defect on the second to last round, and so forth, which reinstates defection as the dominant strategy for all rounds.

8. It will be recalled that they argue: "Three answers come to mind: because they can't; because they don't want to; or because nobody asked." (Verba, Schlozman, and Brady 1995: 269).

Chapter 3

1. "Not at all" = 1; "Rarely" = 2; "Occasionally" = 3; "Frequently" = 4. These scales applied to all the variables except the last two in table 3.3, which are dummy variables scoring 1 = yes; 0 = no.

2. In LISREL modeling this statistic measures the difference between the observed and fitted correlation matrix (see Jöreskog and Sörbom 1993: 122) and is a goodness-of-fit measure, the smaller the better. In the case of Labour the one-factor solution produced a chi-square goodness-of-fit test of 4,264.91 with twenty-seven degrees of freedom, whereas the two-factor solution was 3,796.18 with twenty-six degrees of freedom. Thus the chi-square goodness-of-fit statistic improved by 468.7 for the loss of one degree of freedom. The corresponding figures for the Conservatives were 1,971.61 for a one-factor solution with twenty-seven degrees of freedom and 1,963.66 for a two-factor solution with twenty-six degrees of freedom. In this case the chi-square statistic improved by 7.95 for the loss of one degree of freedom. Clearly the two-factor solutions are superior in both cases.

3. This is measured by the contact scale in one model and the activism scale in the second.

4. These are statements that are coded using a five-point scale that varies from "strongly agree" to "strongly disagree" with "neither" as the midpoint.

5. Individuals who strongly agree with the two indicators score five for each, and individuals who strongly disagree with them score one for each measure.

6. The measure is a dummy variable, scoring one if the individual was recruited in this way and zero otherwise.

7. In earlier work we have argued that, since much policy-making takes place at the local level in Britain, a highly active individual may have a significant influence over collective outcomes in his or her locality, since there are relatively few such individuals in local politics. Under these circumstances actors have an incentive *not* to free ride, making participation motivated by collective incentives rational (see Whiteley, Seyd, Richardson, and Bissell 1994).

8. For a discussion of different conceptions of rationality and the problems they pose see Elster 1983.

9. The number of households with incomes below 50 percent of the average increased from 9.4 percent in 1979 to 19.4 percent in 1987, the last year for which statistics were available under the Conservative government (see Bradshaw 1992).

10. In the foreword to the Labour party's 1992 election manifesto Neil Kinnock set out various objectives that he argued were "fundamental to improving the quality and quantity of provision in health and social services, and to combatting poverty" (Labour Party 1992: 7), indicating that public spending to alleviate poverty was a priority for Labour at that time.

11. On this subject see Wistow 1992.

12. Again in the 1992 election manifesto Neil Kinnock wrote: "We have absolute commitment to a high-quality National Health Service, free at the time of need and not fractured or weakened by under funding" (Labour Party 1992: 7).

13. In practice the Conservative government has had little success in achieving this goal, but it was still committed to it.

14. Labour party members were asked about the effectiveness of these activities in helping the party achieve its goals, whereas Conservatives were asked whether they could personally influence politics by undertaking the activity. This difference of wording affects the reliability but not the validity of the indicators, since, as mentioned earlier, in social psychological theory no distinction is made between individual and group effectiveness. Thus the underlying scales should be accurate measures of the individual's sense of the effectiveness of different types of participation.

15. It can be seen that only one of the social norms indicators is common to both parties. Additional tests (not shown) were conducted to see whether this influenced the findings in the later models. When one common indicator is used in both the Labour and Conservative models, this did not significantly affect the estimates.

16. The critical value of χ^2 with five degrees of freedom at the 0.05 level is 11.1.

17. Note that the negative sign on the social class variable is merely an artifact of the coding—the salariat in table 3.6 are coded one and the working class five.

18. In the case of social norms the negative coefficient implies that respondents

who disagree with the statements in table 3.11 participate more than those who agree with them, a finding that accords with expectations.

19. Each of the indicators of the collective benefits scale was multiplied by the two indicators of the personal influence scale, and the twelve resulting measures were used to estimate a personal influence times benefits scale, which was substituted for these measures in the model. The results were:

$$\text{Activism} = 0.06(\text{influence*benefits}) + 0.01(\text{costs}) + 0.25(\text{outcome})$$
$$(2.5) \qquad\qquad (0.8) \qquad (13.7)$$
$$+ \ 0.11 \ (\text{process}) -0.02(\text{ideology}); \ R^2 = 0.14.$$
$$(9.8) \qquad\qquad (1.1)$$

This suggests that the interactive model is inferior to the additive version. There are more elaborate ways of testing interactions in the LISREL framework (see Hayduk 1987: 190–243), and one other approach was adopted. The equality of the coefficients of the benefits scale variable was tested for groups of respondents in different categories of the personal influence variables. If interactions exist then these coefficients should shift over the separate groups (e.g., benefits becoming more important for high-efficacy groups). Tests indicated that these coefficients did not significantly change between groups, suggesting that no significant interactions occurred between the benefits and personal influence variables. The correlation of 0.09 between these variables in the additive model reinforces this point.

Chapter 4

1. The methodological details of the panel surveys are discussed in the appendix.

2. The National Trust is an organization devoted to the preservation and maintenance of Britain's heritage, including parks, castles, large country estates, and sites of historical importance.

3. Probabilities were calculated from Butler and Butler 1994: 219.

4. In 1959 individual membership of the Labour party was 847,526, although this figure was distorted by the constitutional requirement that parties affiliate with a minimum of 800 members (Seyd and Whiteley 1992: 16). There are no records of individual membership of the Conservative party in that year, but Webb, writing in Katz and Mair's handbook on party organization, asserts that the national membership in 1960 was 2,800,000 (1992: 847). By 1992 this picture had changed rather dramatically, with Labour having a published individual membership of 280,000 (Butler and Butler 1994:147) and the Conservatives an estimated membership of about 750,000 (Whiteley, Seyd, and Richardson 1994: 25).

5. Note that we have to assume that contemporaneous and longitudinal effects do not exactly cancel each other out, thereby producing a nonsignificant effect.

6. The way to avoid this problem would be to have the two waves of the panel

surveys conducted very close together in time, which should reduce the effects of longitudinal factors. However, the price paid for this is that the lagged endogenous variable would become very dominant in such a model, potentially eliminating important effects.

7. Another way of interpreting this is to say that the first wave variables apart from activism drive the system and ensure that 12 percent of the gap (i.e., 1–0.88) between an equilibrium level of participation and actual participation is closed over this two-year period. Thus the system is characterized by high levels of inertia.

8. Obviously, a shorter period of time between the two waves of the panel might well have produced significant effects.

9. Note that income was not statistically significant in any of the models and so is excluded from table 4.7.

Chapter 5

1. The party captured only 27.6 percent of the vote, the worst result since 1918, which itself was a unique postwar election in which the British party system fragmented (see Butler and Butler 1994: 218).

2. Prior to 1989 members were recruited only at the local constituency level and there were no central membership records.

3. The source of the information about the "Active Labour" campaign is interviews with party officials at Labour party headquarters at Millbank in London.

4. This is despite the fact that the letters accompanying the survey asked people to respond even if they no longer considered themselves to be Labour party members.

5. The mean score refers to the eight activities in table 4.3. The mean score is calculated by adding together the responses for each individual on the scales, where "not at all" = 1; "rarely" = 2; "occasionally" = 3; "frequently" = 4 (see also Seyd and Whiteley 1992: 95–97).

6. Again the total activity score for a party member is the sum of the scores for each of these eight activities, with the same coding as described in note 5.

7. We are assuming that expressive incentives are exogenous in this model.

8. The Tote is a lottery scheme run by many local parties for fund-raising purposes. Activists typically call around to see inactive party members to collect their lottery payments.

9. If the individual cited expressive motives for joining, the dummy variable scored one, otherwise it scored zero.

10. The scale explained 67.3 percent of the variance in the indicators with an eigenvalue of 1.35.

11. The scale explained 55.8 percent of the variance in the measures with an eigenvalue of 2.23.

12. The scale explained 42.1 percent of the variance in the measure with an eigenvalue of 1.26.

13. The scale explained 58.9 percent of the variance in the indicators with an eigenvalue of 1.77.

14. If an individual is New Labour he or she scores one, and Old Labour scores zero.

Chapter 6

1. That is, voter utilities only have one modal point or maximum value along the left-right continuum (see Mueller 1989: 179–85).

2. This assertion, however, can be exaggerated (see Seyd and Whiteley 1992: 214–17 and Whiteley, Seyd, and Richardson 1994: 63–64).

3. The Granger causality tests differ in this case from those in chapter 4, since we cannot estimate the effects of exiting at time one on the predictor variables at time two. With a two-wave panel it is only possible to measure exiting at time two.

4. The membership went from 405,000 in 1997 to 388,000 in 1998 (see table 1.1).

5. Each of the independent variables involving two or more observable indicators is the factor score derived from a factor analysis of the indicators with the extraction criterion restricted to one factor.

6. The Wald statistics for process and outcome incentives are significant at the 0.14 level in each case.

Chapter 7

1. Objective efficacy as discussed in this model should not be confused with subjective efficacy, or the feelings that individuals might have about their ability to influence politics and the political system. Survey work suggests that many people have a sense of political efficacy, but there is no basis for this sense in objective reality when it comes to voting (see Margolis 1982).

2. For example, the election study has no indicators of the probability that an elector will vote Conservative, Labour, or for another party; it merely records party preference. This has changed in the 2001 British Election Study, which now carries such measures.

3. The Gallup Political Index contains aggregate indicators from monthly surveys of the British electorate. The data used in the present chapter are taken from report 377 (January 1992) and every subsequent report through to 424 (December 1995).

4. A research grant from the U.S. National Science Foundation allowed a team of researchers to buy in questions on the Gallup Political Index from the start of 1992. This represents the start of the party identification series in the Gallup Political Index, a variable that had not been measured on a continuous basis before that time. Thus earlier observations cannot be used to estimate these models. The team consisted of Marianne Stewart and Harold Clarke, from the University of Texas at Dallas; and Paul Whiteley from the University of Essex (see Clarke, Stewart, and Whiteley 1998).

5. Versions of the models that included prospective and egocentric economic evaluations were tested as alternative measures of the subjective economy. How-

ever, none of these proved to be statistically significant predictors of voting intentions.

6. Formally a stationary series has a mean and variance that is time invariant, such that $E(x_t) = \mu$ and $E(x^2_t) = \sigma^2$ for all t, and the autocovariances are a function only of the time lag separating observations (see Vandaele 1983: 12–28).

7. Hendry (1980) provides an amusing example of this when he demonstrates a highly statistically significant relationship between cumulative rainfall in Britain and the rate of inflation.

8. Two series are cointegrated if they are in long-term equilibrium, such that a deviation from the long-run growth of one series produces a deviation from the long-run growth of the other. If this is true, then the difference between the two series measured over time must be stationary or constant, since if this difference grew larger (or smaller) they could not be in equilibrium. See Engle and Granger 1987 for a formal discussion of cointegration.

9. The RESET test is Ramsey's (1969) test of functional form; the normality test is the Jarque-Bera test (1980) of the normality of the regression residuals; the ARCH test is the autoregressive-conditional heteroscedasticity test developed by Engle (1982); and the heteroscedasticity test is the Breutsch-Pagan test (1979).

10. The RESET test suggests, however, that the functional form of the model is problematic. Further analysis with a logarithmic version of the most parsimonious model renders the RESET test nonsignificant. However, there is no substantive difference between the logarithmic and the original version of the model; accordingly the former is not reported or analyzed.

11. Although many of them do!

Chapter 8

1. Kavanagh (1998: 42) argues in a similar vein: "people wishing to be active and to promote a cause seem more willing to engage in an interest group than in a political party."

2. Maloney and Jordan (1997) suggest that members of the "protest business" organizations are more accurately "financial supporters" only and that their continuity of support is unlikely to be maintained for long.

3. Such a claim would be possible to verify in Italy, where such a regular audit of group life is carried out.

4. These acronyms stand for the Automobile Association and the Royal Automobile Association, both of which have members but strongly restrict their participation.

5. Central government in Britain funds a large proportion of local government spending, such that changes in national policies have large implications for changes in local policies. Thus the provision of national and local collective goods is significantly related.

References

Abelson, Robert P., Elliot Aronson, William J. McGuire, Theodore M. Newcombe, Milton J. Rosenberg, and Percy H. Tannenbaum, eds. 1968. *Theories of Cognitive Consistency: A Sourcebook.* Chicago: Rand McNally.

Abramson, Paul R., and Ronald Inglehart. 1995. *Value Change in Global Perspective.* Ann Arbor: University of Michigan Press.

Aish, A. M., and K. G. Jöreskog. 1990. "A Panel Model for Political Efficacy and Responsiveness: An Application of LISREL 7 with Weighted Least Squares." *Quality and Quantity* 24:405–26.

Aldrich, John H. 1993. "Rational Choice and Turnout." *American Journal of Political Science* 37:246–78.

———. 1995. *Why Parties? The Origin and Transformation of Party Politics in America.* Chicago: University of Chicago Press.

Almond, Gabriel A., and Sidney Verba. 1963. *The Civic Culture.* Princeton: Princeton University Press.

American Political Science Association. 1950. "Toward a More Responsible Two-Party System." *American Political Science Review* 44, supplement.

Arnold, R. Douglas. 1990. *The Logic of Congressional Action.* New Haven: Yale University Press.

Axelrod, Robert. 1984. *The Evolution of Co-operation.* New York: Basic.

———. 1997. *The Complexity of Cooperation.* Princeton: Princeton University Press.

Azjen, I., and Martin Fishbein. 1969. 'The Prediction of Behavioral Intentions in a Choice Situation." *Journal of Experimental Social Psychology* 5:400–416.

Barnes, Samuel H., and Max Kaase. 1979. *Political Action: Mass Participation in Five Western Democracies.* Beverly Hills and London: Sage.

Barr, N., and F. Coulter. 1990. "Social Security: Solutions or Problems?" In *The State of Welfare*, ed. Jill Hills, 274–337. Oxford: Clarendon.

Barry, Brian. 1970. *Sociologists, Economists, and Democracy.* London: Collier-Macmillan.

Bartle, John. 1999. "Improving the Measurement of Party Identification in Britain." In *British Elections and Parties Review*, ed. Justin Fisher, Philip Cowley, David Denver, and Andrew Russell, 9:119–35. London: Frank Cass.

Beer, Samuel. 1965. *Modern British Politics*. London: Faber.

Berelson, Bernard, Paul F. Lazarfeld, and William N. McPhee. 1954. *Voting*. Chicago: University of Chicago Press.

Birch, A. H. 1964. *Representative and Responsible Government*. London: Allen and Unwin.

Black, Duncan. 1958. *The Theory of Committees and Elections*. Cambridge: Cambridge University Press.

Blair, Tony. 1994. *Change and National Renewal*. London: Labour Party.

Blake, Robert. 1966. *Disraeli*. London: Eyre and Spottiswoode.

Bochel, John, and David Denver. 1972. "The Impact of the Campaign on the Results of Local Government Elections." *British Journal of Political Science* 2:239–43.

Bogdanor, Vernon. 1994. "Western Europe." In *Referendums around the World*, ed. David Butler and Austin Ranney. London: Macmillan.

———. 1997. *Power and the People: A Guide to Constitutional Reform*. London: Gollancz.

Bradshaw, Jonathan. 1992. "Social Security." In *Implementing Thatcherite Policies*, ed. David Marsh and R. A. W. Rhodes, 81–99. Buckingham: Open University Press.

Brennan, Geoffrey, and James Buchanan. 1984. "Voter Choice: Evaluating Political Alternatives." *American Behavioral Scientist* 28:185–201.

Breutsch, T. S., and Adrian R. Pagan. 1979. "A Simple Test for Heteroscedasticity and Random Coefficient Variation." *Econometrica* 47:1287–94.

British Election Study. 1997. University of Essex: ESRC Data Archive.

British Election Study website. 2001. <http://www.essex.ac.uk/bes/>.

Brody, Richard A. 1978. "The Puzzle of Political Participation in America." In *The New American Political System*, ed. Anthony King. Washington, DC: American Enterprise Institute.

Brynin, Malcolm, and David Sanders. 1997. "Party Identification, Political Preferences, and Material Conditions: Evidence from the British Household Panel Survey, 1991–92." *Party Politics* 3:53–77.

Budge, Ian. 1999. "Party Policy and Ideology: Reversing the 1950s?" In *Critical Elections*, ed. Geoffrey Evans and Pippa Norris, 1–21. London: Sage.

Budge, Ian, Ivor Crewe, and Dennis J. Farlie. 1976. *Party Identification and Beyond: Representations of Voting and Party Competition*. New York: John Wiley & Sons.

Budge, Ian, and Dennis J. Farlie. 1983. *Explaining and Predicting Elections*. London: George Allen and Unwin.

Butler, David, and Gareth Butler. 1994. *British Political Facts, 1900–1994*. London: Macmillan.

Butler, David, and Denis Kavanagh. 1988. *The British General Election of 1987*. London: Macmillan.

———. 1992. *The British General Election of 1992*. London: Macmillan.

———. 1997. *The British General Election of 1997*. London: Macmillan.

Butler, David, and Anthony King. 1966. *The British General Election of 1966*. London: Macmillan.

Butler, David, and Donald Stokes. 1974. *Political Change in Britain*. London: Macmillan.

Campbell, Angus, Philip E. Converse, Warren E. Miller, and Donald E. Stokes. 1960. *The American Voter*. New York: Wiley.

Carter, John R., and Stephen D. Guerette. 1992. "An Experimental Study of Voting." *Public Choice* 73:251–60.

Charezma, Wojciech W., and Derek F. Deadman. 1992. *New Directions in Econometric Practice*. London: Edward Elgar.

Charter News. 1998. 53:1–4. Charter Movement: Twickenham Middlesex.

Chong, Dennis. 1991. *Collective Action and the Civil Rights Movement*. Chicago: University of Chicago Press.

Clarke, Harold D., and Allan Kornberg. 1992. "Do National Elections Affect Perceptions of MP Responsiveness? A Note on the Canadian Case." *Legislative Studies Quarterly* 17:183–204.

Clarke, Harold D., Euel W. Elliott, William Mishler, Marianne C. Stewart, Paul F. Whiteley, and Gary Zuk. 1992. *Controversies in Political Economy: Canada, Great Britain, the United States*. Boulder: Westview.

Clarke, Harold D., and Marianne C. Stewart. 1995. "Economic Evaluations, Prime Ministerial Approval, and Governing Party Support: Rival Models Reconsidered." *British Journal of Political Science* 24:597–622.

Clarke, Harold, Marianne Stewart, and Paul F. Whiteley. 1995. "Can the Tories Win Again? The Dynamics of Conservative Support and the Next General Election." Paper presented at the PSA specialist group conference Elections and Public Opinion of the Political Studies Association, September 15–17.

———. 1997. "Tory Trends: Party Identification and the Dynamics of Conservative Support since 1992." *British Journal of Political Science* 27:299–331.

———. 1998. "New Models for New Labour: The Political Economy of Labour Party Support, January 1992–April 1997." *American Political Science Review* 92:559–75.

Coates, Ken, and Hugh Kerr. 1998. *The Need for An Independent Network*. Nottingham: Russell Press.

Cole, G. D. H. 1948. *A History of the Labour Party from 1914*. London: Routledge and Keegan.

Conover, Pamela Johnson, and Stanley Feldman. 1986. "Emotional Reactions to the Economy: I'm Mad as Hell and I'm Not Going to Take It Anymore." *American Journal of Political Science* 30:50–78.

Conservative Party. 1992. *The Best Future for Britain: The Conservative Manifesto 1992*. London: Conservative Central Office.

———. 1997. *Our Party: Blueprint for Change*. London: Conservative Central Office.

———. 1998. *Constitution*. London: Conservative Central Office.

Converse, Phillip. 1964. "The Nature of Belief Systems in Mass Politics." In *Ideology and Discontent*, ed. D. Apter. New York: Free.

Cook, Thomas D., and Donald T. Campbell. 1979. *Quasi-Experimentation—Design and Analysis Issues for Field Settings*. Boston: Houghton Mifflin.

Cox, Gary W., and Samuel Kernell. 1991. *The Politics of Divided Government*. Boulder: Westview.

Crewe, Ivor, Bö Sarlvik, and James E. Alt. 1977. "Partisan Dealignment in Britain, 1964–1974." *British Journal of Political Science* 7:129–90.

Crewe, Ivor, and Brian Gosschalk. 1995. *Political Communications: The General Election Campaign of 1992*. Cambridge: Cambridge University Press.

Crewe, Ivor, and Anthony King. 1995. *The SDP*. Oxford: Oxford University Press.

Crotty, William J. 1971. "Party Effort and Its Impact on the Vote." *American Political Science Review* 65:439–50.

Crouch, Colin. 1990. "Industrial Relations." In *Developments in British Politics*, vol. 3, ed. Patrick Dunleavy, Andrew Gamble, and Gillian Peele. London: Macmillan.

Cutright, Phillip. 1963. "Measuring the Impact of Local Party Activity on the General Election Vote." *Public Opinion Quarterly* 27:372–85.

Daalder, Hans. 1992. "A Crisis of Party." *Scandinavian Political Studies* 15, no. 4: 269–88.

Dalton, Russell J., Scott C. Flanagan, and Paul Allen Beck. 1984. *Electoral Change in Advanced Industrial Democracies*. Princeton: Princeton University Press.

Debnam, Geoffrey. 1994. "The Adversary Politics Thesis Revisited." *Parliamentary Affairs* 47, no. 3: 420–33.

Demos. 1994. "Lean Democracy." *Demos* 3: 1–40.

Denham, Andrew. 1996. *Think Tanks of the New Right*. Aldershot: Dartmouth.

Denver, David, and Gordon Hands. 1985. "Marginality and Turnout in General Elections in the 1970s." *British Journal of Political Science* 15:381–98.

———. 1997. *Modern Constituency Electioneering*. London: Frank Cass.

Denver, David, Gordon Hands, and Simon Henig. 1998. "Triumph of Targeting? Constituency Campaigning in the 1997 Election." In *British Elections and Parties Review*, ed. David Denver, Justin Fisher, Philip Cowley, and Charles Pattie, 8:171–90. London: Frank Cass.

Dicey, A. V. 1885. *An Introduction to the Study of the Law of the Constitution*. London: Macmillan.

Dickey, David A., and Wayne A. Fuller. 1979. "Distribution of the Estimators for Autoregressive Series with a Unit Root." *Journal of the American Statistical Association* 74:427–31.

Downs, Anthony. 1957. *An Economic Theory of Democracy*. New York: Harper and Row.

Dunleavy, Patrick. 1980a. "Some Political Implications of Sectoral Cleavages and the Growth of State Employment, Part 1: The Analysis of Production Cleavages." *Political Studies* 28:364–83.

———. 1980b. "Some Political Implications of Sectoral Cleavages and the Growth of State Employment, Part 2: Cleavage Structure and Political Alignment." *Political Studies* 28:527–49.

Dunleavy, Patrick, and Christopher T. Husbands. 1985. *British Democracy at the*

Crossroads: Voting and Party Competition in the 1980s. London: Allen and Unwin.

Duverger, Maurice. 1954. *Political Parties*. London: Methuen.

Eckstein, Harry. 1992. "Rationality and Frustration." In *Regarding Politics: Essays on Political Theory, Stability, and Change*, ed. Harry Eckstein. Berkeley: University of California Press.

Elster, Jon. 1983. *Sour Grapes: Studies in the Subversion of Rationality*. Cambridge: Cambridge University Press.

———. 1989. *The Cement of Society*. Cambridge: Cambridge University Press.

Engle, Robert F. 1982. "Autoregressive Conditional Heteroscedasticity with Estimates of the Variance of United Kingdom Inflation." *Econometrica* 50:987–1007.

Engle, Robert F., and Clive W. J. Granger. 1987. "Co-integration and Error Correction: Representation, Estimation, and Testing." *Econometrica* 55:251–76.

Epstein, Leon. 1967. *Political Parties in Western Democracies*. London: Pall Mall Press.

———. 1986. *Political Parties in the American Mold*. Madison: University of Wisconsin Press.

ESRC (Economic and Social Research Council). 1992. British Election Study Dataset. University of Essex: ESRC Archive.

Evans, Geoffrey. 1999. "Economics and Politics Revisited: Exploring the Decline in Conservative Support, 1992–1995." *Political Studies* 47:139–51.

Ferejohn, John A., and Morris P. Fiorina. 1974. "The Paradox of Not Voting: A Decision Theoretic Analysis." *American Political Science Review* 68:525–36.

———. 1975. "Closeness Counts Only in Horseshoes and Dancing." *American Political Science Review* 69:920–25.

Festinger, Leon. 1964. *Conflict, Decision, and Dissonance*. Stanford, CA: Stanford University Press.

Finer, Samuel, ed. 1975. *Adversary Politics and Electoral Reform*. London: Anthony Wigram.

Finkel, Steven E. 1985. "Reciprocal Effects of Participation and Political Efficacy: A Panel Analysis." *American Journal of Political Science* 29:891–913.

———. 1987. "The Effects of Participation on Political Efficacy and Political Support: Evidence from a West German Panel." *Journal of Politics* 49:441–64.

Finkel, Steven E., and Edward N. Muller. 1998. "Rational Choice and the Dynamics of Political Action: Evaluating Alternative Models with Panel Data." *American Political Science Review* 92:37–50.

Finkel, Steven E., Edward N. Muller, and Karl-Dieter Opp. 1989. "Personal Influence, Collective Rationality, and Mass Political Action." *American Political Science Review* 83:885–903.

Finkel, Steven E., and Karl-Dieter Opp. 1991. "Party Identification in Collective Political Action." *Journal of Politics* 53:339–71.

Fiorina, Morris. 1981. *Retrospective Voting in American National Elections*. New Haven: Yale University Press.

Fishbein, Martin. 1967. "Attitude and the Prediction of Behavior." In *Readings in Attitude Theory and Measurement*, ed. Martin Fishbein. New York: Wiley.

Fisher, Justin. 1994. "Why Do Companies Make Donations to Political Parties?" *Political Studies* 42:690–99.

———. 1995. "The Institutional Funding of British Political Parties." In *British Elections and Parties Yearbook, 1994*, ed. David Broughton, David M. Farrell, David Denver, and Colin Rallings, 181–98. London: Frank Cass.

Flanagan, Scott C., and Russell J. Dalton. 1984. "Parties under Stress: Realignment and Dealignment in Advanced Industrial Democracies." *Western European Politics* 7:7–23.

Forrester, Tom. 1976. *The Labour Party and the Working Class*. London: Heinemann.

Frank, Robert H. 1988. *Passion within Reason: The Strategic Role of the Emotions*. New York: W. W. Norton.

Frendreis, John P., James L. Gibson, and Laura L. Vertz. 1990. "The Electoral Relevance of Local Party Organisations." *American Political Science Review* 84:225–35.

Gallagher, Michael. 1996–97. "The Single Transferable Vote—An Assessment." *Representation* 34, no. 1: 2–6.

Gamble, Andrew. 1994. *The Free Economy and the Strong State*. Basingstoke: Macmillan.

Gamble, Andrew, and Stuart Walkland. 1984. *The British Party System and Economic Policy, 1945–1983*. Oxford: Clarendon.

Goldthorpe, John H. 1980. *Social Mobility and Class Structure in Modern Britain*. Oxford: Clarendon Press.

Goodhart, C. A. E., and R. J. Bhansali. 1970. "Political Economy." *Political Studies* 18:43–106.

Granger, Clive W. J. 1988. "Some Recent Developments in a Concept of Causality." *Journal of Econometrics* 39:199–211.

———, ed. 1990. *Modelling Economic Series*. Oxford: Clarendon Press.

Granger, Clive W. J., and Paul Newbould. 1974. "Spurious Regressions in Econometrics." *Journal of Econometrics* 2:111–20.

———. 1986. *Forecasting Economic Time Series*. San Diego: Academic.

Green, Donald P., and Ian Shapiro. 1994. *Pathologies of Rational Choice Theory*. New Haven and London: Yale University Press.

Grofman, Bernard. 1995. "Is Turnout the Paradox That Ate Rational Choice Theory?" In *Information, Participation, and Choice*, ed. Bernard Grofman. Ann Arbor: University of Michigan Press.

Gyford, John. 1983. *National Parties and Local Politics*. London: Allen and Unwin.

Habermas, J. 1976. *Legitimation Crisis*. London: Heinemann.

Hain, Peter. 1999. "Interview." *New Statesman*, June 7, 18–19.

Harrop, Martin. 1980. "The Urban Basis of Political Alignment: a Comment." *British Journal of Political Science* 10: 388–97.

Hayduk, Leslie A. 1987. *Structural Equation Modeling with LISREL*. Baltimore: Johns Hopkins University Press.

Heath, Anthony, John Curtice, Roger Jowell, Geoff Evans, Julia Field, and Sharon Witherspoon. 1991. *Understanding Political Change*. Oxford: Pergamon.

Hendry, David. 1980. "Econometrics—Alchemy or Science?" *Economica* 47: 387–406.

———. 1995. *Dynamic Econometrics*. Oxford: Oxford University Press.

Hendry, David F., and Jean-Francois Richard. 1990. "On the Formulation of Empirical Models in Dynamic Econometrics." In *Modelling Economic Series*, ed. C. W. J. Granger, 304–34. Oxford: Clarendon Press.

Himmelweit, Hilde, Patrick Humphries, Marianne Jaeger, and Michael Katz. 1981. *How Voters Decide*. London: Academic.

Hindess, Barry. 1971. *The Decline of Working Class Politics*. London: MacGibbon and Kee.

———. 1988. *Choice, Rationality, and Social Theory*. London: Unwin Hyman.

Hinich, Melvin J. 1981. "Voting as an Act of Contribution." *Public Choice* 36:135–40.

Hirschman, Albert O. 1970. *Exit, Voice, and Loyalty: Responses to Decline in Firms, Organizations, and States*. Cambridge: Harvard University Press.

HMSO. 1976. *The Report of the Committee on Financial Aid to Political Parties*. London: Her Majesty's Stationary Office.

———. 1993. *Home Affairs Committee: Funding of Political Parties*. London: Her Majesty's Stationary Office.

———. 1995. *Standards in Public Life: Evidence to the Nolan Committee*. London: Her Majesty's Stationary Office.

Hobson, J. A. 1907. *The Economics of Distribution*. New York: Macmillan.

Hodge, Margaret, Steve Leach, and Gerry Stoker. 1997. *More than the Flower Show: Elected Mayors and Democracy*. London: Fabian Society.

Hollis, Christopher. 1949. *Can Parliament Survive?* London: Hollis and Carter.

Huckfeldt, Robert, and John Sprague. 1990. "Social Order and Political Chaos: The Structural Setting of Political Information." In *Information and Democratic Processes*, ed. John A. Ferejohn and James H. Kuklinski, 23–58. Urbana and Chicago: University of Illinois Press.

———. 1992. "Political Parties and Electoral Mobilization: Political Structure, Social Structure, and the Party Canvass." *American Political Science Review* 86:70–86.

———. 1995. *Citizens, Politics, and Social Communication*. Cambridge: Cambridge University Press.

Hughes, Colin, and Patrick Wintour. 1990. *Labour Rebuilt*. London: Fourth Estate.

ICPSR (International Consortium for Political and Social Research). 1992. *American National Election Study Dataset*. Ann Arbor: University of Michigan.

Jackman, Robert W. 1993. "Response to Aldrich's 'Rational Choice and Turnout': Rationality and Political Participation." *American Journal of Political Science* 37:279–90.

Jarque, C. M., and A. K. Bera. 1980. "Efficient Tests for Normality, Homoscedasticity, and Serial Independence of Regression Residuals." *Economic Letters* 6:255–59.

Johnston, Ronald J. 1987. *Money and Votes: Constituency Campaign Spending and Election Results*. London: Croom Helm.

Johnston, Ronald. J., and Charles J. Pattie. 1995. "The Impact of Spending on Party

Constituency Campaigns at Recent British General Elections." *Party Politics* 1:261–73.

———. 1997. "Fluctuating Party Identification in Great Britain: Patterns Revealed by Four Years of a Longitudinal Study." *Politics* 17, no. 2: 67–77.

Johnston, Ronald. J., Charles J. Pattie, and Lucy C. Johnston. 1989. "The Impact of Constituency Spending on the Result of the 1987 British General Election." *Electoral Studies* 8:143–55.

Johnston, Ronald. J., Charles J. Pattie, and David Rossiter. 1996. "The UK's Antiquated Electoral System: Bringing It (Belatedly) into the Twentieth Century." *Radical Statistics* 63:7–16.

Jones, G., and J. Stewart. 1983. *The Case for Local Government*. London: Allen and Unwin.

Jones, Tudor. 1996. *Remaking the Labour Party*. London and New York: Routledge.

Jöreskog, Karl. 1990. "New Developments in LISREL: Analysis of Ordinal Variables Using Polychoric Correlations and Weighted Least Squares." *Quality and Quantity* 24:387–404.

Jöreskog, Karl, and Dag Sörbom. 1993. *LISREL 8: Structural Equation Modeling with the SIMPLIS Command Language*. Hillsdale, NJ: Lawrence Erlbaum Associates.

Kandiah, M. D., and Antony Seldon, eds. 1996. *Ideas and Think-Tanks in Contemporary Britain*. London: Frank Cass.

Katz, Richard S., and Peter Mair. 1995. "Changing Models of Party Organization and Party Democracy: The Emergence of the Cartel Party." *Party Politics* 1:5–28.

———, eds. 1992. *Party Organizations: A Data Handbook on Party Organizations in Western Democracies*. London: Sage.

Kavanagh, Dennis. 1995. *Election Campaigning: The New Marketing of Politics*. Oxford: Blackwell.

———. 1998. "R. T. McKenzie and After." In *Britain in the Nineties*, ed. Hugh Berrington, 28–43. London: Frank Cass.

Kelly, Richard. 1989. *Conservative Party Conferences*. Manchester: Manchester University Press.

———, ed. 1999. *Changing Party Policy in Britain*. Oxford: Blackwell.

Key, V. O., Jr. 1966. *The Responsible Electorate: Rationality in Presidential Voting, 1936–1960*. New York: Vintage.

King, Desmond. 1993. "Government beyond Whitehall." In *Developments in British Politics*, vol. 4, ed. Patrick Dunleavy, Andrew Gamble, Ian Holliday, and Gillian Peele. London: Macmillan.

Kirchheimer, Otto. 1966. "The Transformation of the Western European Party Systems." In *Political Parties and Political Development*, ed. Joseph LaPalombara and Myron Weiner. Princeton: Princeton University Press.

Kitschelt, Herbert. 1989. "The Internal Politics of Parties: The Law of Curvilinear Disparity Revisited." *Political Studies* 37:400–421.

Klingemann, Hans-Dieter, Richard Hofferbert, and Ian Budge. 1994. *Parties, Policies, and Democracy*. Boulder: Westview.

Kramer, Gerald H. 1970. "The Effects of Precinct-Level Canvassing on Voter Behavior." *Public Opinion Quarterly* 34:560–72.

———. 1983. "The Ecological Fallacy Revisited: Aggregate versus Individual-

Level Findings on Economics and Elections and Sociotropic Voting." *American Political Science Review* 77:92–111.

———. 1992a. *Labour's Election Manifesto: It's Time to Get Britain Working Again.* London: Labour Party.

———. 1992b. *Conference Report 1992.* London: Labour Party.

———. 1997a. *National Executive Committee Report.* London: Labour Party.

———. 1997b. *Partnership in Power.* London: Labour Party.

———. 1998. *National Executive Committee Paper (23/1/98).* London: Labour Party.

Lawson, Kay, and Peter Merkl, eds. 1988. *When Parties Fail.* Princeton: Princeton University Press.

Leamer, Edward E. 1983. "Let's Take the Con out of Econometrics." *American Economic Review* 73, no. 1: 31–43.

LeDuc, Lawrence. 1980. "The Dynamic Properties of Party Identification: A Four Nation Comparison." *European Journal of Political Research* 9:257–68.

Leighley, Jan. 1995. "Political Participation: A Field Review Essay." *Political Research Quarterly* 48:181–210.

Lewis-Beck, Michael S. 1988. *Economics and Elections: The Major Western Democracies.* Ann Arbor: University of Michigan Press.

Lipset, Seymour, and Stein Rokkan. 1967. "Cleavage Structures, Party Systems, and Voter Alignments: An Introduction." In *Party Systems and Voter Alignments: Cross-National Perspectives,* ed. Seymour Lipset and Stein Rokkan, 1–64. New York: Free Press.

Lowi, Theodore J. 1992. "The State in Political Science: How We Became What We Study." *American Political Science Review* 86:1–7.

MacIntyre, Donald. 1999. *Mandelson.* London: Harper-Collins.

Mandelson, Peter, and Roger Liddle. 1996. *The Blair Revolution.* London: Faber and Faber.

Maine, Henry. 1885. *Popular Government.* London: John Murray.

Mair, Peter. 1997. *Party System Change.* Oxford: Clarendon.

Maloney, William, and Grant Jordan. 1997. *The Protest Business.* Manchester: Manchester University Press.

Marcus, George E. 1988. "The Structure of Emotional Response: 1984 Presidential Candidates." *American Political Science Review* 82:737–61.

Margolis, Howard. 1982. *Selfishness, Altruism, and Rationality.* Chicago: University of Chicago Press.

Markus, Gregory B. 1979. *Analyzing Panel Data.* Newbury Park, CA: Sage.

Marr, Andrew. 1996. *Ruling Britannia.* London: Penguin.

Marsh, Alan. 1977. *Protest and Political Consciousness.* Beverly Hills and London. Sage.

May, John D. 1973. "Opinion Structure of Political Parties: The Special Law of Curvilinear Disparity." *Political Studies* 21:135–51.

Mayhew, Christopher. 1969. *Party Games.* London: Hutchinson.

McKelvey, Richard D. 1976. "Intransitivities in Multi-dimensional Voting Models and Some Implications for Agenda Control." *Journal of Economic Theory* 18: 472–82.

―――. 1986. "Covering, Dominance, and Institution Free Properties of Social Choice." *American Journal of Political Science* 30:283–314.

McKenzie, Robert. 1955. *British Political Parties*. London: Heinemann.

McKenzie, Robert, and Alan Silver. 1968. *Angels in Marble*. London: Heinemann.

Meadowcroft, James, and M. Taylor. 1990. "Liberalism and the Referendum in British Political Thought, 1890–1914." *Twentieth-Century British History* 1, no. 1: 35–57.

Meehl, P. E. 1977. "The Selfish Citizen Paradox and the Throw-Away Vote Argument." *American Political Science Review* 71:11–30.

Michels, Robert. [1902] 1962. *Political Parties*. New York: Free.

Mill, John Stuart. [1861] 1946. *Representative Government*. Oxford: Blackwell.

Miller, Warren, and J. Merrill Shanks. 1996. *The New American Voter*. Cambridge: Harvard University Press.

Miller, William L. 1991. *Media and Voters*. Oxford: Clarendon.

Miller, William L., Harold D. Clarke, Martin Harrop, Lawrence LeDuc, and Paul F. Whiteley. 1990. *How Voters Change: The 1987 British Election Campaign in Perspective*. Oxford: Clarendon Press.

Minkin, Lewis. 1978. *The Labour Party Conference*. London: Allen Lane.

―――. 1991. *The Contentious Alliance: Trade Unions and the Labour Party*. Edinburgh: Edinburgh University Press.

Mizon, Grayham E. 1984. "The Encompassing Approach in Econometrics." In *Econometrics and Quantitative Economics*, ed. David F. Hendry and Kenneth F. Wallis, 211–52. Oxford: Basil Blackwell.

Moloney, William, and Grant Jordan. 1997. *The Protest Business? Mobilizing Campaign Groups*. Manchester: Manchester University Press.

Mueller, Denis C. 1989. *Public Choice II*. Cambridge: Cambridge University Press.

Mulgan, Geoff. 1994. *Politics in an Anti-Political Age*. London: Polity.

Muller, Edward N. 1979. *Aggressive Political Participation*. Princeton: Princeton University Press.

Muller, Edward N., Henry A. Dietz, and Stephen E. Finkel. 1991. "Discontent and the Expected Utility of Rebellion: The Case of Peru." *American Political Science Review* 85:1261–82.

Muller, Edward, and Karl-Dieter Opp. 1986. "Rational Choice and Rebellious Collective Action." *American Political Science Review* 80:471–89.

―――. 1987. "Rebellious Collective Action Revisited." *American Political Science Review* 81:561–64.

Newton, Kenneth. 1992. "Do People Read Everything They Believe in the Papers? Newspapers and Voters in the 1983 and 1987 Elections." In *British Elections and Parties Yearbook, 1991*, ed. Ivor Crewe, Pippa Norris, David Denver, and David Broughton, 51–74. London: Harvester Wheatsheaf.

Nie, Norman, Sidney Verba, and John R. Petrocik. 1976. *The Changing American Voter*. Cambridge, MA: Harvard University Press.

Niemi, Richard G. 1976. "Costs of Voting and Non-Voting." *Public Choice* 27:115–19.

Noelle-Neumann, Elizabeth. 1984. *The Spiral of Silence: Public Opinion—Our Social Skin*. Chicago: University of Chicago Press.

Norpoth, Helmut. 1992. *Confidence Regained: Economics, Mrs. Thatcher, and the British Voter*. Ann Arbor: University of Michigan Press.

Norris, Pippa. 1993. "Has Labour Become a Catch-All Party?" Paper presented to the European Consortium for Political Research joint sessions, University of Leiden.

Norris, Pippa, and Joni Lovenduski. 1995. *Political Recruitment*. Cambridge: Cambridge University Press.

Norton, Phillip. 1975. *Dissension in the House of Commons: Intra-Party Dissent in the House of Commons' Division Lobbies, 1945–1974*. London: Macmillan.

———. 1980. *Dissension in the House of Commons, 1974–1979*. Oxford: Clarendon.

Olson, Mancur. 1965. *The Logic of Collective Action*. New York: Schocken.

———. 1982. *The Rise and Decline of Nations*. New Haven: Yale University Press.

Opp, Karl-Dieter. 1990. "Postmaterialism, Collective Action, and Political Protest." *American Journal of Political Science* 34:212–35.

Ostrogorski, Moisie. 1902. *Democracy and the Organization of Political Parties*. London: Macmillan.

Palfrey, Thomas, and Howard Rosenthal. 1985. "Voter Participation and Strategic Uncertainty." *American Political Science Review* 79:62–78.

Panebianco, Angelo. 1988. *Political Parties: Organization and Power*. Cambridge: Cambridge University Press.

Parry, Geraint, George Moyser, and Neil Day. 1992. *Political Participation and Democracy in Britain*. Cambridge: Cambridge University Press.

Pattie, Charles J., and Ronald J. Johnston. 1996. "Paying Their Way: Local Associations, the Constituency Quota Scheme, and Conservative Party Finance." *Political Studies* 44, no. 5: 921–35.

Pattie, Charles J., Ronald J. Johnston, and Edward Fieldhouse. 1995. "Winning the Local Vote: The Effectiveness of Constituency Campaign Spending in Great Britain, 1983–1992." *American Political Science Review* 89:969–83.

Pattie, Charles, Paul F. Whiteley, Ronald J. Johnston, and Patrick Seyd. 1994. "Measuring Local Campaign Effects: Labour Party Constituency Campaigning at the 1987 General Election." *Political Studies* 42:469–79.

Pelling, Henry. 1965. *A Short History of the Labour Party*. London: Macmillan.

Pindyck, Robert S., and Daniel L. Rubinfeld. 1991. *Econometric Models and Economic Forecasts*. New York: McGraw-Hill.

Pinto-Duschinsky, Michael. 1983. *British Political Finance, 1830–1980*. Washington, DC: American Enterprise Institute.

Popkin, Samuel L. 1994. *The Reasoning Voter: Communication and Persuasion in Presidential Campaigns*. Chicago: University of Chicago Press.

Putnam, Robert. 1993. *Making Democracy Work: Civic Traditions in Modern Italy*. Princeton: Princeton University Press.

———. 1995. "Tuning In, Tuning Out: The Strange Disappearance of Social Capital in America." *Political Science and Politics* 28, no. 4: 664–83.

Rallings, Colin, and Michael Thrasher. 1997. *Local Elections in Britain*. London: Routledge.

Ramsey, J. B. 1969. "Tests for Specification Errors in Classical Linear Least Squares Regression Analysis." *Journal of the Royal Statistical Society* B, 31:350–71.

Ranney, Austin. 1965. *Pathways to Parliament*. Madison: University of Wisconsin Press.

Richardson, Jeremy. 1994. *The Market for Political Activism: Interest Groups as a Challenge to Political Parties*. Bologna: European University Institute.

Riker, William, and Peter Ordeshook. 1968. "A Theory of the Calculus of Voting." *American Political Science Review* 62:25–42.

———. 1973. *An Introduction to Positive Political Theory*. Englewood Cliffs, NJ: Prentice-Hall.

Rose, Richard. 1984. *Do Parties Make a Difference?* London: Macmillan.

Rose, Richard, and Ian McAllister. 1986. *Voters Begin to Choose*. London: Sage.

———. 1990. *The Loyalties of Voters: A Lifetime Learning Model*. London: Sage.

Rosenstone, Steven J., and John Mark Hansen. 1993. *Mobilization, Participation, and Democracy in America*. New York: Macmillan.

Routledge, Paul. 1998. *Gordon Brown*. London: Simon and Schuster.

Rush, Michael. 1969. *The Selection of Parliamentary Candidates*. London: Nelson.

Salisbury, Robert. 1969. "An Exchange Theory of Interest Groups." *Midwest Journal of Political Science* 13:1–32.

Samuelson, Paul. 1954. "The Pure Theory of Public Expenditure." *Review of Economics and Statistics* 36:387–89.

Sanders, David. 1991. "Government Popularity and the Next General Election." *Political Quarterly* 62:235–61.

———. 1993. "Why the Conservatives Won—Again." In *Britain at the Polls 1992*, ed. Anthony King et al. Chatham, NJ: Chatham House.

Sarlvik, Bö, and Ivor Crewe. 1983. *Decade of Dealignment*. Cambridge: Cambridge University Press.

Scammell, Margaret. 1995. *Designer Politics: How Elections Are Won*. Basingstoke: Macmillan.

Scarborough, Elinor. 1984. *Political Ideology and Voting*. Oxford: Clarendon.

Scarrow, Susan. 1990. "The Decline of Party Organization? Mass Membership Parties in Great Britain and West Germany." Paper presented to the Annual meeting of the American Political Science Association, San Francisco.

———. 1996. *Parties and Their Members*. Oxford: Oxford University Press.

Scarrow, Susan, and Thomas Poguntke. 1996. "The Politics of Anti-Party Sentiment." *European Journal of Political Research* 29, no. 3:257–62.

Schofield, Norman. 1978. "Instability of Simple Dynamic Games." *Review of Economic Studies* 45:575–94.

Seldon, Anthony, and Stuart Ball, eds. 1994. *Conservative Century*. Oxford: Oxford University Press.

Seyd, Patrick, and Paul F. Whiteley. 1992. *Labour's Grass Roots: The Politics of Party Membership*. Oxford: Clarendon.

———. 1995. "Labour and Conservative Party Members: Change Over Time." *Parliamentary Affairs* 48, no. 3:456–71.

———. 1999. "Liberal Democrats at the Grass Roots: Who Are They?" Paper presented at the annual conference of the Elections, Public Opinion, and Parties Group, University College, Northampton.

Shaw, Eric. 1994. *The Labour Party since 1979*. London: Routledge.

———. 1996. *The Labour Party since 1945*. Oxford: Blackwell.

Shonfield, Andrew. 1965. *Modern Capitalism*. Oxford: Oxford University Press.

Silberman, Jonathan, and Gary Durden. 1975. "The Rational Behavior Theory of Voter Participation: The Evidence from Congressional Elections." *Public Choice* 23:101–8.

Sims, Christopher A. 1980. "Macroeconomics and Reality." *Econometrica* 48:1–48.

Smith, John. 1993. "Membership Is Vital." *Labour Party News* 4 (September/October): 5.

Sniderman, Paul M., Richard A. Brody, and Philip E. Tetlock. 1991. *Reasoning and Choice: Explorations in Political Psychology*. Cambridge: Cambridge University Press.

Spanos, Aris. 1990. "Towards a Unifying Methodological Framework for Econometric Modelling." In *Modelling Economic Series*, ed. C. W. J. Granger, 335–68. Oxford: Clarendon.

Stewart, J., E. Kendall, and A. Coote. 1994. *Citizens' Juries*. London: Institute for Public Policy Research.

Stewart, J., and G. Stoker. 1989. *The Future of Local Government*. London: Macmillan.

Taylor, Michael. 1976. *Anarchy and Co-operation*. London: Wiley.

Times Guide to the House of Commons, 1997. 1997. London: Times Newspapers.

Topf, Richard. 1994. "Party Manifestoes." In *Labour's Last Chance?* ed. Anthony Heath, Roger Jowell, and John Curtice, 149–72. Aldershot: Dartmouth.

Travers, T. 1986. *The Politics of Local Government Finance*. London: Allen and Unwin.

Tsebelis, George. 1990. *Nested Games: Rational Choice in Comparative Politics*. Berkeley and Los Angeles: University of California Press.

TSO. 1998a. *Fifth Report of the Committee on Standards in Public Life, Volume 1*. London: The Stationary Office.

———. 1998b. *Government Annual Report, 1997*. London: The Stationary Office.

———. 1998c. *Report of the Independent Commission on the Voting System*. London: The Stationary Office.

Tullock, Gordon. 1967. "The Welfare Costs of Tariffs, Monopolies, and Theft." *Western Economic Journal* 5:224–32.

———. 1971. "The Paradox of Revolution." *Public Choice* 11:89–99.

Uhlaner, Carol. 1989. "Rational Turnout: The Neglected Role of Groups." *American Journal of Political Science* 33:390–422.

Vandaele, Walter. 1983. *Applied Time Series and Box-Jenkins Models*. San Diego: Academic Press.

Verba, Sidney, and Norman Nie. 1972. *Participation in America: Political Democracy and Social Equality*. New York: Harper and Row.

Verba, Sidney, Norman Nie, and Jae-On Kim. 1978. *Participation and Political Equality: A Seven Nation Comparison*. Cambridge: Cambridge University Press.

Verba, Sidney, Kay Lehman Schlozman, and Henry Brady. 1995. *Voice and Equality: Civic Voluntarism in American Politics*. Cambridge: Harvard University Press.

Verba, Sidney, Kay Lehman Schlozman, Henry Brady, and Norman Nie. 1993. "Citizen Activity: Who Participates? What Do They Say?" *American Political Science Review* 87:303–18.

Webb, Paul. 1994. "Party Organizational Change in Britain." In *How Parties Organize*, ed. Richard S. Katz and Peter Mair, 109–33. London: Sage.

———. 1995. "Are British Political Parties in Decline?" *Party Politics* 1, no. 3: 299–322.

———. 2000. *The Modern British Party System*. London: Sage.

Webb, Paul, and David Farrell. 1999. "Party Members and Ideological Change." In *Critical Elections: British Parties and Voters in Long-Term Perspective*, ed. Geoffrey Evans and Pippa Norris, 44–63. London: Sage.

Weir, Stuart. 1995. "Questions of Democratic Accountability." *Parliamentary Affairs* 48, no. 2: 306–22.

Weir, Stuart, and David Beetham. 1999. *Political Power and Democratic Control in Britain*. London: Routledge.

Whiteley, Paul. 1982. "The Decline of Labour's Local Party Membership and Electoral Base 1945–79." In *The Politics of the Labour Party*, ed. Dennis Kavanagh, 111–34. London: Allen and Unwin.

———. 1983. *The Labour Party in Crisis*. London: Methuen.

———. 1986. *Political Control of the Macroeconomy*. London: Sage.

———. 1995. "Rational Choice and Political Participation—Evaluating the Debate." *Political Research Quarterly* 48:211–34.

Whiteley, Paul F., and Patrick Seyd. 1992. "The Labour Vote and Local Activism: The Impact of Local Constituency Campaigns." *Parliamentary Affairs* 45:582–95.

———. 1994. "Local Party Campaigning and Voting Behavior in Britain." *Journal of Politics* 56:242–51.

———. 1998. "The Dynamics of Party Activism in Britain: A Spiral of Demobilization?" *British Journal of Political Science* 28:113–38.

———. 1999. "How to Win a Landslide by Really Trying—The Effects of Local Campaigning on Voting in the British General Election of 1997." Paper presented at the annual meeting of the American Political Science Association, Atlanta.

Whiteley, Paul F., Patrick Seyd, and Jeremy Richardson. 1994. *True Blues: The Politics of Conservative Party Membership*. Oxford: Clarendon Press.

Whiteley, Paul F., Patrick Seyd, Jeremy Richardson, and Paul Bissell. 1994. "Explaining Party Activism: The Case of the British Conservative Party." *British Journal of Political Science* 24:79–94.

Wielhouwer, Peter W., and Brad Lockerbie. 1994. "Party Contacting and Participation, 1952–90." *American Journal of Political Science* 38:211–29.

Windlesham, Lord. 1966. *Communication and Political Power*. London: Jonathan Cape.

Wistow, Gerald. 1992. "The National Health Service." In *Implementing Thatcherite Policies*, ed. David Marsh and R. A. W. Rhodes, 100–116. Buckingham: Open University Press.

Wolfinger, Raymond. 1963. "The Influence of Precinct Work on Voting Behaviour." *Public Opinion Quarterly* 27:387–98.

Index